RECEIVING SPIRIT

THE PRACTICE OF FIVE ELEMENT ACUPUNCTURE

Best Wishes

Della

2015

RECEIVING SPIRIT
THE PRACTICE OF FIVE ELEMENT ACUPUNCTURE

DEBRA KAATZ

CALLIGRAPHY

HARRISON XINSHI TU

THE PETITE BERGERIE PRESS

RECEIVING SPIRIT
THE PRACTICE OF FIVE ELEMENT ACUPUNCTURE

Published by
The Petite Bergerie Press
Les Horts, 30460, Soudorgues, France
and 27 Ondine Road, London SE15 4ED

Copyright © 2009 by Debra Kaatz

ISBN 978-0-9549166-4-0

All rights reserved. No part of this book may be reproduced in any form or by any means, electronic or mechanical, including photocopying, recording, or by any information storage or retrieval system without permission in writing from the publisher and copywrite holder except in the case of brief quotations embodied in critical articles and reviews.

Designed and typeset in Garamond by Debra Kaatz
Printed on Five Seasons recycled paper
by the MPG Books Group in the UK

TABLE OF CONTENTS

Foreword	9
Mythology	11
The Way of the Tao	19
The Art of Acupuncture	33
Spiritual Five Element Theory	45
Supporting Spirit - Eight Extraordinary Meridians	71
Opening Our Senses	119
Treatment and the Five Elements	127
Healing Touch for Children	219
Prayers and Healing	227
The Energy and Spirits of European Medicinal Plants	261
Inner Alchemical Healing Cycle	295
Further Reading	315
Author and Calligrapher	319

LE - JOY

A THANK YOU

Joy is what I hope this book will bring to many people. *Le* or joy in Chinese is written as a drum with bells, over a music stand. It is a ceremonial drum that is used in sacred rites and ceremonies. The sound of these large drums were used to invite the spirits to come and join in the ceremony. In this way, the ancestors and gods were invited to come to earth for a brief time. In their presence everyone could feel their greatness and receive their wisdom. When we are blessed with the presence of the ancient ones, we feel a profound harmony inside. It is a joy of deep understanding that brings inspiration. We touch those things that are beyond ourselves and glimpse the infinite beauty of life. There is no limit to our love and compassion for others when we are filled with the wisdom and greatness of joy. May the spirits of the acupuncture points bring this joy to our lives.

I would like to thank with a heart full of joy, my parents who brought me into the world, numerous scholars for all the wonderful translations of old texts, all the students interested in this healing medicine and the immortals themselves who watched over my shoulder and tempted me with insights.

LING - SPIRIT

FOREWORD

The Chinese character for spirit is *Ling*. It is drawn as the rains of heaven falling into the mouths of three shaman women who are dancing between heaven and earth. They are offering their prayers to the heavens in order to bring the rains of prosperity to the earth to bring creativity and fertility to life. As they pray to the heavens they receive the inpirations and wisdom of the gods. When we live our lives with this grace and presence, then we too receive these gifts. Our lives become filled with the vibrant spirit of life. Each of the acupuncture points links us to these gifts that flow between heaven and earth. If we are truly centered and present when we contact these points, we touch *Ling*, this open place between heaven and earth. The patient then receives the energetic gift of the point we use. We become the shamanessses and bring this healing to the patient in the same way the rain brings alive the earth. Then PC8, *Lao Gong*, becomes a palace full of the love and riches of the heart. SP4, *Gong Sun* opens the granary of the royal prince's inheritance. HT5, *Tong Li* takes us to the flowering of our inner nature. LU3 *Tian Fu* brings us to the riches of the heavenly palace, KI6 *Zhao Hai* fills us with the shining sea of illumination and LIV14 *Qi Men* takes us to the gateway of hope. This book is about using the spirits of the points to bring joy, wonder and good health back to those who come to us for help with the dis-eases in their lives.

DEBRA KAATZ
SOUDORGUES FEBRUARY, 2009

極泉

JI QUAN - UTMOST SOURCE

YOU ASK WHY I LIVE ALONE IN THE MOUNTAIN FOREST
AND I SMILE AND AM SILENT,
UNTIL EVEN MY SOUL GROWS QUIET.
IT LIVES IN THE OTHER WORLD, ONE THAT NO ONE OWNS
THE PEACH TREE BLOSSOM, THE WATER CONTINUES TO FLOW
LI PO

MYTHOLOGY

It is said that in the beginning there was only the Tao. It was one, a swirling chaos of unity, still, yet containing all. For thousands of years the Tao existed alone and complete. Then in a single movement, in the middle of this chaos, was born a being called P'an Ku. P'an Ku lived in the chaos of the Tao, sleeping for eighteen thousand years. He fed on the greatness of the Tao that surrounded him. Finally he opened his eyes. There was nothing to see but darkness and confusion.

He raised his arms and struck out at the darkness around him and scattered the elements of chaos. Things began to change. P'an Ku, with this mighty swing of his arms had freed the heavens from the earth. The light and pure rose upwards and became the heavens, and the dark and heavy moved downwards and became the earth. He stood between them, holding the sky on his head and the earth under his feet. P'an Ku grew taller and the heavens and earth moved further apart until they were finally fixed firmly in place. Then P'an Ku laid down on the earth to rest and died. His destiny was complete.

His body made the earth rich and fertile. His breath created the winds and clouds. His voice became the deep thunder and his eyes became the sun and the moon. Each of the hairs on his head became a twinkling star. The sweat of his brow flowed and became the rain and the dew. His body created the mountains, his hands the north pole and his feet the south pole. The rivers of the earth came from his blood. The fields came from his flesh. The hairs on his body grew into trees and flowers. P'an Ku was transformed into the splendours of the earth and the glory of the heavens. Then Nü Kua came to earth and created mankind from the rich clay of the soil.

Many years later a great emperor appeared. He was called Huang Di or the Yellow Emperor. It was he who discovered the great medicine of acupuncture. His father Yu brought the great floods of China under control by opening waterways and creating channels. Yu knew how to flow with the waters of life and in such a way brought balance and harmony to the world. Huang Di, the Yellow Emperor, was his first son and Yen Di, the Flame Emperor, was his second son. When Yu died the world was divided between the two sons. Huang Di followed the way of the Tao seeking peace and harmony for his kingdom. Yen Di however wanted all of the world for himself. He began to use his great powers of fire against his brother. Huang Di called on mythical beasts and birds to put out the flames. They poured water on the fires. He then called on the wind and the rains to cool his brother's fiery nature. Finally Yen Di challenged his brother to a battle on the great plains below the Kunlun mountains. He gathered all the fires of earth. After many days, Huang Di was finally able to extinguish Yen Di's fire power using the great forces of water he had inherited from his father Yu. Huang Di became emperor of the world and Yen Di was banished to the great north. Huang Di had become master of balancing water and fire, and the great forces of yin and yang.

Yen Di's best friend was the god of war, Ch'ih Yu. Ch'ih Yu had watched the battle between the two brothers and knew he could do better. He challenged Huang Di to another battle on the same plain in a month's time. The great day arrived. Ch'ih Yu brought his friends the rain master, Yu Shih and the wind god, Feng Po to control the power of water. However Huang Di brought the Responding Dragon and Drought Fury, his own daughter. They have the ability to cause drought by holding back water. The battle went on for nine days and nights. Each day Ch'ih Yu would send the wind god and the rain master to create huge storms and floods. Each night, the Dragon and Drought Fury would store the water in the cave of Deep Resources. Huang Di felt he needed help. So on the ninth night he went to the Deep Cave of the Dark Mountains. There he waited in the darkness. Finally the Dark Lady greeted him. He bowed in respect and asked for her help. She then fully appeared to him in the shape of a beautiful woman and the body of a bird. She taught him the art of war and its strategies. The next day as the violent storms came, the Dragon and Drought Fury distracted Ch'ih Yu, while Huang Di charged at his heart and killed him in a single stroke. Huang Di had mastered the art of war and peace came to the world.

Several years later a man arrived at the palace, his clothes torn and his eyes fearful. He said to Huang Di, 'You must save us from the mighty monster, K'uei who is bringing terror to the countryside.' K'uei was a great ox with a blue body and one hoof. As he moved in and out of water he produced severe storms all over the kingdom. It was said his eyes would send out a beam as strong as the sun and moon and it would light up the sky. His voice was said to sound like one giant drum that would thunder across the sky. Hunag Di mounted the Great Dragon of the East and travelled to the Eastern Seas and the Flowing Wave Mountain. In the Valley of Immortal Vines he cut several lengths of vine. When he met K'uei in the high plateau he sent the vines flying in all directions towards K'uei. The more K'uei struggled the more tightly the vines held. When the beast could no longer move, Huang Di killed it. He then took its skin and made it into a drum. When Huang Di would strike this drum with a bone from the thunder beast, all the world would stand in awe. Huang Di now had the power of the forces of nature to bring balance to the world.

Huang Di was now able to rule his kingdom in peace and harmony. However his kingdom was surrounded by four other Emperors. These were the Emperors of the North, South, East and West. They did not know how to follow the Tao and became jealous of the harmony of Huang Di's kingdom. They sent their soldiers to harass the people of the middle kingdom. Finally Huang Di rode out with his troops to each of the Emperors. When they would not accept the way of the Tao, he exiled them to the Western seas. From this time forward the whole kingdom was ruled by the way of the Tao and the calm peace of Huang Di's heart. The world was at last in harmony.

One day Huang Di was wandering in the palace garden when his minister Cang Ji, the Noble One, came up to him

MYTHOLOGY

with great excitement in his heart. He had discovered the way of writing. He explained that as he had been walking looking at the footprints of animals, he suddenly realized each footprint was distinct. Then he realized that distinctive marks could be used as symbols for words. He drew a heart for the Emperor. He then represented water with flowing lines. The word for mother was drawn as a woman's full breasts. These symbols became the radicals of Chinese writing. For example one radical is the heart. If the symbol for heart and the symbol for centre are drawn together they mean loyal, faithful, devoted, sincere, honest and right. If the radical characters for mother and child are drawn together the combination means goodness. In this way each Chinese character becomes a fascinating story.

The characters are formed out of the magical seven strokes which are known as the seven mysteries. The strokes are the horizontal, the vertical, the sweeping to the right or left, the dots, the hooks and the diagonal strokes. Children practice these strokes by copying the work of masters until their strokes are fluid and alive. It is said that the horizontal stroke should be like a cloud that slowly drifts across the sky. The dot should be drawn as a falling rock, The vertical stroke should have the growth of a strong vine stem. The sweeping stroke should rise and fall like the ocean waves. The hook should be like an animal's claw. The diagonal stroke should have the dynamic energy of an arrow. It is said that the person who has mastered all of these strokes is able to write the characters for eternity, for they have learned how to write with the seven mysteries. For the Chinese, the act of writing a character is like the process of creation. Every character derives from the first stroke of the brush and mirrors the idea that the universe was created from this original oneness, the great Tao. This one stroke determines the nature of the others that follow. The stroke grows as it is made and becomes, in that instance, a thing that is in spirit, the heart, mother, mountain or stream. This outer form reveals the inner life of the tree or river or whatever is being expressed.

Using these characters, Huang Di wrote the book of Chinese Medicine and Acupuncture called the Way of Heaven and Earth. In this great work Huang Di asks his ministers questions on how to maintain balance and harmony in life. They tell him that health is maintained by being balanced in life. They explain to him that to develop this balance we need to be in harmony with the energy of the Tao by being centered in spirit and by not misusing energy. Everything should be done in moderation and in accordance with the cycles of nature and its seasons. All the seasons stimulate, subdue, tonify and sedate the natural life force. How a person lives and the changes in nature are what affects health. If we move along the path nature gives us, then life is full and harmonious. When all is in harmony and balance with the universe then there will be health. When there is imbalance, either in our lives or in the seasons around us, it is then that injury and weakness occur.

Huang Di would go each year to his tower in the inner palace gardens. There he would rest in quiet contemplation with the Gods. He would hear in his heart how to keep his kingdom in harmony and in balance for the following year. Then he would see to it that whatever was needed was done.

The Chinese healers of his court mapped out the seas, rivers and points of energy on the human body. These energy channels and points are constantly bringing energy to us from heaven and earth. They help to keep our lives in balance and good health. When there are outside forces such as extreme weather conditions, pollutions or bad spirits, then these can create imbalances. Today we often create the imbalances in ourselves by not eating well, living in polluted environments, losing our contact with nature and its spirit, and by filling our minds with stressful worries. When this happens a healer can feel the energy pulses of the twelve meridians and choose points to bring our energy back into balance and harmony. We can also meditate on the points, calling on their spirits to bring back harmony to our hearts. These amazing meridians and energy points are capable of bringing resources of vitality to our mind, body and spirit when it is needed.

> *One must remain in the vastnesss, alert and lucid,*
> *Letting one's gaze encompass the infinity of the sky,*
> *As though seated on the summit*
> *Of a mountain open to all the horizons.*
> **SHABKAR - TIBETAN SAGE**

*MY LUTE SET ASIDE ON THE LITTLE TABLE
LAZILY I MEDITATE ON CHERISHED FEELINGS
THE REASON I DON'T STRUM AND PLUCK?
THERE'S A BREEZE OVER THE STRINGS
THEY PLAY THEMSELVES*
PO CHU-I

THE WAY OF THE TAO

*Something whole and complete was born
Before heaven and earth
Silent and formless, standing alone and unchanging
Moving in an endless cycle.
It is mother to the world.
I do not know its name, so I call it the Tao.
If I put a name to it, I call it great.
Greatness means it moves through everything.*

LAO TZU

The ancient ones would take their students walking through the world. By experiencing the sun rising in the morning creating each new day and feeling its warmth and love throughout its passage from east to west and by watching the cycles of the moon at night, these students gradually learned how to follow the Tao. They began to see its spirit in each rock and tree and in the movement of the winds and rains. Each of us has our own special path to walk through life. This path is a part of all paths that are guided by the great oneness of the Tao. When we open our spirit to this great wonder, we not only find our true path but are each day inspired by the wonders that surround us.

The Chinese character for the Tao has two short slanting lines on top. The line on the left represents the sun and the line on the right is the moon. In heaven, yin is the moon and yang is the sun. On earth the sun is the golden boy and the moon is the jade rabbit. In the body they are the two eyes. These two lines represent the inner and outer light. Under these two lines is a longer horizontal line that means one, wholeness and emptiness. It represents the horizon that is both a part of heaven and earth. When heaven receives this oneness it is pure and when earth receives this oneness it is peaceful. When we receive this oneness, we become inspired. These two slanting lines and one horizontal lines together mean the oneness of the Tao. Below is a symbol that combines the sun and the moon. It means self. All of these lines together mean foremost or priority. In other words, the Tao must be our priority in life. Next to this combined character is the symbol for walking on a path. The Tao is our path in life. When we know and follow this path we are at peace and in harmony both within and without. The Tao is both the way of heaven and our original nature. It has no form and is the mysterious energy of the universe. It gives life to heaven and earth, and moves the sun and moon. It is devoid of all emotion, empty, but nourishes all beings.

道

THE TAO

THE WAY OF THE TAO

The great Tao is everywhere, flowing right or left.
All things depend on it for growth in life
It does not refuse them.
It does its work with humility
Its accomplishments fulfilled, it does not dwell on them.
It lovingly nourishes all things, but does not control them
As it has no desire or aim, it can be called small
All things are embraced by it without being dominated
In this way it is called great.
It can accomplish what is great.

LAO TZU

We do not know many things in the world. Some animals and plants need help to survive and others survive on their own. Some can live in very hostile conditions and others can grow only in the most mild conditions. But we can say that everything naturally grows and has its place in the balance of the universe. If we try and change the ways of life, we upset the balance of things and the order of the universe is disturbed. Everything plays a part in the cycles of creating, nourishing, transforming and destroying. In every moment there is birth and death. Thoughts, colours, shapes and feelings also come and go. Where these things go we do not know. We can say however that all things are born from the Tao. When the spirit is empty and clear then all beings return to the Tao. When the spirit is distracted by the dust of the world, all beings stray from their natural course. This is not because the Tao has distanced itself from humanity, but because humanity has distanced itself from the Tao.

RECEIVING SPIRIT

Look, you will not see it, it is unfathomable.
Listen, it can not be heard, beyond sound, precious.
Grasp it and you will not feel it, it is subtle and ungraspable.
Even these cannot be completely known for they merge into one.
Up above it is not bright and down below it is not dark
Infinite and continuous it returns again to nothing.
A shape without shape, its form is without object
It is elusive and fleeting, indefinable.
When you face it, you do not see its head
When you follow it, you will not see its back.
Use the ancient way to master the present situations and
To know the origins of the universe and understand the Tao.

LAO TZU

To find the Tao we must practice listening to the stillness within. By practicing emptiness in the heart we will eventually find true emptiness and be able to see the mysteries in all things. See through these illusions and find your true path and become one with the Tao. It is our intuitive nature that holds the essence of our precious inner spark of the Tao. If we are natural and true to our own original nature, then we will find the wonder and beauty in all things. When we sit quietly in stillness, we find this wisdom within.

Quietly sitting listening to music or walking out in the park or forest brings an inner calm. The mind can let go of the business of the day and enjoy the space of having nothing to think about. When we enter these moments of reverie, we allow our inner intuitive nature to begin to surface and find moments of inner peace. We touch a world that is greater

THE WAY OF THE TAO

and full of wisdom. It is through cultivating this stillness that we are given the time and space for inspiration. We are able to experience a wholeness with all living beings. Rather than passing each day organizing the world around us, if we become still and experience the quality of each moment, we can find a greatness that goes beyond ourself. In this way each moment become precious. Everything is sensed in its fullness. Our ego fades and we let go. It is by meditating that we find our way back to the infinite Tao and dissolve in its unity.

We begin by simply sitting in stillness and watch how our thoughts come and go. Gradually we begin to realize that the problems these thoughts bring to us are created by the mind. Therefore if we can still the mind, these problems will go away. It is like a glass with muddy water. At first the glass is filled with muddy water. But if we allow this water to sit in the glass undisturbed, gradually the sediment falls to the bottom and the water clears. When we can sit calmly and leave behind both the distraction of the outer world and our inner world, then we can focus on the inner source within and find deep inspiration and inner wisdom.

The myriad differences resolved by sitting, all doors opened.
In this still place I follow my nature, be what it may.
From the one hundred flowers, I wander freely,
The soaring cliff, my hall of meditation
Sitting on this frosty seat, no further dream of fame.
The forest, the mountain, follow their ancient ways,
And through the long spring day, not even the shadow of a bird.

REIZAN

RECEIVING SPIRIT

In the great mountain of the Shensi province there is a cliff face. Carved on this great face of rock is the diagram of life called the Wu-chi diagram. It was first revealed to a hermit known as the Sage of the River. He had studied the river path for many years and realized all rivers returned to their mother the great sea. Read one way, the Wu-chi diagram explains how life is created. Read in the opposite direction it explains how we return to the Tao. Wu-chi means the origin or source of all things.

When we read the Wu-chi diagram from top to bottom it describes the path of life in this way. From the Wu-chi or source of all things comes Tai-chi or the great Qi energy of both yin and yang. From the movements of yin and yang are created the five elements of water, wood, fire, earth and metal. These nourish all things with their cycles that also create the five seasons. From heaven the male is said to be born and form earth the female is said to be born. The union of heaven and earth produce the ten thousand beings that live in the world. All of life contains a spark of the original Wu-chi and its wholeness. In this way each being has its own purpose as well as a connection to the whole.

When we read the Wu-chi diagram from bottom to top it describes the process of transformation that returns us to our source of wholeness or the Tao. First by meditation we open the mysterious gateway. We then heat the fires of our internal energy in the lower Tan-tien with exercises. This energy purifies our spirit and Qi energy and revitalizes our inherited energy. When these energies are united they can be used to purify our five elements within. We then bring these five energies together by bringing the fire raven and water turtle together and the green tiger of wood and the white tiger of metal. They all meet in the centre of earth and form the golden elixir. We then cultivate this energy with the energy of the sun, moon and stars. When all is ready we enter the immortal realms and become one with the Tao.

In ancient Taoist texts it is said to practice meditation in a quiet room with the body like a tree receiving all nature gives it, and the mind like ash with all distractions burnt away. The light of your spirit will then be your guide. When this stillness reaches its height, it is then that you feel the movement of the infinite begin. This movement is the root and leaf of the Tao. When energy swirls within you draw it inwards and conserve it. This substance that emerges from nothingness renews life.

Build a sacred internal environment and a hundred rays of light will come from the head and a thousand petaled lotus will be created from the light. Call on the fires of the warrior and the scholar. If the monsters appear, the warrior fires will drive them away. Then your true inner pearl will come and give you intuitive wisdom. The scholar will teach the heart and you will return to your original nature. When your spirit emerges with the Tao, the celestial mind shines, the waters of the ocean are clear and the moon is reflected in the deep lake. You will then find yourself in the sacred hall of Buddha light and the immortals.

Be master of your own life, holding onto nothing, craving nothing. By cultivating the Tao there will be gods to help you with your difficulties. By not losing your original nature, the dust of the world will vanish. The sky then reveals the bright moon. You will see the many coloured clouds. When you are hungry, the dragon woman will bring you your tea. You will far surpass the three thousand families at the mouth of the Han river. You will far out distance the hundred thousand families in the capital city. Let all mortals of the world hurry and awaken and sweep away their anxieties and stress cutting through the yellow grass. Buddhas, God, ancestors, sages, angels and immortals are in your original nature. Returning to the Tao is both mysterious and wonderful. By doing nothing we achieve all things.

> *Each day I bath my body*
> *I watch the moon to cultivate my form*
> *I sense the immortals*
> *The western lady above*
> *And the twenty-eight constellations are with me*
> *The Celestial Lord Ling-pao protects my soul*
> *He guards the human spirit*
> *And sees the internal organs are bright and whole*
> *Oh, Green Dragon and White Tiger*
> *Weave your force around me*
> *Oh, Red Raven and Blue Tortoise*
> *Protect my inner spirit*
>
> **TAOIST PRAYER**

By meditating we can find our inner source of health and vitality. We can touch the inspirations of the wonders around us and see deeper meanings in the messages that come to us each day. We can also bring healing energy to our five elements that keep us balanced throughout the five seasons of the year. The following five healing colour exercise can purify and heal the mental, emotional and physical energy pathways in the body. By visualizing these healing colour forces, the imbalanced Qi will be transformed and brought into harmony.

Begin by closing your eyes and imagining you are in one of your favourite places in the world. Then place your hand on the area of the liver. Smile into your liver and feel it smile back at you. Imagine the liver is a green rose slowly opening. This activates the kindness of the liver. Watch as your liver fills with this green healing light of kindness. Inhale this healing green light and exhale any cloudy stressful energy. Repeat this until the liver feels clear and full of kindness. Then imagine this healing green light being formed into a beautiful green dragon. Fill your entire being with this full green dragon energy as you breathe in and out for several cycles. Then place this green dragon in your liver.

Next go to the heart and place your hands on your heart. Smile into your heart and imagine it smiling back. Imagine the heart as a red rose slowly opening. This opens the love and warmth of compassion in the heart. Watch as your heart fills with this red healing light of love and joy. Inhale this healing red light and exhale any cloudy stressful energy. Continue with this until the red light of compassion starts to radiate out from your heart with love and joy. Now imagine this red healing light being transformed into a beautiful phoenix.

Fill your entire being with this full red phoenix energy as you breathe in and out for several cycles. Then place this red phoenix in your heart.

Next go to the spleen and place your hand there. Smile into your spleen and feel it smile back at you. Imagine the spleen to be a golden yellow rose that slowly opens. This activates the sympathy and care of the spleen. Watch as it radiates the golden healing light of nourishment and care. Inhale this golden nourishing light and exhale any worries and cares. Continue to do this until you feel filled with golden nourishing light. Then imagine this golden healing light being transformed into a golden ox. Fill your entire being with this healing golden ox. Then place it in your spleen.

Next go to the lungs and place your hand there. Smile into your lungs and feel them smile back. Imagine the lungs to be a white rose that slowly opens. This activates the courage and inspirations of the lungs. Watch as your lungs fill with this white healing energy of inspiration and encouragement. Inhale this white inspiring light and exhale any doubts and cloudy energy. Continue to do this until you feel filled with white inspired, encouraging light. Then imagine this white healing light being transformed into a white tiger. Fill your entire being with this healing white tiger light. Then place it in your lungs.

Next go to the kidneys and place your hand there. Smile into your kidneys and feel them smile back. Imagine the kidneys to be a blue rose that slowly opens. This opens their healing energy of gentleness and reassurance. Watch as your kidneys fill with this blue healing energy of vitality and reassurance. Inhale this blue light and exhale any fears and cloudy energy. Continue to do this until you feel filled with blue gentleness. Then imagine this blue healing light being transformed into a blue turtle. Fill your entire being with this healing blue turtle light. Then place it in your kidneys.

When we do this exercise it brings balance and harmony to our inner yin organs and to our five elements. This keeps our energy flowing well and brings vitality to our mind, body and spirit. By meditating we find the jewels of Tao as well as the health and well being of our five elements and their healing energies.

The story of the ox is a search for the elusive invisible force of nature, the Tao. In this search, we have to try and find the ox or the Tao, by cutting a path through brambles and undergrowth. We search over mountains and across wide rivers. The path is ever longer and the mind is exhausted. We can't find the ox, but there is a rustling of leaves and the songs of crickets. Suddenly by the water, deep in the forest there are traces of its footprint. Slowly you have to follow the signs and tracks and enter the endless mountains. There is distant sky and perhaps the hidden tip of its nose. In the morning light there is a singing yellow bird on a branch. In the quiet of the warm sun the mind drifts. You rest. Gentle breezes come and caress your cheek, as you are lost in thought. In the brambles the ox is glimpsed. You see a faint outline and its eyes. By supreme concentration and tremendous effort you catch the ox. Sometimes it runs onto high ground and sometimes it vanishes in the mist for its will is strong and body vigorous. With kindness and patience you tame the ox to walk alongside you with gentleness. Following the winding path you ride the ox home. Playing your flute the notes soar and the sound is beyond the lips and mouth. Finally at home and at rest you forget the ox. Under warm bright sunshine you daydream in bliss and let go of the rope. The vast blue sky cannot be reached by ideas. The ox and you are empty. How can the fire's flame sustain the snowflakes? You are a part of the ancient way forgetting all. Your effort is over for you have returned to the source. The self is blind and deaf. Inside the hut, nothing outside is seen. Waters are boundless, flowers red. You go to the market place barefooted and in old clothes, smeared with mud, covered with dust, but smiling. Using no other power you bring the withered trees to bloom.

It is said that the three forces and supreme medicines for all physical and spiritual ills are *Ching*, *Qi* and *Shen*. Gathered together they create the great medicine. The Chinese character for *Ching* is drawn as uncooked rice and a newly sprouting plant. Together they mean the regenerative and creative force in the body inherited from our parents. This energy gives the body strength and vitality. Our inherited energy is normally lost during life. It is said that in order to return to the vitality, mental alertness and spiritual brightness we had as children, we have to replenish *Ching*. We do this through energy exercises as *Tai Chi*, calm meditation and diet. In this way our youthfulness, vigour, strength and stamina return and the skin soften and glows.

THE WAY OF THE TAO

The Chinese character for *Qi* is drawn as rice being cooked in a pot with vapour coming off. The pot is like the abdomen where the food is cooked and formed into energy. The vapour is the breath or *Qi* energy. It represents the energy and power of *Qi* to nourish and drive the mind, body and spirit. Breath is what brings nourishment and spirit into the body. By working with the breath we enter into an inner stillness that allows us to reach the quiet contemplation of our inner wisdom. This breath also feeds the body with the energy of the air of heaven that permeates all things in the universe. The more deeply and longer the breath can be held, the more this heavenly breath can be absorbed in to the body. Gradually this true breath can penetrate every element of the body. It is as if the whole body breathes in a vital, expansive and lively way. *Qi* is the life force of nourishing energy that permeates all beings from the highest stars to the smallest dust.

Shen is drawn as the sun, moon and stars and two hands extending a rope. It means spirit. It is where we have the intention to draw this spirit into ourselves. This is the origin of all things that connects us to heaven and earth. When our hearts are open and calm, we find the wisdoms and inspirations of spirit. When we are filled with spirit our life is guided by the Tao.

When these three jewels are joined, it is said that our spirit is capable of entering stone and of taking flight. It is also said that when this supreme harmony is full, the sacred sun and moon will illuminate the golden court of our hearts and the body will become youthful and we will have long life.

SHEN TAO - SPIRIT PATH

NOT LAST NIGHT,
NOT THIS MORNING
MELON FLOWERS BLOOMED
BASHO (1644-1694)

THE ART OF ACUPUNCTURE

Acupuncture is an ancient healing art. By intuitively listening to the twelve pulses on a person's wrists, we can begin to understand what is not in balance and harmony for that person. By respectfully and deeply listening to the person, we can begin to understand where the person is in their life and how they might like to change. By using the spirits of the acupuncture points, we can both balance the person's energy as well as help them along their path in life. Each acupuncture point contains a rich source of vital energy that can create opportunities to open a person's life, allowing it to blossom forth with richness. Spiritual five element acupuncture is not about matching a point to a symptom. It is about helping someone to become full of balance and harmony in their energy, so they can stride forward and realize their dreams. When we as acupuncturists help to bring someone back into harmony and balance, this also balances and harmonizes the energy around them. We not only help the person to become happier, but the world as well.

Five element acupuncture is an ancient art of healing the mind, the body and the spirit. A healer will deeply listen to the patient and also sensitively read their twelve Chinese pulses. He or she will then balance that person's energy and give them the acupuncture points of spirit that will help the them to move forward along their path in life. All of the acupuncture points are palaces of energy that are described by the Taoist tales of their Chinese characters. By using these points we not only balance the person's energy but are also able to give them the wonderful healing spiritual energy contained in many of the points. In this way life can then open for the person and they have the energy and courage to change their life.

The ancient Chinese healers knew that when a person suffered an illness or shock it would affect their energy during one of the five seasons, and the corresponding element within that person would be weakened. The cause of this weakness could be an illness, a loss, an accident, an emotional upheaval, a fright, or even a natural disaster like a hurricane or flood. This energetic trauma would cause a weakness in the element within the person of the season in which it happened. This afterwards shows in the person's energetic colour, sound of the voice, odour and emotion. When we support this weakness on the corresponding acupuncture meridians of that element, the person's energy comes back into balance and the person returns to health.

There is a very simple assumption in the theory of spiritual five element acupuncture. This is that at sometime, probably early in life, our energy became imbalanced. This threw our system out of hamony in a certain season. This then produced a weakness in our energetic system. When a person comes to me I can see this in their energetic colour, detect it in the odour, feel it in their energy, and hear it in their voice. If this energetic weakness is not helped it continues to weaken our energy especially in the season when it happened. This weakness is shown in a tint to our energetic colour, in the sound pattern of the voice, in a flavour to our odour, and in an emphasis in certain emotions. For example if the imbalance occurred in the spring, there would be a greenish tint to the energetic skin colour, a shout or lack of shout in the voice, a sharp flavour to the odour and some inappropriate anger. This is not a personality thing but an energetic weakness that we can support with treatment so the person feels whole again. By treating on the two wood meridians of the gallbladder and liver, the energy of the person, with an imbalanced in spring, can be strengthened and brought back into harmony. The person's spirit can be further helped by using the wonderful points on the eight extraordinary meridians, the outer bladder line, and the kidney chest points. This way of treating is both simple and profound in its healing strength and power.

If the seasons of the year are in harmony then spring brings to life the smallest seeds and the world is filled with greenness, the smell of cut grass like sharp souring cheese, the energy of dynamic growth and the shouting voices of a thousand insects. Summer brings sunshine and long days. There is the smell of roasted dried grasses, fields full of beautiful flowers bringing great joy and laughter, birds celebrating with vibrant songs, and the warmth of the heat of hours of full sunlight. The harvest season or late summer brings the rich ripe golden yellow colours of the harvest, the smell of sweet fruits and vegetables at their peak, the soft song of mother earth offering her bounty without reserve to all and the security of knowing there will be food to survive the winter.

RECEIVING SPIRIT

In autumn the cold comes with the north winds and all life goes back into the earth to await the next spring. The leaves turn magnificent colours until they too fall back into the earth to nourish her for the next year. The autumn brings the smell of rotting compost, the sighs of letting go and falling leaves, the whiteness of clear skies and the rich metals in the rains to nourish the soil. The bare limbs of trees open the spaces of the sky, giving inspiration in the sharp clear air. By letting go of each old breath, we breathe in the next moment of absolute newness and find the essence of each moment.

Winter then comes with the rains and the snows. These fill the reserves of springs, rivers, lakes and seas. Without this water the spring seeds will not germinate. Winter brings the smell of water and snow, the odour of rain in the air, blue water in lakes, the constant rushing sound of a river passing by and the freshness of spring water. Winter is the time of drawing inwards and guarding our reserves. It is a time when these resources need to be nourished with warmth and contemplation by meditation, to find our deep inner reserves. Here we can reach the profound mysteries of the depths of our inner spirit in the quiet stillness of winter.

It is out of these natural observations that the Chinese learned to live in harmony within themselves. When one of these seasons was out of harmony within a person, then those colours or smells would also be out of balance and a healer would know by using his senses how to help that season flourish again in that person. When a season itself was out of balance, then the Emperor would go to his tower in the inner gardens of the palace and rest in meditation until he understood what to do, by listening to his heart and allowing it to fill with heavenly wisdom.

When the seasons within us are not in harmony, then our hearts have to struggle and our lives do not have the vitality and freshness of each change of weather. We then become stuck in old patterns and beliefs and cannot flow in harmony with the changes around us. When we are in balance, the hope of a new seed opens each day in spring. The warmth of the summer sun gives joy to relationships. The harvest gives security and balance to our very centre. In autumn we are able to let go of the old and take in the new. In winter our reserves are filled with the energy we need for each endeavour.

When the spring is cold or frosts or floods then the plants are delayed in their growth. In times of drought many seeds will not flower at all in that year. If the spring inside us has been imbalanced, then we may not have the energy to put our plans into action or we may lose the vision of the direction in our lives. Like an old tree we may become covered in old growth and can no longer find the flexibility and vitality of new growth. Each spring gives us the chance to renew our vision. The spring with its freshness inspires us to create the next year. With this direct energy we are able to move forward and our spirit is filled with hope.

If our energetic imbalance occurred in the spring, there would be a greenish tint to the energetic skin colour, a shout or lack of shout in the voice, a sharp flavour to the odour and some inappropriate anger. By treating on the two wood meridians of the liver and gallbladder, the person's energy, which was imbalanced in spring, can be strengthened and brought back into harmony.

When the summer arrives with all of its warmth, longer days and abundance of flowers, there is an ease and fluidity to life. We are able to enjoy our families and others late into the evening. For the Chinese the summer warmth is the time of the heart. It is when the gateways to relationships open with generosity and warmth. When we have this warmth inside, we can love freely and completely. The sun itself gives its warmth to everything that is on the earth. When this warmth comes at the right time then the garden is a splendid display of flowers. This warmth within us needs to be balanced so we can be at the right temperature for each person. If the summer is cold then there will not be as many flowers. If we are too cold then we will distance people and our hearts will not flourish. If we have too much heat then we may overwhelm another with our own needs. With summer sunshine in our heart and with the gateways well oiled, those around us will be filled with love and understanding. Without this sunshine within we lack joy and laughter in our lives and the world clouds over. But when the sun comes out again we are able to see the richness all around us and give love where it is needed with compassion and understanding.

If the imbalance happened in summer, there is either a reddish or greyish tint to the energetic skin colour, a laugh or lack of laugh in the voice, a scorched odour and some inappropriate over joyfulness or lack of joy. The fire element has four meridians. By treating on one pair of the fire meridians, either the heart and small intestine or the heart protector and triple burner, the energy is brought back into balance. If the person has a difficulty sorting the pure from the impure we treat on the heart and small intestine. If the person has difficulty regulating their fire and joy we treat on the heart protector and triple burner.

As the flowers lose their petals and become rich ripe fruits and golden grains, we have a sense of wholeness. This is the harvest season or what the Chinese call late summer. At this time of the year all fruits and vegetables are harvested and stored for the winter. In late summer we have the security and stability of knowing mother earth has provided for our nourishment for the hard winter months. We are taken in her lap and fed with all we need. When the harvest is poor, then there is not enough to share and the distribution becomes uneven. When we are hungry we cannot take in what is all around us. Some will have more than others and there will be fights and arguments. When we are well fed, we are comfortable, and centred. From that centre we can care for ourselves and others with the abundance of the earth.

If the imbalance happened in late summer as the harvest is being brought in, then we can sense a yellow energetic colour on the skin, a sing in the voice, a sweet odour and an inappropriate need for care and sympathy. By treating on the two earth meridians of the stomach and spleen, the energy of the person, whose energy had an imbalance in late summer or the harvest season, can be strengthened and harmonized.

What cannot be used at harvest time decays back into the earth as rich fertile compost. Autumn is a time when the growth of summer dies back into the earth. The skies are no longer shaded by leafy green canopies but reveal the inspirations of the heavens. All the growth of summer needs to sink back into the earth to enrich it for the next year. In this same way we need to let go of what is no longer valuable to find the essence of ourselves. As we let go, then we too can see the sky overhead in its full wonder and be inspired by what life brings. We can let go of all the stale and unuseful air and breathe in the new fresh breezes. Our way becomes inspired and special. Here is our Tien Fu or heavenly palace as the Chinese call our inner essence.

If the imbalance occurred in autumn then there is a white tint to the skin colour, a sigh in the voice, a rotten flavour to the odour and some inappropriate grief. By treating on the two metal meridians of the lungs and large intestine, the energy of the person can be rebalanced.

In winter we retire inside. The Chinese believed we should live in harmony with the five seasons. Winter was a time to conserve reserves and survive the cold. When we can not find our reserves we struggle in our efforts to find our way. The energy is not there when we really need it. When all is flowing within us, we have these deep reserves to draw on and our deep inner drives can be fueled with the force of the waters that fill the reservoirs in winter. It is winter that gives us the time of quiet contemplation within a warm home if we have guarded our reserves well. By meditating in the quiet stillness of winter, we can find and follow the way of our lives. The rivers then will flow and nourish the next flowers of spring.

If the imbalance happened in winter, then there is a blue tint to the energetic skin colour, a continuous groan in the voice, a putrid flavour to the energetic odour and some inappropriate fear or lack of fear. By treating on the two water meridians of the bladder and the kidneys, the energy can be brought back into harmony.

Thousand of years ago the Chinese mapped out the seas and rivers of Qi energy on the human body. If you place your hands facing each other and slightly apart and gently move them back and forth you can feel this energy. This is the energy that creates life and is nourished by all that feeds the body. It is called Qi energy. Although Qi is the energy of life there are many forms of Qi. There is *Tien Qi* or heavenly Qi, *Ren Qi* or the Qi of human life and *Tu Qi* or the Qi of mother earth among many others. Qi flows from the heavens and earth through man creating and nourishing his life. It is through the Qi channels that this energy is constantly flowing while we are alive. It is said all of life is fed by the heavens and earth, the eternal father and mother.

Chinese healers refined their senses and touch until they could feel the channels of energy flowing through the body. The twelve channels can be felt on the left and right wrists. It is said that a master healer can read the life of a person just by feeling the pulses. By seeing the colour on a person's face or by smelling their odour, a healer can know which season is out of balance within a person. Points on those channels are then used to rebalance the energy. Just like a river these channels have bends and turns and pools where the energy gathers. These places of points were each given a spirit name and are used to move energy in various ways to help rebalance a person's inner seasons. This can be done in many ways. For example it can be done by using needles or pressure or gentle tapping or with plants or by calling on the spirit of the point itself, or by meditating on a point.

When we take the twelve pulses we are listening to what each pulse has to say. The heart maybe unhappy and strained, the stomach maybe full and happy just having had lunch, the liver maybe unsettled and frustrated at not having a clear plan, the large intestine may not be able to let go of a problem. By intuitively listening to the pulses and not judging them we are able to deeply listen to the strains and flows of a person's energy. We can then ask the questions that will encourage the person to help us in deciding which points they need for the next step in their lives. By taking in the sound, colour, odour and emotion we can know which paired meridians will bring harmony to the imbalanced element of the person.

All the changes of the season were felt to stimulate, subdue, tonify or sedate one's natural life force. It was both how a person lived and the changes in nature that affected his health. Life for the Chinese was not fragmented but a part of everything else. If we move along the path nature has given, then life is full and harmonious. When all is in harmony and balance with the universe then there will be health, but if there is imbalance, then injury and weakness can occur. The ancient

Chinese mapped out the body into seas, river and points that naturally provided health by bringing balance and harmony of the Qi energy of each individual As healers we use our senses to hear, smell, see and feel the imbalance and then use certain points to help re-establish the harmony that has been lost. The Emperor himself would go deep into his palace gardens and meet the gods in quiet contemplation until he could hear in his heart how to keep his kingdom in harmony and balance for the next year. When we as healers listen carefully we can hear how to bring the person who comes to us back into balance in their lives.

> *The difficulties of winter and autumn,*
> *The heat of summer, and spring's changes*
> *Are the spirit of life*
> *Winds, clouds and lightening*
> *All these help to make distinctions clear*
> *So the dust coloured earth*
> *May bring forth all it holds in its heart*
> *Whether ruby or dull stone.*
> **MEVLANA JELALUDDIN RUMI**

火
FIRE

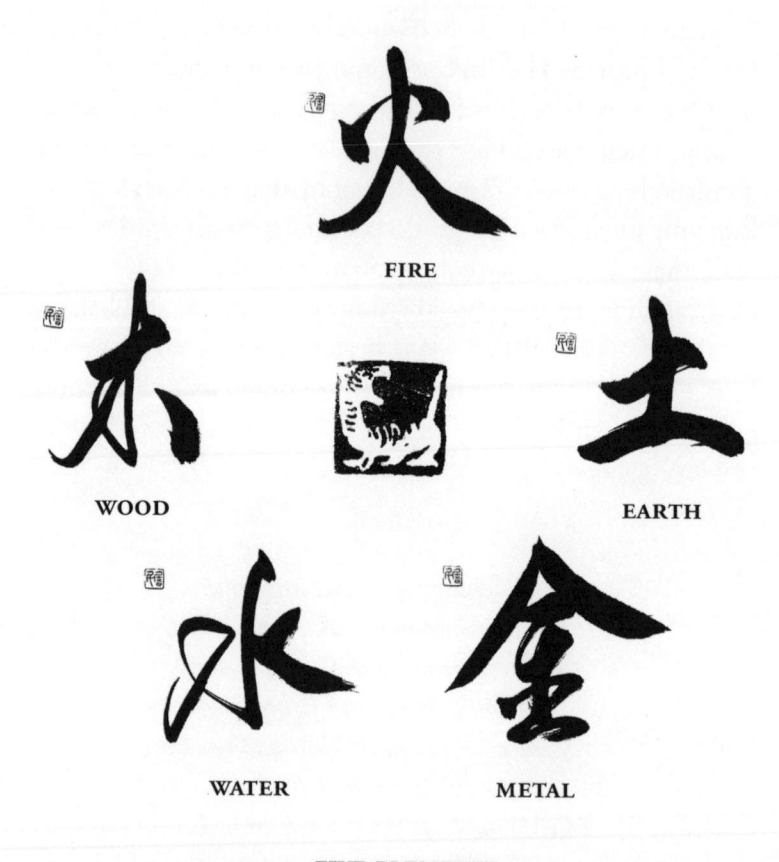

木　　　土
WOOD　　　**EARTH**

水　　　金
WATER　　　**METAL**

FIVE ELEMENTS

The world is ruled by letting things take their course
It cannot be ruled by interfering.
LAO TZU

SPIRITUAL
FIVE ELEMENT THEORY

People come to us because their lives are uncomfortable. This maybe a physical illness, an emotional depression, or some other dis-ease in their life. They know themselves what they need to tell us. So we simply listen to what they need to tell us and sometimes ask questions to help us understand better what they are saying. At the same time we are looking for the colour, sound, odour and emotion that is out of balance and displaying itself to us. If we try too hard we miss what our senses are telling us. Sometimes it is not until people are on the couch that they reveal what is really deeply troubling them and we can sense the imbalanced element.

When people lie on the couch I give them a minute to relax and sink into the soft couch and its support. I then gently take their hand and begin to read their pulses. This is a deep listening to their spirit. What does their heart feel? How is the vision of their liver? Is the stomach well fed or empty? Are the lungs able to breathe in fresh inspiration or is the large intestine unable to let go? How are their ancestral reserves of the kidneys? Each of the twelve pulses gives a wonderful energetic story of the person if we listen carefully. We are there to bring harmony and balance to the pulses. So we listen to hear if there are blocks between the pulses. This is where one pulse is pounding because the gateway is hardly open into the next pulse on the daily cycle of energy, and this next pulse has hardly anything in it. We listen to the spirit of the person to see if they are full of life or if there is a cloud over all that they do. Sometimes the person is not there because something has possessed them. In this case there is no sparkle in the eyes and the person does not seem to be at home.

Taking in all this information, we then decide where we start on the protocol of five element treatment. The first thing that would be done is possession if the person is possessed. Possession is a deep disturbance in the energy of the person that acts as an invading force that the person has to struggle against. When we look into a person's eyes we can see if their spirit is clouded over with this possession, or if it is still shining through their eyes. When the possession is cleared we do an aggressive energy drain.

If they are not possessed, we then start with an aggressive energy drain. This usually is just done once unless there is a subsequent shock or there has been a long gap in treatment. Aggressive energy is when the flow of Qi energy becomes polluted in one or more of the yin organs. It can occur when there is a severe shock or repeated battering to the energy. This can then spread to the other yin organs. An aggressive energy drain is a check to see if the energy of the yin organs are clear. It clears the energy of any sediment. When the energy is clear, we can then move it cleanly through the system. We always do an aggressive energy drain in the first treatment.

We then check for blocks. These can be entry/exit blocks, husband/wife blocks, ren mai/du mai blocks, or akabanis. We then clear any blocks. If there are no blocks then we look at the spirit. If the spirit needs support we can use the kidney chest points, the outer bladder line points or the extraordinary meridian points. If the spirit is well, we may look at points to enhance it or open a person's life further.

We then treat on the two paired meridians of one of the elements, where, because of sound, colour, odour and emotion, we feel the original imbalance is. The points on each of the paired meridians supply us with all the possibilities for treating any symptom. Normally we end the treatment with points on the lower arms and hands or the lower legs and feet depending on the meridian. These elemental points give a good grounding to the treatment. Let us now look at each of these areas in more detail.

Below is a summary of the treatment protocol.
Check pulses and determine if there is possession.
Clear possession if it is there.
Clear aggressive energy on everyone in the first treatment
Check pulses again and clear any other blocks to energy.
Check pulses again and choose points to help the person
  open their lives by supporting the spirit using points
  on the eight extraordinary meridians,
  outer bladder line points and kidney chest points.
Ground the treatment with points on the paired
  meridians of the elemental imbalance.
Remember each point is a rich palace of spiritual energy.
For possession and aggressive energy we sedate
For anything else we use moxa and tonify
  Except in the rare case when energy is excessive

RECEIVING SPIRIT

PULSES

We take the hand of our patient with tenderness, respect, and compassion. We embrace them with our love and offer them our entire attention. We then listen with the utmost care to their pulses. There is nothing more important at that point in time than listening to the twelve pulses and giving the patient the fullness of our understanding.

We listen to the general energy flow. Is there an agitation over the pulses? This could be stress, medication or emotional difficulties. We allow our fingers to feel the quantity in each pulse. Are there blocks between the meridians along the wei cycle. The wei cycle is the optimum time cycle for all the elements. For example the heart works best from 11AM-1PM. It is followed by the small intestine from 1PM-3PM, etc.. This cycle tells us the order in which the meridians follow each other and feed energy into each other. We check the pulses to see if the heart and small intestine are pounding, while the bladder and kidneys have nothing in them. If this is the case we open the gates of the fire meridians with small intestine 19, *Ting Gong* and open the gates of the water meridians with bladder 1, *Jing Ming*. This is called an Entry/Exit block. Another kind of block occurs when the right hand pulses are pounding and the left hand pulses are empty. This is a Husband/Wife block. If there nothing in the system then this is a block between the Ren Mai and Du Mai meridians. When these blocks occur we simply clear them and then listen to the pulses again.

We also listen to each pulse in a qualitative way. Is the heart full of quiet calm energy, or is it agitated or empty? Is the small intestine sorting well or is it unable to make good decisions? Are the kidneys full of rich energetic movement and good ancestral reserves, or have they lost their vitality? These questions and more we ask as we listen intently to what the pulses have to say.

Each of us needs to develop our own way of describing the pulses as we develop our sensitivity and understanding. We need to listen and not judge the qualities that each of the pulses is giving us. In this way we truly listen to the soul of the person. When we have emptied ourselves of all presumptions, then, it is then, and only then, that we truly hear another's energy and understand why it is not in balance. It is said masters read a lifetime in the pulses. This listening is healing in itself. We are listening for this energetic history. If we try and listen to specific characteristics, we may miss what is truly being asked for. We must empty ourselves so water flows freely through us and the winds imprint their messages on our hearts.

Should the patient respond to your listening with a question or a comment, then ask them more about what they have felt and discovered within themselves. This is their deep inner voice helping you to understand what they need to heal themselves. By listening we are able, through the choice of acupuncture points, to help nature and the person themselves return to health and balance. We too can ask them questions. What shocked your heart? How do you see the future? Where do you feel your reserves have gone? How are you nourished? What inspires you? In this way our understanding deepens.

When the patient first enters the room, we may still slide into assumptions. But when we touch the pulses, we have the opportunity to let go and really listen.

POSSESSION

Chinese acupuncture comes from an ancient shamanic tradition, and there is the belief that ill health may come from external forces, such as the weather, a ghost, or even negative wishes. Ill health internally may come from over indulging in food, drugs, late nights and other stresses. It may also come from worry, depression, a sudden loss, a wandering spirit or an emotional shock. Somehow the mind, body and spirit has become imbalanced and ill health is the result. Often if the person learns how to live with moderation in all things, and brings stillness back to their heart so their *shen* spirits return, the balance of life also returns. Sometimes, however, there are external forces that have shocked the system excessively or there are internal difficulties that have attached themselves and more intervention is needed. When the illness or shock is great, the system can become overwhelmed by negative energy that is very draining on the person's spirit. In this instance, the person may struggle greatly to even be present with an emptiness in the mind, body and spirit. Sometimes it is as if the person is not actually there at times. It is as though the imbalance or external or internal force has taken possession of part of the person. Then what happens is that a person has to struggle against this invasive energy while still trying to be present in their ordinary lives. The struggle can sometimes be overwhelming. Fortunately the Chinese healers knew that this possession could occur and developed a way of calling in the dragons to chase out this invasive energy.

First a series of points are used to activate the internal dragons to clear anything internally. The needles are placed in the points, right and then left and turned counterclockwise to drain the energy. After we sense that the energy has cleared or lightened, then the needles are tonified, left and then right and turned clockwise. If the brightness of the eyes has not returned and there is a sense that something is still there, the external dragons are sent in to clear the external energies.

INTERNAL DRAGONS

The internal dragons heal with earth energy by energizing the follow points: the master point, a tear drop below REN MAI 15, *Jui Wei*, dove tail, ST25, *Tian Shu*, heavenly pivot, ST32, *Fu Tu*, Swift flexible hare, and ST41, *Jie Xi*, released stream.

The first point, REN MAI 15 is *Jui Wei* or the loving protection of the dove. The Chinese regard the sternum as being in the shape of a dove. It is believed that the dove protects her young with peace and love. *Jui Wei* is the tail of the dove. The dove is a bird of spirit. The ancients often talked to birds and would ask for their wisom and insights. *Jui Wei* is a place of loving protection. *Jui* is drawn as the number nine and a bird with a long tail. It is said that this turtle dove produces nine young and protects them with love, peace and tranquility. They grow in her safe, warm nest of security. *Wei* is made of a body and a tail, meaning a tail, end, extremity and behind. Here is a very protected place, and sacred space, to contact the unwanted spirit and send it on to where it will find peace. The Chinese say that we find love when we again become part of the Tao and find our inner home. This love is said to be our greatest protection. So by activating this point we are helping the person to again be in touch with that wholeness within, which was disrupted by whatever happened. A dove tail is also a joint made between two pieces of wood. It is so well fitted that changes in the weather never affect the joint. The sternum protects our heart and lungs, our emotions and our inspirations. From this safe, snug, well fitting place, our spirit can take wing and fly again.

ST25 is called *Tian Shu*, meaning to pivot with the heavens. Here we contact the heavenly beings to help clear our spirit. *Tian Shu* is the axis of a central point that turns with the heavens. This is the axis of our earth within, where we can turn in harmony with the heavens in the same way the earth turns through the heavens to create each beautiful day. With this flexibility, we can see all around and move through the seasons in balance. When we can't go the old way any longer, this point gives us the strength and security of earth so our lives can pivot in a new direction. It is said that when we reach the limit of one way, we have to pivot in a new direction. *Tian Shu* is this great pivot in perfect balance with the heavens. *Tian* is drawn as a mature man who is reaching for the heavens, signified by a line drawn above him. The heavens are a vast expanse of space that govern and inspire mankind. It means the highest of all things, nature, sky, heaven, the seasons, weather, celestial and the Supreme Being. *Shu* is drawn as wood and to dispose of, or stow things away. *Shu* means pivot, axis, the central point and fundamental. Here we can move in a new direction, to rediscover flexibility and stability so we can move easily where life takes us.

ST32, *Fu Tu*, means the hiding hare of swift flexibility. A hare has a great nose to sniff out danger. With great speed, it can out run its enemies and hide. It knows the wisdom of living together in a group and has the humility to run when it needs to save itself. Its thigh offers great strength, flexibility and movement. Here we can refind strength and movement to untangle the snares of being caught. *Fu Tu* is a humble yielding hare who can hide with great swiftness and flexibility. *Fu* is drawn as a man and a dog. It symbolizes a man imitating a dog by crouching down. It means to lie, prostrate, hide, humble, yield, suffer, lie in ambush, conceal and secret. *Tu* is drawn as a hare squatting down with its tail perked upwards. It means a rabbit or hare. Here we become alert, enabling us to sense danger. At this point we are able to bounce through life with vibrant instincts and a keen sense of when everything is alright, and when it is not.

ST41, *Jie Xi*, means to untie the flow force of a mountain stream. It has the warmth of the sun that ripens the harvest on earth. Fire is the mother of earth, feeding her with great loving warmth so the harvest can mature and ripen. This is the fire point of the meridian where warmth and love can flow into relationships, supporting life with love and understanding.

RECEIVING SPIRIT

Here the streams of sunshine bring the fruits to ripeness. With this warmth, we too can mature and flow towards ripened thoughts, ideas and feelings. When we are cared for and warm within, then we have the maturity and stability to move outward, offering what we have harvested to others. In this way, we are able to flow like a revitalized stream full of warm sunlight. *Jie Xi* is a free flowing mountain stream, vibrantly moving through a ravine. Here we feel the warmth rushing through us, bringing joy and a rich harvest. *Ji* is drawn as a horn and a bodkin. Bodkins were used for untying knots. It means to get rid of, to get free from, to loosen, to divide, to solve, to undo, to untie and to release. *Xi* is drawn as water and a person who works threads. It means a mountain stream, a torrent, a creek, a ravine, a rivulet, a small valley, and a deep gorge. Here warmth and nourishment can again flow with free abandonment, allowing our hearts to blossom with love.

When these seven points are used, the seven internal dragons come to the person in support, chasing out the invading energies and sending them onwards to the light.

EXTERNAL DRAGONS

The external dragons heal with heavenly energy and the vibrant cleansing energy of water. They consist of the following points: DU MAI 20, *Bai Hui*, meaning the meeting of grand unity, BL11, *Da Zhu* meaning the great important weaving of the shuttle, BL23, *Shen Shu* meaning the vital transfer of energy to the kidneys and BL61, *Pu Can*, meaning to serve with counsel.

SPIRITUAL FIVE ELEMENT THEORY

Du Mai 20, *Bai Hui*, is the grand meeting of unity. The Tao is a part of everything and this is the meeting place of all the meridians. It is the point between posterior and anterior, the yin and the yang, and the light and the dark. It is where all things can be directed from the one Tao and become whole. Here is where all the rivers and seas of energy can be directed, and guided, from the original source of life. The grand unity for the Chinese is the number one hundred, called *Bai*, and drawn as the number one over the sun. *Hui* is a meeting of words brought together and is drawn as words under a roof. It means to meet, assemble, collect, co-operate, to understand and to be in the habit of. *Bai Hui* is a place that calls on the wisdom of the ancients to bring the entire life of the person back into harmony where all is again working together. This place, where the ancestors reside, is the point at the top of the head nearest to the heavens, which directs and inspires all life. In ancient times the Emperor would go to the gods and his ancestors at times of upheaval, or natural disasters, for advice and to pray for harmony and balance to return. This is just such a place, to visit in times of extreme disharmony to open a person's own inner wisdom, recreating the calm and harmony of balance within. It is this unity that we need when our external energy has been invaded.

BL11, *Da Zhu*, is a great and important weaving of a shuttle. When a tapestry is woven, a shuttle is used to weave the patterns of design. It is the shuttle that guides and creates the details that will weave the overall picture of the tapestry. Here our way in life can be woven in harmony with the cycles and patterns of life. This point is both the vision and organization of the inner bladder line, which contains the points having direct contact with each of the vital organs. Here is the first opening along that line of points of a delicate network of Qi that is both able to rejuvenate and revitalize each organ. This offers the movement and force of a shuttle, which is able to weave dynamic patterns that enrich the working cycles and patterns of the organs so their efforts work in harmony. *Da Zhu* is an important full shuttle, receiving the influences and enriching their working cycles. *Da* is drawn as a grown man standing upright with the stature of an adult. It means to make great, full grown, extensive, vast, important, eminent, best in quality, noble, elder, tall and great. *Shu* is drawn as wood and an object. It means a work of masonry, the movement of a shuttle and the shuttle of a loom. Here is a quality of movement that is all encompassing, great and important, enabling the organs to create the cycles necessary for a balanced life, enriching the working cycles of the meridians.

BL23, *Shen Shu*, is the vital transfer point to the kidneys. The Chinese believe that from the spirit of the Tao, and the generative essences of our parents, the kidneys are created, which then create all the other organs and elements of the new embryo. This point is on the extraordinary meridian of the Dai Mai. The Dai Mai circulates the pattern of life, bringing all the meridians into harmony with each other. It keeps the movement of life well arranged so it functions in a well ordered and balanced way, like a sheep dog looking after its sheep. It brings together the connections and relationships of all the meridians so they act for the same purpose. It harmonizes the five elements, both within and without. The kidneys are the energetic movers of the vitality of water that is needed for every cell of the body. They are the inner powerhouse, out of which comes will, purpose, vitality and strength. Within the kidneys, lie our source of ancestral inheritance that can be drawn on in times of endurance. *Shen Shu* is where direct contact can be made with this vitality.

Shen is drawn as flesh and a minister who is under the hand of his prince, lord or master. In ancient times slaves were not just ordinary workers, but often skilled men and women who were of great use to the Emperor. They served him and his ministers well, equipped with acquired knowledge and abilities, as well as their inherited knowledge. Our inheritance is what we are given by our lord. With it, we can serve life itself with the wholeness of our goodness and abilities. Here we are filled with virtue, experience and knowledge. This is where our deepest reserves are found, directing life and revitalizing the spirit. *Shen* means the kidneys. *Shu* is drawn as a small boat or primitive barge that is going upstream and being united. Here is a uniting transfer of energy. It means to report to a superior, to submit, to exhaust, to lose, an offering, to bring what is due, to introduce, to transport, a vital transfer and a transporting movement. It is a place of direct communication with the kidneys, bringing the vitality of inherited energy and energetic movement to the other organs so that all is in harmony again with the five seasons.

RECEIVING SPIRIT

BL61, *Pu Can*, means to serve with counsel. This point is on the extraordinary meridian of the Yang Qiao Mai. This meridian enables energy to run from the earth, through our body, to the heavens in the same way growth naturally takes place. This dynamic growth and movement brings our inner being into harmony with the outer world. This meridian helps the other meridians to follow the cycles of the seasons, night and day, and the year so we are well nourished and maintained in all the rhythms of life. In this way a vital, powerful and graceful dancing movement comes out of the constantly changing flow of life's energies. Here we can receive nature in all her influences and be enriched in their endlessly changing cycles. By receiving and serving, we can hear the flight of stars and glimpse their pathways. We can see the growth of the earth and grow ourselves through those changes.

Pu Can is to serve oneself to the counsel of the stars and to penetrate their wisdom. To serve is to follow, and to follow is to see that both misfortune and good fortune are a part of life, and equally rich in wisdom. Through both, we can learn to understand and utilize what comes our way. If we can follow the cycles of the Tao like a trusted friend, then we will never be lost in the cycle of happiness and disaster. *Pu* is drawn as a man, two hands and branches. It is a servant who gathers twigs in order to make a faggot. It means someone who serves, oneself, a driver, a servant and a slave. *Can* is drawn as wings under three stars of a constellation. It means to penetrate, to blend, to mix, aid, to consult together, to counsel, and a group of three. By serving, we can find the counsel and aid of heaven, and follow the invisible threads of the guidance of the heavenly influences above.

When these seven points are activated, the seven external dragons appear and chase out the invasive energies, transforming them back into light energy.

If we do not want to needle the points, artemesia vulgaris can be called upon to energize each point via moxa. We can also use crystals and acupressure or call on the spirits of the points themselves. A shaman simply grabs hold of the entity and pulls it out. Journeying to the entity can help but the patient then needs back-up by clearing the internal organs and bringing the spirit back to life so they are no longer vulnerable to such an influence. Clearing and re-energizing the internal organs can also be done with Qigong exercises such as the Eight Brocades. Supporting the spirit to return to a natural state of vitality can also be enhanced by the patient committing to a regular spiritual practice that they enjoy.

AGGRESSIVE ENERGY DRAIN

We clear aggressive energy after possession. If there is no possession we begin the first treatment with an aggressive energy drain. In Chinese medicine we have what is called the Ko cycle or the cycle of how the elements control each other. For example the wood element controls the earth by keeping her soil held in her roots. Earth controls water by keeping water within her banks. Water controls fire by keeping it at the right temperature. Fire controls metal by heating it and allowing it to take what form it needs. Metal controls wood by being able to cut it back when it needs to be. If Earth can not hold water then water gets out of control and the system starts to break down. In the same way if our earth element within becomes weak our water element can become out of control and the energy begins to go the wrong way around the system. This is when aggressive energy forms. When we die one of the elements in our system breaks down and then the others follow back through the Ko cycle in the opposite direction so everything loses control until the body no longer functions.

Checking for aggressive energy is a very simple and very profound treatment. If there is no possession we start with the aggressive energy drain. We go directly to the yin shu points on the back. The yang organs are constantly moving body fluids through the system so naturally clear any energy. The yin organs are more inner and are likely to contain any energy that is not flowing in its natural cycle. To clear this energy we simply place needles very shallowly, first left and then right, into BL13, the lung shu point, *Fei Shu*, BL14, the heart protector shu point, *Jue Yin Shu*, BL15, the heart shu point, *Xin Shu*, BL18, the liver shu point, *Gan Shu*, BL20, the spleen shu point, *Pi Shu*, and BL23, the kidney shu point, *Shen Shu*. If there is 'muddy' energy in any of these organs it shows as a redness around the needle. We also place a test needle somewhere nearby that is not on a point to check for the natural redness reaction of the skin. We then simply wait until the redness goes which clears this energy. We then remove the needles. This is a treatment that should be used in all traditions of acupuncture as it clears the energy so when we move energy it is pure and vital. Normally we only need to do it in the first treatment.

ENERGETIC BLOCKS
REN MAI/DU MAI

This is an energy block between the Ren Mai and Du Mai meridians. The Ren Mai is the sea of our inner yin energy. The Du Mai is the guiding governor of all the meridians. If there is a block in these two meridians it means that there is no energy coming from these two seas of energy into the twelve ordinary meridians. This means that when we feel the pulses there is hardly any energy in any of the pulses. This block is cleared by needling and tonifying the following points left and then right in the following order, REN MAI 1, *Hui Yin*, the meeting of the inner seas of vitality, REN MAI 24, *Cheng Jiang*, receiving the rich broth of life, DU MAI 1, *Chang Qiang*, a vigorous thrust of energy and then DU MAI 28, *Yin Jiao*, the river mouth crossing into the sea. When this is done then once again the oceans of yin at *Hui Yin* flow into the mouth receiving fluids of *Cheng Jiang*, which flow into the great strength of *Chang Qiang* that flows into *Yin Jiao* or the crossing of all rivers. After needling, the energy is able to flow into all the other meridians both nourishing them with what they need as well as directing them from our utmost source of vitality.

HUSBAND/WIFE BLOCK

When all the right hand pulses are pounding and there is nothing in the left hand pulses then this is what is called

RECEIVING SPIRIT

a Husband/Wife imbalance. The left hand pulses being the husband and the right hand pulses being the wife. In order to bring them back into balance we draw energy from the right side back to the left side. We do this by using the following points. We needle left to right and tonify each of the points in the following order.

BL67, *Zhi Yin*, meaning to reach our inner nature, which is the metal point of the bladder meridian drawing energy from metal on the right side pulses into the water element on the left hand side of the pulses.

KI 7, *Fu Liu*, meaning to return to the constantly flowing currents of life, which is the metal point of the kidney meridian drawing energy from metal on the right side pulses into the water element on the left hand side of the pulses.

KI3, *Tai Xi*, meaning the strength, stability and source of a great forceful torrent, which is the earth point of the kidney meridian drawing energy from the earth pulses on the right into the water pulse of the left.

LIV4, *Zhong Feng*, meaning the middle or essence of our inner seal, which is the metal point of the liver meridian drawing energy from the metal pulses on the right into the wood pulses on the left.

SI4, *Wang Ku*, meaning the flexibility of the wrist and our inner structure, which is the source point of the small intestine used to bring stability back to the fire element.

HT7, *Shen Men*, means the gateway of spirit, filling the heart with love. It is the source point of the heart that brings stability and harmony to the mind body and spirit.

SPIRITUAL FIVE ELEMENT THEORY

ENTRY/EXIT BLOCKS

In Chinese medicine there is what is called the Chinese Clock. This is the optimum time in each day when each of the organs functions best. The heart functions best between 11H-13H, the small intestine from 13H-15H, the bladder from 15H-17H, the kidneys from 17H-19H, the heart protector from 19H-21H, the *san jiao* or triple burner from 21H-23H, the gallbladder from 23H-1H, the liver from 1H-3H, the lungs from 3H-5H, the large intestine from 5H-7H, the stomach from 7H-9H, and the spleen from 9H-11H. This cycle is also the cycle for entry/exit blocks. These blocks occur between the elements. So if the stomach and spleen pulses are pounding and there is nothing in the heart and small intestine pulses then there is a block between earth and fire. To clear this we tonify the exit points of the small intestine and then tonify the entry points of the heart.

If the metal pulses are pounding and there is nothing in the stomach pulses then there is probably a block between the large intestine and stomach meridians. In this case we needle left to right and tonifying the exit points of the large intestine, LI20, *Ying Xiang*, and then the entry points of the stomach, ST1, *Cheng Qi*. Then once again the welcome fragrances and rich compost of autumn nourish the earth. Here the enriching nutrients of *Ying Xiang* flow into the receiving mouth of *Cheng Qi*.

If the earth pulses are pounding and there is nothing in the fire pulses of the heart and small intestine then we needle left to right and tonify the exit points of the spleen meridian, SP21,

Da Bao and then the entry points of the heart meridian, HT1, *Ji Quan*. Then, once again, the great enveloping nourishment of the spleen contained in *Da Bao* can flow again into the heart's utmost source at *Ji Quan*.

If the fire pulses of the heart and small intestine are pounding but there is nothing in the pulses on the water element, then we needle left to right and tonify the exit points of the small intestine meridian, SI19, *Ting Gong*, and then the entry points of the bladder meridian, BL1, *Jing Ming*. Then once again the purity and understanding of love in the listening palace of treasures of *Ting Gong* can again flow and nourish the reserves of the bladder so we can see with great brightness at *Jing Ming* translated as eyes full of illumination.

If the water pulses are pounding but there is nothing in the pulses of the heart protector and the *san jiao* or triple burner (these pulses are the right wrist medial pulses), then we needle left to right and tonify the exit points of the kidney meridian, KI22, *Bu Lang*, and then the entry points of the heart protector meridian, PC1, *Tian Chi* (for men) or PC2, *Tian Quan* (for women). Then, once again, the vitality of the kidneys at *Bu Lang* or the refreshment of the garden courtyard can flow into *Tian Chi* or *Tian Quan* the reservoir and spring of heavenly wisdom and love.

If the heart protector and *san jiao* or triple burner are pounding but there is nothing in the pulses of the gallbladder and liver, then we needle left to right and tonify the exit points of the *san jiao* or triple burner meridian, TB22, *He Liao*, and then the entry points of the gallbladder meridian, GB1, *Tong*

Zi Liao. Then, once again, the harmony of warmth and love of *He Liao*, the singing bone of harmony can again flow into *Tong Zi Liao* or the bone of fresh innocent eyes that brings the vision and newness of springtime.

If the wood pulses are pounding but there is nothing in the metal pulses, then we needle left to right and tonify the exit points of the liver meridian, LI14, *Qi Men*, and then the entry points of the lung meridian, LU1, *Zhong Fu*. Then, once again, the gateway of expectation and hope of *Qi Men* can flow into the middle palace of heaven or *Zhong Fu* and we are taken by the hand of our heavenly father and can feel his support and love.

If there is a difference between the meridians of the same element we can use the junction point or luo points of the two meridians to bring balance back. We simply tonify the points in the order of the Chinese clock. This however is rare.

AKABANIS

Akabani points are the entry or exit points at the ends or beginnings of the meridians on the fingers and toes. We check to see if the two sides of a single meridian are in balance by waving a moxa stick across these points just above the surface of the skin and counting the number of crossings. If the crossing are about the same the two sides of the same meridian are in balance. If they differ, for example if we find the left side of ST45 is five passes and the right side of ST45 is twenty passes we simply tonify the junction or luo point on the deficient side or the one with twenty passes.

RECEIVING SPIRIT

POINTS FOR SPIRIT AND THE ELEMENTAL IMBALANCE

Once any blocks have been cleared we can then begin to move the person's Qi into harmony and build up its reserves by using the spirit points of the kidneys, the outer bladder line, and the eight extraordinary meridians. These points we use with anyone. For example we may see the person has suffered over a long time so we may use KI24 *Ling Xu*, the wild lands of spirit to bring the spirit back to life. KI24 is the wild lands of spiritual power where our inner being and our spirit can be revived. It is said that if one practices Tai Qi or calligraphy, they bring the Tao into oneself just as the heavenly rains fall to earth and penetrate her with heavenly nourishment. When calligraphy is done with grace and presence, it is then that it shows a vitality with un-erring movement. When this happens, it is said that *Ling*, or spirit, has entered the person. *Ling* is drawn as rain falling from the heavens into the mouths of three shaman women who are dancing between heaven and earth. They are offering their prayers to heaven in order to bring the rain of prosperity to the earth. In this way, our spirit is within the harmonies of the heavens. It means spiritual, mysterious, supernatural, power, transcendence, marvelous, spiritual, divine, the power of a medium and ingenious. *Xu* is the wild lands of nature. This point contains a rich resource of energy that is able to deeply rejuvenate the spirit when the way of life has been hard.

If we see the person has some reserves but needs a resource of support for their spirit we may use KI25, *Shen Cang*, the treasure house of spirit. When someone is feeling well and are ready to open at another level we may use KI26 *Yu Zhong*, the center of elegance. If someone's vitality is lacking we may go to the outer bladder line and use BL46(51), *Huang Men*, the gateway to the vital centre. If someone really needs nourishing we may use BL45(50) *Wei Cang*, the golden granary of the stomach. If someone needs a lot of energy we may use REN MAI 6 *Qi Hai*, the sea of abundantly flowing Qi. If we need to nourish the spirit and feed it we may use REN MAI 8, *Shen Que*, the inner gateway tower of spirit. These are only some of the choices we have on all the extraordinary meridians, outer bladder line and kidney chest points talked about later.

We then ground this with the wonderful points on the paired elemental meridians where the original imbalance is. If the person is a wood elemental imbalance, and it is spring we may want to use the wood points, GB41 *Zu Lin Qi* or to walk out of winter's tears into spring and LIV1 *Da Dun*, the fullness of good esteem. These two points will balance and harmonize the wood element and bring good health back to the person. It maybe in talking to the person that their heart fires are low and we may want to go to the fire points. Or it maybe that their confidence and sense of themselves is not there and we may want to use one of the metal points on the wood meridians. We go to the points on the meridians where the elemental imbalance is, to more quickly and effectively bring back balance to the entire system, by supporting where it became imbalanced in the first place.

To summarize we clear possession if it is there first of all. We then clear aggressive energy after possession or as the first treatment. We then clear any other blocks. After this, the spirit is supported with KI24 or other spirit points on the extraordinary meridians, the outer bladder line or the kidney chest points. We then go to the meridians of the elemental imbalance and choose the points that will help bring balance to the pulses and the person's life. In the first treatment this is often the source points. The source points give the person exactly what they need at that point in time. GB40, *Qiu Xu* means a wilderness tumulus. This point brings the vibrant energy of spring and fresh vision to all the decision making of the gallbladder. Here we can see all viewpoints as we look over the wholeness of life. LIV3, *Tai Chong* means a supreme rushing forward. Here is the vision of our life moving us forward with flexibility and courage. HT7, *Shen Men* is the gateway of spirit. At this point we can find the nourishing love that brings security and stability to the tender feelings of the heart. This love deeply touches our spirit. SI4, *Wang Ku* means the flexibility of the wrist bone. Here in the depth of our bones we can find the clarity, structure, distinction and flexibility to respond to what life brings. We see clearly what is useful and what is not.

PC7, *Da Ling* means a great important ancient tumulu. This is a meeting place of our ancestors who can be called upon to protect our hearts and give us guidance. It fills us with warmth, love and protection. TB4, *Yang Chi* means a sunfilled pool of yang. Here we have the warmth and yang energy we need to resource our lives with the fullness of fire's loving embrace. ST42, *Chong Yang* means the rush of the warmth and movement of the sun. Here we are filled with the nourishment of earth and given a full harvest that gives us the stability and care we need. SP3, *Tai Bai* means the great movement of pure clear energy. Here we have a full granary of energy to nourish our mind, body and spirit. LU9, *Tai Yuan* mean a supremely profound pool. Here we are filled with the fresh breaths of the inspirations of life. LI4, *He Gu* means a valley of united harmony. This is the source of the great letting go ability of the large intestines. BL64, *Jing Gu* means the bone of the empire. Here are the resources, vitality and force of water bringing fluidity to life. KI3, *Tai Xi* means a great forceful torrent. Here are the inherited reserves and dynamic vitality of the kidneys. I find if I am on the correct element these points bring a full stength to the pulses. In subsequent treatments I choose the points that will help the person in their life. These are explored in the following chapters.

This way of working gives us a wonderful and creative way of choosing points to support and help someone to grow into a richer and fuller life. After we give the person each point, we check the pulses and slowly build up the openness, ease and harmony between the pulses so everything comes into harmony and balance. It is like taking the patient on a journey to support their life. They move from being anxious, distracted, or dull into a space that is rich, mature and full of potential. This is the difference from just treating symptoms to engaging with the person and helping them to be the fullness of who they are, with the energetic resources they need to blossom.

奇經八脈

EIGHT EXTRAORDINARY MERIDIANS

THE MOON ABIDING IN THE MIDST OF SERENE MIND,
BILLOWS BREAK INTO LIGHT.
DOGEN

SUPPORTING SPIRIT EIGHT EXTRAORDINARY MERIDIANS

The eight extraordinary meridians are responsible for the development of the embryo before birth. They give life its primitive vital structure and act as the oceans that both guide and energize the twelve ordinary meridians. These twelves ordinary meridians come into action when we are born giving us harmony and balance as we grow and develop in the world surrounding us. The Chinese believe that there is something invisible that guides life. It is called the Tao. This path or way of life is full of a constant flow of mysteries if we choose to listen carefully. The eight extraordinary meridians are said to be guided by this breath of nature. These are like the eight winds who are said to be the spirit guides of the Tao. The eight extraordinary meridians come from a deeper more ancient source of energy that directs and organizes the yin and yang of the body and its five elements.

The twelve ordinary meridians are constantly protected and resourced from this older part of life expressed in the eight extraordinary meridians. Here lies the organizational power that gives the twelve ordinary meridians their structure, stability and resources so they can flow well by being perfectly linked to each other and the seasons. It is from the deep inner sources of the eight extraordinary meridians that the twelve ordinary meridians can be guided to work in harmony with each other, the original source of the Tao, the cycles of life, and the natural seasons.

Any of the points on any of these meridians can be used to help a person move further and deeper into their lives. For example we might use Du Mai 4, the gate of life when a young person is looking for a direction in life. We might use Du Mai 13, kiln path when someone needs more passion in life. We might use Ren Mai 6, sea of chi when someone is in need of a great resource of energy. Each of these points is serving us each day, but at times we may need to call on the spirit of one of the points of the eight extraordinary meridians to help a person open and resource their life. Let us begin by looking at the Ren Mai in more detail in this context.

REN MAI, THE VESSEL OF CONCEPTION

When the sperm and egg unite to form a new and unique embryo, the Ren Mai comes into being to nourish this new life. It nourishes and forms the organs of the body. It is like an inner sea, out of which life is formed and nourished. It is a sea of energy that both creates and feeds our inner resources so life is balanced and whole. It is the regulator and protector of all the yin meridians. It creates, nourishes, protects and regulates our inner energy. It is a sea that feeds the other meridians with life and energy like a rich warm loving mother's milk. It also brings unity and harmony to the entire mind, body and spirit. When we need this profound unity and nourishment, the points along this meridian can be called upon to bring great reserves and harmony where it is needed.

SUPPORTING SPIRIT

REN MAI 1, *Hui Yin*, is the meeting of the inner seas of vitality. When a person is drowning in their life, having no energy to support them, this point can be used to bring back tremendous vitality. This point unites our inner yin energy when there is little or no energy in the system. It can be used to bring back the full force of a unity of vital energy. It is where there is the full nourishment of our inner united yin energy. This is a united transformative energy that happens when the egg and sperm meet and form a new embryo. When there is a severe lack of energy on all the pulses, *Hui Yin* can be used to bring the person back up to the surface so they swim through life with new vitality. When this point flows freely there is tremendous resources of energy to feed our inner most depths and all the other meridians. This brings a wholeness to life.

REN MAI 2, *Qu Gu*, means the maze of bone structure. It is our bones that give structure to the body and this point energizes, creates and unifies that entire structure. The point lies on the beautifully curved pubic bone giving both structure and flexibility to the wholesome nourishing energy of the sea of Ren Mai. It gives our entire structure a unity and profound nourishment and is used when our inner core or entire structure needs this full sea of nourishing vitality.

REN MAI 3, *Zhong Ji*, means the utmost limit of balance. This point gives the utmost balance and harmony to our entire being. Zhong means middle or centre and is drawn as either two halves of a whole or an arrow hitting the exact centre of its target. Night is a part of day, light is a part of the dark and inner is a part of the outer. These opposites make and balance the whole. So *Zhong* is the middle essence of life that keeps all things balanced and moving towards the central target. *Ji* means to reach the utmost limit. *Zhong Ji* is the utmost limit of balance. This is also the third point on the meridian. Three for the Chinese symbolized man in balance between heaven and earth. When we need to go back to our utmost centre, this point can be used to bring us deeply into harmony again, so like an arrow we can fly straight and true to our purpose in life.

REN MAI 4, *Guan Yuan*, means the gateway of origin. This gateway is a vast balanced network that is nourished and guided by the unity of our original source. It is the fourth point of the meridian where we stand balanced by the four directions. When we use this gateway it opens all our inner and outer connections and brings them into harmony. When trauma such as a miscarriage or accident has sent our system reeling and there is a rupture of this deep sense of where we are in the world, then this point can open the gateway and bring nourishment and harmony back to the system. It opens our inner creative gardens again bringing fertility, wisdom, clarity and inspiration to life.

REN MAI 5, *Shi Men*, is an ancient stone gateway. It is the fifth point on the meridian and five for the Chinese represents the five seasons that nourish all life throughout the year. This gateway is naturally nourishing our elements within with the fertile harmony of the seasons surrounding us. It also helps us to remain balanced through all the seasonal changes of the year. This point can deeply nourish our five inner seasons or elements when times have been difficult and the years have deprived us of gathering the wonders around, or when the stress of life has pulled us out of contact with the richness of the natural world. Here our energy can be given the rich nourishment of all the five seasons so the next year enables us to flourish with its wonders.

Ren Mai 6, *Qi Hai*, is the abundant sea of nourishing Qi. *Qi* is drawn as the five grains of life boiling into a rich vapour. *Hai*, or sea, is drawn as a mother's breast, the abundance of growing grass and water. We can meditate on this point to bring nourishing Qi energy to the entire body. The Chinese say that by meditating here, both our heart Qi and spirit Qi can be generated and united to bring joy and harmony to life. This point holds an abundance of Qi. We can use lots of moxa on this point when the energy is low and needs enriching and revitalizing. It is like filling the entire mind, body and spirit with an ocean of rich, loving mother's milk.

Ren Mai 7, *Yin Jiao*, means the united crossing of yin. This point is a full flowing river of nourishing yin energy. At this point the Ren Mai that unites all our yin energy is joined with the inherited energetic reserves of the kidneys as well as the Chong Mai which brings together and harmonizes all our yin and yang energy. This point moves and builds nourishment throughout all the body and spirit. It gives a dynamic thrust to our reserves and builds up nourishment throughout all the meridians. It unites the nourishment of the Ren Mai with the inherited reserves of the kidneys and the good circulation of the Chong Mai. When our energy needs a good enriching boost and thrust forward this point can be called upon to build and enrich.

REN MAI 8, *Shen Que*, is the palace tower of our inner gateway of spirit. Shen is drawn as two hands reaching for the sun, moon and stars for guidance and inspiration. It is our inner connection to the invisible spirit world of the Tao. The point is on the navel which is sometimes described as our lotus blossom. It is said that at birth the *shen* spirits of heaven enter through this point and we become our unique individual selves. We use moxa on this point over salt. As the moxa warms it gives us great nourishment for our spirit and we then remember the dreams of life and have the courage to put them into action. It gently opens us up so we can see more deeply into the wisdoms of our life. Here we contact and are held in the lap of the great mother spirit of earth. This point gently opens the flowers of our inner essence so we can live in the world with creative wholeness.

REN MAI 9, *Shui Fen* means the flowing division of water. The number nine is composed of three sets of three. The harmony of heaven, earth and man is compounded three times bringing great harmony. This point contains a dynamic flow of energy from the very centre of our essence. When we need to go out into the world and use our creative forces, this point can help us find our inner resources and give us the courage to stride forward out into life. This point gives all the other meridians the nourishment and wholeness of the source enriching them with vitality. It helps all the developing organs of the embryo receive the vitality they need.

REN MAI 10, *Xia Wan*, means our lower earthly core and regulates our lower *jiao* which is composed of the bladder, kidneys and large and small intestines. This point brings nourishment and harmony to the entire area of the lower *jiao* which lies in the area on the body between the belly button and the legs. It is here we let go of what is no longer needed and build up our reserves from a reservoir of inherited and stored energetic Qi. When we let go of what is no longer needed we are open to new experiences and what is no longer needed is taken back into the earth and transformed into nutrients for new life. In this point the Po guardians create the organs that allow us to let go and transform nutrients into rich nourishing Qi. This point has the ability to deeply regenerate the organs of our lower *jiao* and bring them into harmony.

REN MAI 11, *Jian Li*, means an established cultivation or to organize and establish a hamlet. This point regulates all of the three *jiaos* through the *san jiao* or triple burner and brings them into harmony and balance so that the whole energetic community works for the common good. It gives a sense of wholeness and goodness to the three *jiaos*. It is like a community meeting in the village square where everyone meets for good discussions and agreements. This point can bring a profound fine tuning to all the pulses or be used when the three *jiaos* are completely out of balance.

REN MAI 12, *Zhong Wan*, means the central core. It regulates our middle *jiao* containing the stomach, spleen, gallbladder and liver and which lies between the belly button and the lower ribs. Here is our central core bringing nourishment to our wood and earth elements. It brings us a feeling of well nourished harmony. It is where all the meridians are fed with what they need and have the vision to put life into action with good decisions. This point brings us back to the very centre of our being, giving depth to our vision to guide us through life. Here we are nourished in the full basket of mother earth. It is also where we see the wonders of our inner and outer world with fresh vision.

REN MAI 13, *Shang Wang*, means the upper heavenly core. This point deeply and profoundly nourishes our upper *jiao* of the heart, heart protector, and the lungs, our fire and metal elements. The upper *jiao* lies in the region of the chest. Here we are inspired by the heavens and filled with the passions of the heart. When we empty our hearts of troubles and distractions, then the wisdom of heaven can enter our soul and fill it with inspiration. At this point we gain a natural connection to the vast wisdom of the heavens. This we receive deep within our hearts. This point calms the fire within filling it with the warmth and love it needs. It helps to give us the courage to unveil our hearts, allowing the invisible to penetrate deep within our soul.

REN MAI 14, *Ju Que*, means the tower gateway of the great palace. Great for the Chinese represents the great ruler or Emperor. For us this great ruler is the heart, for within the stillness of our hearts we can listen to the *shen* spirits and grow with their wisdom. This gateway leads to the royal chambers within our hearts. When we put our hearts into what we do, then life flourishes. The opening and emptying of our hearts is not an easy task. Therefore as practitioners, it is only with great respect we should touch this sacred place. When the time is right, this point can be used to put us back into touch with our inner potentials and dreams so that we can flower with great compassion.

REN MAI 15, *Jui Wei*, means the loving protection of the dove. The dove is a bird of spirit that protects her young with love, peace and tranquility. This point gives us that warm, protected nest which is safe and secure. When we have lost this trust and security, then this point can be used to bring us safely back to the nest again. A dovetail is also the name of a joint between two pieces of wood. It is so well fitted that any changes in the weather do not affect the joint. This point is on the dove tail of the sternum. The sternum protects our heart and lungs, our emotions and inspirations. When we contact this point we can feel a warm loving safe snug place within. Out of that security we grow the confidence to spread our wings and fly on the currents of life wherever they take us.

REN MAI 16, *Zhong Ting*, is the middle palace courtyard. This point is a beautiful inner terrace full of refreshing fountains, flowers and trees. It is a place to rest and find our inner courtyard of spirit. When we are balanced and ready to enter into a higher spiritual level, then this point can open the doorway of our lives. In an expanded awareness we can experience the spiritual energy deep in our own inner wisdom and in the messages of the world. This point takes us to a beautiful, calm, resting place within ourselves and we are refreshed in elegance. Here we taste the spirit messages of the winds, understand the songs of birds, feel reflections in the moonlight. and glimpse the treasures of each day.

REN MAI 17, *Dan Zhong*, means the centre of our inner storehouse of life. As we move upwards along the Ren Mai meridian the points contain deeper and richer experiences of our spiritual potential. This point is a place of great tenderness. It lies in between the breasts. When we moxa this point we can feel a great sensitive tender loving warmth. It is as though pure light is pouring into our spirit, nourishing it with love. When we need to grow and open with tenderness, it is this point that nourishes the peace and harmony within. It enables us to expand our love of others. Here we are nourished with the purest grains of light, love and warmth which opens our compassion for others.

REN MAI 18, *Yu Tang*, means the ancestral hall of jade. Yu is drawn as three pieces of jade strung together. Jade is a milky opaque stone of great beauty. It is said to come from the dragon's sperm and contains the spirit of the dragon. Jade is honest by revealing its flaws. It is both hard and soft at the same time showing balance. Each shape it is made into is said to become a living being. When struck it makes a beautiful musical sound. At this point we enter the ancestral hall of jade where we find the deep ancient resources to help us deepen our lives. All of our ancestors have helped to form us into what we are today and this point takes us to that rich ancestral heritage that lies within. These resources are always there to help and support us into becoming a beautiful unique piece of jade. Here we can contact the creativity of the dragon's sperm and create our world from a place of deep inheritance and rich, vibrant, inner essence.

REN MAI 19, *Zi Gong*, means the royal palace of purple. Here we find our imperial robes and our noble nature. When we are balanced, receptive and open, then this point can take us to the royal chambers of our Emperor. It is then that life takes on a new dimension and we have an understanding of how dreams become reality. It is as though our path opens before us and we walk forward into a rich, bright new day. In this point lies the riches of the kingdom and the beauty of our inner soul.

REN MAI 20, *Hua Gai*, which means the hidden opening of our inner flower. The immortals walked on earth but never for an instant lost their connection with heaven. They knew spirit was everywhere. Each colour change, each new wind, or each leaf on the tree was a miracle full of meaning. With this point, we open the special blossom of our spirit flower and feel as though the most wonderful spring has brought us alive. We burst open like the flowers in springtime with laughter and joy. Like a new bud we become delicate, fragile and see the wonders of the world with fresh new eyes. This point gives us the feeling of being a wonderful flower as it opens in the sunshine. We become beautiful, irresistible, fragrant and full of sweet nectar.

REN MAI 21, *Xuan Ji*, is the jade within the pearl. This is the centre of our soul, the jewel within the stone. This point takes us to the absolute pearl of our being. It is like finding the precious pearl in the ocean of life. This pearl then needs to be polished with faith, humility, benevolence and moderation. Out of that polishing can come the radiance and beauty of who we really are. This point holds our precious inner gem that allows us to be uniquely who we are in the great expanse of life's possibilities.

REN MAI 22, *Tian Tu*, is the sudden opening of the heavens. This point is a chimney or window to the heavens point. Each of the elements has a window point that opens our vision. This point is like walking out of winter into a bright spring day of wild flowers and new growth. It is as though the haze we have been seeing the world through, is lifted and everything now delights us with its vibrance and beauty. These heavenly heights can be frightening or unuseful unless we have the balance, courage and stability to move ourselves into new dimensions. We can use this point when someone is asking to see further or wanting to experience more. This point can also give us a more balanced vision through all cycles of life.

REN MAI 23, *Lian Quan*, is full of correctly angled spring waters. When we want our vision to flow, widen and develop then this point can give us the vitality of a gushing spring pouring out of a mountain rock. Here we are given the ability to craft our vision through skill and experience. We feel vibrant, alive and flow with the skilled understanding of why we are here and what we may achieve. This point gives us the flowing stream to move our visions into action.

REN MAI 24, *Cheng Jiang*, means receiving the rich broth of life. This is the exit point of the Ren Mai, where the vitality of the rich energy of our inner yin ocean flows into the Du

SUPPORTING SPIRIT

Mai. It is a rich full fluid supporting point giving us the vitality of life and enables us to flow further into what life is offering us. This rich broth flows into the Du Mai which will direct its flow. It is a concentrated, nourishing milk to move life forward. When this point is used, it is as though we have been filled with the ocean of the Ren Mai. With this vital force we can finally swim in the ocean of life receiving and giving all we are able to bring to life.

DU MAI, THE GOVERNING VESSEL

The Du Mai guides our direction for the mastery of life. It is like a governor who takes the Emperor's warmth and love and distributes it throughout the kingdom as well as keeping an eye and ear on the kingdom to bring any observations back to the Emperor so he is fully informed of what is happening. It is like a main rope holding the other meridians in place as well as giving them strength and guidance. It directs its activity from a unity of power as well as giving it the flexibility of differentiation. It is the river source giving water and movement to all the other tributaries so they can then flow along their proper course with strength. It is the ruling vessel that keeps an eye on all the other meridians and supervises how they are run.

Du Mai 1, *Chang Qiang*, means a vigorous thrust of energy. Here is a strong powerful vigorous energetic thrust of vitality that grows and excels over a length of time and space. This is the entry point of the Du Mai, putting everything into action with a dynamic thrust. This point has the energy of the force of a leaf bursting through the soil reaching for the sun. It gives all the other meridians strength and energy, with structure and control. At this point all the yang meridians are united giving a directive force to the potential activity in life. Here we literally feel a kick up the backside and are thrust into action. It is the very cornerstone of the Du Mai that fills all the other meridians with direct dynamic energy.

Du Mai 2, *Yao Shu*, means the direct energetic transfer to the loins. When a man places his hands on a beautiful woman's waist he feels the force of his desires through his loins. Here we feel our desires warming and with an excitement of life that moves us forward to reach out to what comes. This is a vital transfer to the loins where we can feel a rejuvenated sense of vitality and sensuality. At this point we go directly to the source of loins and their creative drive.

Du Mai 3, *Yao Yang Guan*, means the gateway to our yang vitality. This gateway opens the drive and force of our desires. When we open this gateway the full force of yang strengthens and warms this rich vitality and awakens our hunger for life. It brings the vital sunshine of yang vitality to spark our growth and development. It opens and enriches our vitality and invigorates our very life force. It revitalizes our creative forces and brings expectation and excitement back to life.

Du Mai 4, *Ming Men*, means the gateway of destiny and our unique purpose in life. This is the gateway to an agreement made between heaven and us as we entered life. At this point we have heaven's stamp that enables us to create our unique way in life. How we use this potential depends on how far we can open this gate during our lifetime. This gateway opens a pattern that grows and develops from birth to death. When we have lost contact with who we are, this point can open that gateway and put us on our path again. Opening this gate brings us back to the unique purposeful drive that is individual and special to each of us. At this point we can refind our unique way forward that can open opportunities to develop in the richest way possible.

Du Mai 5, *Xuan Shu*, means the suspended central pivot. This point can help us to pivot in all directions. This gives us the flexibility we need to adjust to the changes in life. It can help us change direction when life is stale or rigid. When we pivot a whole new geometry is formed. Here we can regain the ability to see new angles and move out of stiff inflexible rutted patterns. At this point the spine pivots with great flexibility and enables us to advance along the way in the same way a ballerina can dance and twirl on a single point.

Du Mai 6, *Ji Zhong*, means the balanced middle of the spine. The Du Mai meridian directs life so it flows in a good and balanced way. This point is in the middle of the spine, where we balance between heaven and earth. This is the still calm point that balances all movement. It is a place of stability and security. Without this balance we can not stand erect nor can we move forward. So this point functions all the time keeping the balance. We can meditate on this point to refind the flexibility of our centre and the way of our path in life.

Du Mai 7, *Zhong Shu*, means the balanced central pivot. Here we can balance and pivot from our central core. It is at this point that the pattern of the dance of life is woven enabling us to move in ever changing patterns. Here movement and stillness constantly balance each other so life flows. This point gives us vitality and an ease and strength of dynamic movement so we can move in new directions and grow with life.

Du Mai 8, *Jin Suo*, means the ease and strength of muscles. This point gives us strength when we are too weak to hold the threads of life together, as well as flexibility and ease if we are too rigid and inflexible. Here we have just the right amount of bendability and can allow life to come to us without judgement. We become like the bamboo, adjusting naturally to what nature brings to us. This strength, flexibility and ease is *Jin Suo*. When we have this ease we can benefit from all the opportunities that come to us.

Du Mai 9, *Zhi Yang*, means the peak fullness of yang. This point fills us with the full warmth and love of the longest day of summer. Here we have the fullness, expansiveness and generosity of the full sunshine of summer. At this point we are given the maximum peak of warmth, ease and harmony, so all our relationships in life flourish. It gives us a burst of energy that enables us to fly further in the enjoyment of life and its potential. Here our vital centre is filled with sunshine. We receive the warmth and ease of the long days of summer and feel the sun's love and warmth penetrate deeply within our entire nature.

Du Mai 10, *Ling Tai*, means the tower of spirit. We need spirit to guide our lives. Each year the Emperor would go to his tower in the palace gardens and meditate. He would allow the wisdom of the heavens to penetrate his very essence so he could understand how to keep his country in balance and harmony for the next year. This point takes us to this place of deep guidance and wisdom. It is the heart of the Du Mai meridian giving us the guidance of the heavens. This in turn stirs our inner being and allows us to see the goodness and beauty in all things. By receiving this heavenly inspiration and guidance, we are able to live life in its most sacred way. Here we dance between heaven and earth, receiving heavenly wisdom and grace. This is the point of our precious inner spiritual tower.

Du Mai 11, *Shen Dao*, means the true path of spirit. Here we move along our path in line with the wisdom and guidance of heaven. It is where we sense the heavenly constellations above us and become sensitive to their signs and inspirations. The ancient ones would take their students walking in nature. At first they would notice very little. Gradually over time they became aware of even the most subtle changes in the winds, seasons and animals around them. Soon they could see divine guidance wherever they looked. At this point our senses open to this vastness. When we can listen deeply within, then we can hear the wisdom that can guide us through life, following our true path wherever it leads.

Du Mai 12, *Shen Zhu*, means a supporting and sustaining pillar of life. It is a point that gives us the strength and support to sustain our journey through life. When we have this structure, life is able to survive and flourish. This point gives strength when we are struggling and eases the way when we are stiff and inflexible. It puts backbone into our efforts to grow and develop. When we are wobbly, crumbly or collapsing, this point can give us the structure to rebuild and sustain the house of our life. When we are stuck or rigid this point can move the structure of life into a new framework. It is a very supportive point giving us the energy and support we need for the struggles of life.

Du Mai 13, *Tao Dao,* means the transforming fires of the Tao. It is at this point our lives are transformed in the heart fires. Life becomes dynamic, passionate and transforming. Here with love and passion our creativity opens and our life is filled with its beauty. At this point we are warmed, cooked and ripened. Our nature matures and is shaped with passion and transforming fires giving us the ability to create and flourish with the feelings of elation and joy.

Du Mai 14, *Da Zhui,* means to strike the great vertebrae with importance. This point moves us forward with a full thrust of dynamic yang energy. Here we receive a lightening flash of heavenly energy and inspiration to move us through an opening deeper into life. This is the meeting point of all the yang pathways and their dynamic currents. It is where we can feel this full yang force enabling us to move in all directions. This point moves life forward with a dynamic thrust.

Du Mai 15, *Ya Men,* means the gateway of muteness. This point touches the quiet meditative space within us. The sages do not speak but instead they enter an inner world of meditation and learn. This point joins the Du Mai with the sea of bone marrow which give life its deepest renewal, as well as the Yang Wei Mai that unites all the yang meridians into a vital web that gives great balance and harmony to life. Here our yang energy is directed from our inner original source.

Du Mai 16, *Feng Fu*, means the palace of the wind. This is a window to heavens point that opens our vision to the wonders of life. In this point is stored the great winds of change which when the time is right, can sweep the past away so our vision is refreshed, expanded and becomes fresh and clear. The rooms of life are freshly aired and everywhere is filled with light. This point can often be used when we are in a good place and are ready to shed the habits of the past and move forward into a greater vision of life.

Du Mai 17, *Nao Hu*, means the doorway of the brain. It holds the limitless potential of the brain. This potential comes from heaven and is guided by the compassionate understanding of the heart. Here we are part of the wholeness of all things. It is the place where our understanding comes from intuition. It is a doorway we can open through meditation to develop our intuitive knowledge. Here we can walk with the ancients, hear the voices of the winds and see the messages in nature. By meditating on this point our minds are opened and not cluttered with distractions.

Du Mai 18, *Qiang Jian*, means the strength of a quiet emptiness. *Jian* is drawn as a doorway through which light is pouring. It means empty, quiet and inner light. Here we have the strength of our inner light. This point directs life with a forward thrust coming from the inner light within.

RECEIVING SPIRIT

Du Mai 19, *Hou Ding*, means the summit of earthly life. This is the point of our existence on earth. Here we are brought into balance and harmony with all our earthly influences. When someone has lost an inner sense of their purpose and life on earth, this point can deeply bring back the connection and balance the person. This is also the highest summit, where we can see a full view of life and our potential, and deeply connect to it.

Du Mai 20, *Bai Hui*, means the meeting of the grand unity. This is a place of council, where all the meridians come together to work for harmony and balance of life of the person. Here is the balance between yin and yang, light and dark, and heaven and earth. It is where the meridians are guided from the original source of life. We can use this point when a person is in chaos. It brings the wisdom of the heavenly ancestors to bring the entire life of the individual back into harmony. When we are in balance this point, with meditation, can bring us to a deep inner harmony. Here we can envision and experience the wholeness of life.

Du Mai 21, *Qian Ding*, means the heavenly summit. This point is our heavenly viewpoint. It contains our pre-birth understanding of life where we can refind where we came from and where we will go back in the end. Here is a vast expanse of vision and wonder. At times we glimpse these meanings when ordinary distractions are left behind. When we meditate on this point it brings us insight and spiritual connection.

Du Mai 22, *Xin Hui*, means the meeting of the skull bones. This point lies in the line of the fonteanel. Meditating on this

SUPPORTING SPIRIT

point we can find an open connection with the heavens. The Du Mai is the governor, director and regulator of the other meridians. This point both regulates the flexibility within the bones of the body and their subtle connections, as well as allows the heavens to guide this structure and bring it into balance with the natural world.

Du Mai 23, *Shang Xing*, means our unique heavenly star. When we are born there is a unique heavenly arrangement of stars in the heavens. This point links our development with those heavenly stars to help keep our life in balance with the fortunes written in constellations of the night sky. In this way our voyage through life has the guiding lights of the heavens. *Xing* is drawn as three stars over generating life and means stars, planets, constellations and a point of light. Here is our special star lighting our way in the rich mysterious depths of the night sky. This is our intuitive astrological guide.

Du Mai 24, *Shen Ting*, means the ancestral hall of spirit. When we need the wisdom of our inner sages we can use this point or meditate upon it. Here we can receive light, illumination and wisdom. Time itself is suspended and our expanded vision is open to a universal wisdom. Here we remain present in the moment in audience with the divine.

Du Mai 24.5, *Yin Tang*, means the mysterious pass or hall of seals. It is located where the third eye is said to be on the forehead. Here all the yin is maintained in good, constant proportions to make a harmonious unity. It is said to be like an inner dove of peace that is cooked to perfection with all the warmth and love that it needs. Those who follow the Tao do not delight in the senses or in wealth and gain, but instead find joy in benevolence, justice and happiness. When we are trustworthy, sincere, and have inner harmony then we are joyful and bring joy to others. If we are lured in the wrong direction, try to please people, or are seduced by worldly objects then there is only craving. *Yin Tang* is this mysterious pass and our ancestral stamp. It is where a mark of blessing is traditionally placed for various religions. *Yin* is drawn as taking a badge of authority by the hand. It means a seal or stamp. *Tang* is drawn as dry even soil under a roof. It means a hall, meeting house, court or church. *Yin Tang* is the sacred hall of our inner intuitive vision. It is the vision of our third eye, where we see into the spirit of all things.

Du Mai 25, *Su Liao*, means the ordinary unadorned bone. At this point we are ourselves and nothing more. Here is our pure essence, unadorned and simple. Here we find our simple nature and are free to enjoy life with the freshness of an infant.

Du Mai 26, *Ren Zhong*, means the very centre of man. When we return to our centre, we find a quiet stillness. It is in that balanced stillness where we can envision the true purpose of our nature and its part in the wholeness of nature. When we lose our way, life becomes a struggle. If we are balanced and our aim is straight and true, then we will reach our target. This point brings us back to this great harmony. It also opens our great compassion and connection to all other living beings.

Du Mai 27, *Dui Duan*, means to open with correct reason. Here we speak the good words that dispel grief and rejoice the heart. Here are the wise ways and wholesome directions in life. At this point we are guided to have good exchanges that speak from our own inner truth. A disciplined person acts correctly and in this way action is in perfect symmetry with the vastness of the Tao.

Du Mai 28, *Yin Jiao*, means the river crossing to the sea. Here the active, yang, governing force returns to the inner yin meridian of the Ren Mai. Here the mighty yang river feeds the great mother sea. When we need this great full flowing force, this point can fill us with the greatness of the vast rivers that flow into our inner yin ocean.

CHONG MAI, THE VESSEL OF GREAT CROSSING

The Chong Mai means the vessel of great crossings. It links the eight extraordinary meridians to the twelve ordinary meridians. It unites and gives all the meridians a forward, thrusting vital energy. It gives us a united push forward and allows us to move with great unity. It directs the pattern of the development of life along a straight path that links all the tributaries. It has the ability to gather together all the crossing and tributaries of the yin and yang in the body to create the individual pattern of life and to continually renew that pattern. Here is the vital harmony necessary for the growth of life. The Chong Mai is a guiding vessel of all the great dynamic crossings of life. The meridian begins with a rich nourishing point on the stomach meridian and then goes along the kidney meridian to give it rich energetic vitality and finishes with points along the Ren Mai and Du Mai meridians.

ST30, *Qi Chong*, means a great thoroughfare of Qi. At this point we have a great united force of dynamic Qi that fills all the meridians with the nourishment they need. This vital nourishing Qi gives us abundance enabling life to surge forward. This point nourishes the growth of life within us with the concentrated essence that is contained in a seed to give it all it needs to burst into life. Here is a united wholesome burst of nourishment to feed all the meridians when the energy has been deprived and starved.

KI11, *Heng Gu*, means the great horizontal beam of bone. It is located on the pubic bone. This point gives structure to our vital Qi directing its course through the meridians for good growth. Here we can feel the solid depth of our bones where we have the resources to move through life in a balanced way. This point reaches the very marrow of our bones where life is constantly regenerated and rejuvenated.

KI12, *Da He*, means a full glorious brightness. This point give us the light and warmth of the love of the sun to enable all things to grow. Here is the great vitality, vibrant warmth and inherited creativity of the kidneys. It is like a flame of creative light and love that brings great harmonic movement, spontaneity and fluidity to the inner structure of life. Here we can dance in the fiery enriching vitality of the inherited resources of the kidneys. We can use this point to balance and deeply enrich the vitality of life.

KI13, *Qi Xue*, means the opening of Qi and its other name is the door of infants. This point is where life's creative essence lies and where life's creations can be given birth. This is where

SUPPORTING SPIRIT

our life force enters and where another life can be invited in. It is an opening to the vitality of our own inherited creative essence. When this vitality is blocked or the ability to produce is lost, then this point can be used to bring back our fertility.

KI14, *Si Man*, means the fullness of the balance of four. The four winds create the five seasons. Here is the balanced harmony of the four winds that brings our inner seasons their movements and harmonies. Here our Qi can be balanced and be brought back into harmony with the seasons and we can be brought back to our centre enriched by the changes happening all around us. Here is the full richness of the four directions bringing dynamic changes to life.

KI15, *Zhong Zhu*, means flowing into the centre. This centre holds the balance between day and night, yin and yang, heaven and earth and all other dimensions that make the whole. In this wholeness our life flies straight and true to its goal. We are in balance with the five seasons around us, and our own inner essence flows in harmony enriching our life. Here the very centre of our inner essence and goodness is revitalized and we become distinct and unique.

KI16, *Huang Shu*, means the direct transfer to the vital regions. This point is at the level of the kidney shu points and is a direct transfer to our deep inner reserves of inherited, ancestral energy. This point goes directly to our vital centre that contains the essence of our inherited resources as well as holds the balance between the heart fires and the vital waters of the kidneys. Here our energy can be deeply and profoundly rejuvenated and our will and desires can be brought together.

RECEIVING SPIRIT

KI17, *Shang Gu*, means to accommodate, deliberate and trade. This point brings great vitality to our lives and energy giving it the quality it needs at a particular moment in time. In this way we have the resources we need to remain in balance and harmony. When a person loses their sense of respect, pride and esteem, then this point can take them back to their inner essence and its qualities. We then have the bamboo's ability to move gracefully with quality and flexibility in all exchanges. Here we can adapt without losing contact with our central roots no matter what our fortunes bring.

KI18, *Shi Guan*, means a strong rough stone gateway. This point gives us the strength of an ancient stone gateway. Here is our inner force but with an opening to all the seasons that each give us a different beauty. When we are worn down and grey, this point can bring back the vitality of the seasons to our meridians and harmonize their efforts to keep us bright, alive and balanced.

KI19, *Yin Du*, means our inner capital. Cities contain great resources but can also distract us with their great bustling selling and buying of wares. This point brings us back to our inner resources and restores in us a profound inner tranquility. We refind our inner elegance, beauty and excellence. Here we can experience the riches and dynamic movements of our own inner capital with all its wealth and gifts.

KI20, *Tong Gu*, means an open flowing valley. Here like a great valley we can receive everything that we need to grow and develop. If we are receptive like a valley, then we too can receive the gifts of nature that come to us. When used, this point can help us flow through life in the same way water can flow around any obstacles. This point enables us to flow in the rich fertile valley of our inner riches and harvest the richness around us each day.

KI21, *You Men*, means a dark secret hidden valley. We cannot have darkness without light, nor light without shadows. Here is both an opening into the darker more secret regions of spirit as well as the return of light when life has been difficult. It is a point that opens the shadows, loneliness and darkness. It is also where the light can re-emerge. Here we move out of the darkness into the light.

REN MAI 23, *Lian Quan*, means a correctly angled spring. It is like a special corner out of which flow great vibrant waters that bring vitality. It refreshes our vision and brings us an expanded sense of the greatness of life. It is an inner spring that deepens our experiences and gives life a richer meaning. Energetically it revitalizes us with vibrant flowing spring waters.

REN MAI 1, *Hui Yin*, means the meeting of the seas of vitality. Out of the this sea, all the other meridians are fed and revitalized. Here is the profound energy and depth of resources gathered together in one ocean. When it flows freely, there is tremendous vitality feeding our inner most depths and giving a full life force of Qi nourishment to all the meridians.

DU MAI 4, *Ming Men*, means the gate of our life's destiny and unique purpose. This is the gate that opens us to what will be our individually unique way in life. Here is heaven's stamp that creates our own way in life. How we use this potential depends on how far we choose to develop in life. When we unite with our way, then the rest of life flows with us. It is this sense of destiny that both unfolds and renews life. This gateway brings us back to our path. It also opens a pattern that helps us to develop from birth until death. Here is our unique way forward that can open opportunities for us to develop in the richest way possible.

DAI MAI, THE VESSEL OF GUIDANCE

The Dai Mai is the vessel of guidance. It unites and keeps all the meridians running in good order. It is like the tug boat that guides ships into the harbour or the sheep dog that gathers and leads the sheep home to the barn. The Dai Mai keeps life well arranged so it can function in a well ordered and balanced way. It holds all the meridians together, harmonizing and regulating them so they move well. Here the pattern of life that is established by the Ren Mai, Du Mai and Chong Mai is moved harmoniously forward with good, well ordered vital Qi. It is at this point that the embryo begins to form its arms and legs. It is the following four extraordinary meridians that guide this development. This is also the fourth extraordinary meridian putting us in harmony with the four winds of the four directions that create the five seasons. It prepares us to move forward into the seasons of life. The meridian itself runs around the waist tying the other meridians together so they work in harmony.

BL23, *Shen Shu*, means a vital transfer to the kidneys. The kidneys hold our inherited reserves and bring fertility and vitality to life. They are the energetic movers of our energy. This point goes directly to the kidneys who are the inner powerhouse of reserves out of which comes will, purpose, vitality and strength. Here is where our deepest reserves can be found. This point puts us in touch with our inner knowledge, the wisdom of ancestral experience and the virtues of our life. A beautiful point to resource and guide the other meridians.

LIV13, *Zhang Men*, means the opening of a beautiful composition. This point opens further chapters in our experiences and further possibilities in our book of life. It is also the meeting point of all the yin organs drawing them together so they can contribute to our way forward with a united effort. This point can help when in our lives we may come to the end of a chapter and we need to open another avenue. It can assist when we have many ways to go forward and can not find the right one. This gateway can guide and support new experiences and possibilities. If we have the courage to step forward, then life can develop with greater richness. Here our inner nature and purpose is both united and inspired to help us create a new step forward.

GB26, *Dai Mai*, means to carry the vital circulations. This point is the heart of the gallbladder meridian giving us upright and clear decisions so all the meridians have the guidelines they need to work together. Here is the flexibility and vision of the gallbladder that gives good order to all the decisions needed each day to balance life. These good, upright decisions then flow and direct all the other meridians. At this point the gallbladder connects, directs and binds together all the meridians with its plans and visions. When we need to return to this place of good decisions, this point can act as a guiding ship from the origins of life in the great sea of the Tao.

GB27, *Wu Shu*, means the pivot point of the five. This point is a pivot where we can remain balanced while moving in any direction that is needed. Here we have the ability to move with all the changes that life brings to us. It is the ability to reach the end of one season and then move forward into the next. Here we have the ability to move with all the transformations that we need throughout life to keep our ship on its course through night and day. Nothing is permanent in life and it is *Wu Shu*, that gives us the flexibility to easily adjust to the changes in all the five seasons..We can use this point when the person wants to see more alternatives to life and wants to become more flexible.

GB28, *Wei Dao*, means the binding of one's path. The gallbladder with its upright decisions unites and brings into harmony all the activities of the other meridians. It is the general of our life forces, bringing harmony and balance with its clear sighted decisions. *Wei Dao*, means to hold together, maintain, and uphold the path. It is the essence of the Dai Mai. This point guides us to move from a place where all decisions are united and fed from a central vision. Here we can find our sense of direction and be guided with upright decisions. In this way we can walk our unique path within the great cosmos that is itself a body in constantly changing motion. This point helps to anchor us when we have great changes in our life.

SUPPORTING SPIRIT

YIN AND YANG QIAO MAI,
THE VESSELS OF DYNAMIC AND GRACEFUL MOVEMENT

The Yin and Yang Qiao Mai are the vessels of dynamic and graceful movement. They give us the ability to stand in an upright and dynamic way and guide the development of the arms and legs in the embryo. The energy of these meridians helps us to walk with the great vitality and grace of a stallion. Here we have the well rooted and balanced ability to walk on two legs. The Yin Qiao Mai brings balance, harmony and dynamic movement to our inner yin circulations. It contains points on the kidney, stomach and bladder meridians to direct our dynamic movement through life. The Yang Qiao Mai bring balance, harmony and dynamic movement to our outer yang circulations. It contains a point from each of the yang meridians to direct this dynamic movement. Here we gain our vital, powerful and graceful dancing movements to help us walk erect through life and its constant cycles and changes. These meridians both come into being when the arms and legs of the embryo begin to form.

YANG QIAO MAI

BL62, *Shen Mai*, means the ordering of the vital circulations. The first point on this meridian orders all our vital circulations. The bladder is the reservoir of our water element that revitalizes every cell in our body. When we need this boost of energy this point can help recharge all our vital circulations. It contains a concentration of vital Qi that extends and orders our entire mind, body and spirit. It also orders and vitalizes the growth of the arms and legs in the embryo. Here we have the free flowing energy that gives us a flowing dynamic movement in our lives.

BL61, *Pu Can*, means to serve with counsel. *Pu Can* is drawn as a servant who brings together twigs to form a torch, and wings under three stars. By being a servant to what comes, we can walk our way and be guided by the stars. At this point the stars penetrate our very being and guide our erect, dynamic steps in the world. Here we have the counsel of the constellations to help guide our development through life. When our feet have lost their way, this point can bring us back to our path.

BL59, *Fu Yang*, means to access the movement of yang. Here is a full yang force of movement giving us the confidence to move into the world with our feet firmly on the ground. At this point we can access the dynamic movement of yang. It is the yang impulse that sparks all activity and movement. Here our every action is filled with brightness, sunshine, warmth, heat and movement. When we need this full charge of warm bright dynamic yang movement we can go to this point and fill our strides full of vibrant yang energy.

GB29, *Ju Liao*, means to dwell in the protection and strength of bone. This point lies on the top joint of the leg where it meets the hip. In the embryo it guides the development of the legs. This point is also linked to the Yang Wei Mai which gathers all the movements of yang and co-ordinates them like a giant network. Here is the essence of both graceful power as well as flexible movement. Here the

SUPPORTING SPIRIT

gallbladder co-ordinates all the necessary decisions for how we walk through life, giving us the flexible force we need to meet what comes. Here we can find dynamic strength, protection and graceful movement.

SI10, *Nao Shu*, means a vital transfer to the shoulder. This point develops the arms and balances the body. Our shoulders give structure and support to our central core. They give movement to our arms which reach out into the world to gather its gifts. Here is a place of vital transfer to the whole of the shoulders and the arms. When we use this point we contact this depth of that structure. Here we have the muscle that gives balance and flexibility to accomplish our goals. We can reach out to new experiences and shed our burdens. We find the fluidity and flexibility to shoulder what is necessary and indispensable helping us to reach out to what comes.

LI15, *Jian Yu*, means the monkey bone shouldering and sustaining life. Here we shoulder our responsibilities well. It gives us the strength and good authority to shoulder our tasks in life with a sense of self esteem and pride. Here we can take charge and find the endurance to walk our path with dignity and grace. This point helps us to shoulder our tasks with the strength of character, pride, quality and competence.

LI16, *Ju Gu*, means a very great bone. Bones give the body its structure. They also contain marrow which regenerates the cells that sustain the body. This point directs the growth of the arm from the deepest essence of its structure. Here also we can contact the deep primitive core structure of our lives where we can reach an intuitive sense of where we are going and what goals we may reach in life. Here is the great force of the depth and strength of our bones.

ST4, *Di Cang*, means the gathering of the earthly harvest. This point nourishes the development of our limbs as well as our structure and movement. It gathers, contains and stores the abundance of the harvest of each season. It is a bowl of irresistible goodness where we can find the care, comfort, security and storehouse for achieving our goals. Here we can feed at a deep level whatever hunger or loss we have suffered. At this point our inner earth is fed and satisfied so we can enjoy the world around us. When times are sparse, it is here we can find a bounty of harvested goods and be nourished.

ST3, *Ju Liao*, means the greatness of bone. This point reaches to the very depth of our structure to build and nourish deep within our bones. Here we can find the very marrow of our being bringing us great stability. When we are centered in this great security of earth we can move and adjust to what comes. This points helps to re-establish balance and stability in our life so we can move forward with grace and sensitivity.

ST2, *Si Bai*, means the balanced pure white energy. All movement in nature comes from the four directions of the winds that create the five seasons. This point contains the pure, clear, bright energy of these four winds of change. These winds give energy and direction to our movements. When we are filled with this pure nourishing essence, we have the energy and orientation to move where we need to go. When we are balanced by these four winds we are centered. Out of that centre can come great creativity.

SUPPORTING SPIRIT

ST1, *Cheng Qi*, means to receive the tears of heaven. When earth receives the rains of the heavens, she becomes fertile, soft and receptive. This is the entry point of the stomach meridian that is fed by the large intestine or the metal element with these heavenly rains. At this point we receive these heavenly rains and become enriched, soft, fresh, and vibrant. When this gateway is open we can take in all the nourishment around us. In this way, like the earth, our energy becomes soft, vibrant, rich and nourishing and we become fertile and creative.

BL1, *Jing Ming*, means eyes full of illumination. As students followed their Taoist masters through the mountains, they were at times asked what they saw. At first they would notice very little of what was around them, but over time they began to truly open their eyes until one day they could see the Tao in the winds, trees and pools of water. They could eventually see spirit in all things. At this point our eyes are filled with the wonder of spirit. Here we have both the light of the sun and the moon. It is where we have both an outer and inner vision of the radiance of our spirit. At this point our eyes shine with the light of the sun and the moon illuminating our vision with clarity and opening our hearts to the spirit in all things guiding us along our path in the world.

GB20, *Feng Chi*, means the reservoir of the winds. At this point we have the dynamic energy to move with graceful speed and good decisions wherever our path takes us and with whatever meetings come our way. Winds move with great force, direction and articulation. They adjust to and make the changes that bring the seasons into life. Here is our internal reservoir of wind power and flexibility. When the winds blow, they move around rocks and walls with agility and without losing force or speed. At this point our gallbladder has a reservoir of wind power for all the thousands of decisions it needs to make each day and night. Here we move with clear vision, great organization and dynamic movement.

YIN QIAO MAI

KI2, *Ran Gu*, means a valley full of bright warm sunshine. At this point we can receive what we need by simply being open like a valley that receives the rain and sunshine it needs. Here the vitality of water gives us a flowing, warm, loving energy wherever it is needed. This point brings balance, warmth, love and vitality to our energy so we grow with vitality. Here our relationships grow with warmth and love and we open to the experiences that come our way. When our hearts are filled with this fire water we grow with compassion and mature in life's encounters.

KI6, *Zhao Hai*, means the sea of illumination. This point brings a sparkling vibrancy to life and we have the illumination and wisdom we need to move forward. Here we can experience the light of both the sun and moon and find our inner wisdom. At this point we can bathe in the waters of our inner essence and become enlightened as to the deeper meanings within and around us. Zhao Hai brings us into contact with our vast inner sea of light and love that opens us to the wonders around. Here the reflections and insights of our spirit enrich our life.

SUPPORTING SPIRIT

KI8, *Jiao Xin*, means a sincere, trusting and good exchange. This point gives us the confidence, sincerity and ability to move forward into trusting exchanges. It helps us to build our inner wisdom and faith. When we have these good exchanges, they bring security, integrity, commitment, strength and fortitude. Here we have confidence in our relating to others and our words and actions flow gently with sincerity, faith and trust.

ST12, *Que Pen*, means a broken earthenware pot. This point brings nourishment to whatever needs repairing or help. When we have not had the nourishment we need, we become isolated, disconnected and are unable to accept the love and sharing that comes to us. This needs a transition, so the nourishment bowl can be repaired and made whole again. When repaired this bowl can hold nourishment. We become centered, balanced, open and creative and are able to grow. We can feel the bounty of what nourishes us. When we are full, it is then that we are able to care for others with great compassion.

BL1, *Jing Ming*, means eyes full of illumination. As students followed their Taoist masters through the mountains, they were at times asked what they saw. At first they would notice very little of what was around them, but over time they began to truly open their eyes until one day they could see the Tao in the winds, trees and pools of water. They could eventually see spirit in all things. At this point our eyes are filled with the wonder of spirit. Here we have both the light of the sun and the moon. It is where we have both an outer and inner vision of the radiance of our spirit. At this point our eyes shine with the light of the sun and the moon illuminating our vision with clarity and opening our hearts to the spirit in all things guiding us along our path in the world.

YIN AND YANG WEI MAI
THE VESSELS OF A DYNAMIC NETWORK

The Qiao Mai put life into dynamic motion. The Wei Mai extend this motion into a giant network that joins together and supports the harmonious growth of all the meridians. They protect and support all the influences moving between the meridians. They also guide the embryo in its last months so that all the meridians are in harmony with each other as well as preparing the twelve ordinary meridians which will begin functioning at birth. They keep the twelve ordinary meridians in harmony at a deep level with the world around. They maintain order in the body by seeing to it that all the yin and yang are in constant good proportion making the development of life a continuous and harmonious unity. *Wei* is drawn as threads of silk and a bird being cooked to perfection and perfect harmony. Here our spiritual inner life is given the love and warmth it needs to be in harmony with all that surrounds it. These meridians tie together all the other meridians with their delicate silk connections keeping them well balanced and connected. These two meridians link all aspects of life together to give good relationships and proportions keeping everything at a good level. The Yang Wei Mai bring this network to all our yang meridians. It

SUPPORTING SPIRIT

contains a point from all the yang meridians. It brings our five elements together and links them to our deep profound primitive source. The Yin Wei Mai contains points on the kidneys, spleen and liver. It brings this network of harmony and balance to all our yin meridians and links them to our inner source and essence.

YANG WEI MAI

BL63, *Jin Men*, means the golden gateway. This point is full of liquid gold energy that is vibrant and full. It is a golden gateway that allows the precious gems of life to come to us. Here is the heavy importance of gold, washed of all its impurities. In this way we are brought golden opportunities and bright inspirations. It is a rich gateway of golden nuggets that help our life to connect and benefit from the wealth and gifts of the world we live in.

GB35, *Yang Jiao*, means the crossing network of yang. This point joins the vast yang network of the Yang Wei Mai to the gallbladder. It is where there are the good upright decisions to bring life into harmony and balance. Here is an accumulation of rich, warm, vibrant, active yang energy that gives us strength and brilliance to make good upright decisions. It is like the sun that harmonizes and brings energy equally to all life under its light. This point harmonizes all the yang meridians.

GB29, *Ju Liao*, means to dwell in the protection and strength of bone. This point lies on the top joint of the leg where it meets the hip. At this point the gallbladder, the Yang Qiao Mai and the Yang Wei Mai are united. In this way this point has great united strength that guides our steps in life so we walk our path in harmony and with elegance. Here is an enormous strength coming from our inner structure from which we can move in harmony and unity and find the strength, dynamic movement and protection to stride forward through life. When our entire structure needs to be brought back into harmony, this point can be used to reconnect us to the dynamic network of life where we can receive great vitality.

SI10, *Nao Shu*, means the vital strength of the shoulder. This points links the small intestine with both the Yang Qiao Mai and the Yang Wei Mai. Here our life knows what is pure. It is this point that feeds our arms with dynamic movement so they can reach out for what they need and create. Here we have the dynamic ability and flexibility to accomplish our goals by reaching out for new experiences. It is where we have the strength, protection and fluidity to shoulder what is necessary and indispensable to reach out to both give and receive. This point reaches our deepest structure and can be used to reconnect us to the dynamic network of life giving our entire being great vitality.

TB15, *Tian Liao*, means the bone of heaven. Here the Yang Wei Mai unites with the triple burner to keep the mind, body and spirit in warmth and harmony. At this point we are balanced and aligned with the movement of the heavens. The angels rest on our shoulders and the heavenly ancestors descend to whisper their wisdom and advise. We are enveloped in the guidance of the Tao bringing balance and harmony.

SUPPORTING SPIRIT

GB21, *Jian Jing*, means the well of the shoulder. Here are the refreshing waters of a deep well giving us vitality and inner resources. At this point our energy is rejuvenated from a deep inner source so our decisions come from a place of wisdom and inner insights. Here we can dig deep within ourselves and find the pure spring waters bubbling with clarity and inspirations to guide and unite the networks of our life. Here is the refreshment for our labours so we work with ease. At this point we find the reserves to carry our responsibilities well.

GB14, *Yang Bai*, means the pure clear energy of yang. This point has a reservoir of bright clear yang energy giving all the meridians a great full vital strength. This energy is clear, pure, free and easy. Here is our pure inner self that is warmed and moved into action to fill all our decisions with warmth and activity.

GB13, *Ben Shen*, means the very root of spirit. This point guides our inner and outer network with the vision of our spirit. *Ben Shen* is the established root of our spirit. It is by reaching this root of spirit that a diviner can see the universe in the crack of a turtle shell or an astronomer can predict the future from the stars. When we touch our roots and our spiritual essence, then life becomes full of wonder and all we do works in harmony.

GB16, *Mu Chuang*, means the eye's window. It opens our eyes to the wonders around us and takes us to another level of perception. By opening our eyes, we are able to see spirit in all things and experience the fullness of life. In this way life becomes simple, wonderful and without judgement. Here like students of the Taoist masters we begin to hear the whispers of the winds and understand the language of the seasonal changes.

GB17, *Zheng Ying*, means a correct impartial upright plan. When we are upright and correct in our endeavours, we are balanced and able to see the direction of our life with clarity. This clarity of vision helps us to make centered, just and pure decisions. Here we can put our plans into action in an upright, nourishing and regulated manner. In this way life is walked in harmony and balance.

GB18, *Cheng Ling*, means the receiving of spirit. At this point we contact the spirit of life. Here heaven presents and fills us with spirit. By meditating on this point we bring the unseen and invisible threads of spirit to ourselves to nourish our soul in the same way the rains of heaven nourish the earth. We open to what comes and begin to see the divine in each moment. At times when we are open to these heavenly gifts, our calligraphy can be painted with unerring movements of vitality and songs and poems can be performed with illuminated beauty.

GB19, *Nao Kong*, means the vastness of the brain. Here is the immense potential of our brain that is able to guide our way in life if it follows the understandings of our heart. In this way knowledge becomes intuitive. As we meditate on this point, we receive the illumination that comes by being open to the heavens. When the brain follows the heart opening itself to the heavens then reason comes from intuition, ideas come from action and thinking comes from emotions.

SUPPORTING SPIRIT

GB20, *Feng Chi*, means the reserves of the winds. At this point we can touch the spirit of the winds and all their dynamic directions. In this way we remain in balance through all the seasons and have the flexibility and force to adjust to whatever comes in the fortunes of life. At this point our decisions have the insight, speed, flexibility and articulation of the wind. Here clarity and vision have real wind power so we indeed become a man of all seasons. This point can be used when someone needs either a deep reserve of energy or wants to open their lives with dynamic new directions.

Du Mai 16, *Feng Fu*, means the palace of the wind. This is a window to heavens point that opens our vision to the wonders of life. In this point is stored the great winds of change which when the time is right, can sweep the past away so our vision is refreshed, expanded and becomes fresh and clear. The rooms of life are freshly aired and everywhere is filled with light. This point can often be used when we are in a good place and feel well balanced and able to move ahead. It is used when we are ready to shed the habits of the past and move forward with a greater vision of life.

Du Mai 15, *Ya Men*, means the gateway of muteness. This point touches the quiet meditative space within us. The sages do not speak but instead they enter an inner world of meditation and learn. This point joins the Du Mai with the sea of bone marrow which give life its deepest renewal, as well as the Yang Wei Mai that unites all the yang meridians into a vital web that gives great balance and harmony to life. Meditating on this point gives us a deep inner calm.

YIN WEI MAI

KI9, *Zhu Bin*, means a guest that serves our very foundation. At this point we can find the foundations of our life and our inherited resources. When we can again feel these roots, we are able to open ourselves to others with the goodness and talents we have. In this way we also receive their warmth and our riches increase. At this point we can find our talents and inner riches to build good inner foundations.

SP11, *Ji Men*, means a gateway of a bamboo harvest basket. This is a gateway full of a rich harvest of Qi giving us great nourishment and vitality. Here we can find and access our inner storehouse and find the nourishment we need. At this point our inner yin meridians are nourished and provided for with abundant energy. Here we can feel this nourishment and care flow through our mind, body and spirit.

SP13, *Fu She*, means to dwell in the inner palace. This is our harvest palace full of rich nourishing energy. It is where we have all the comforts of our inner home and the security and stability to build our lives. Here we are laid in the loving, nourishing, caring lap of our mother earth. It is like arriving at an inn where we can rest and find our home comforts and feel the warmth, security and safety of our mother earth and all she provides.

SP15, *Da Heng*, means a great balanced horizontal beam. This point brings balance and harmony to our inner yin energy. We feel the horizon within us balancing between heaven and earth where we experience the changes from night to day and season to season. At this point we can gather what we have accomplished and envisage the next step forward. Here we can feel the fullness of our horizons and bring that richness into our lives.

SP16, *Fu Ai*, means to caress our laments with compassion. When we have sorrows as the loss of life, the loss of opportunity or the loss of love and care, we are filled with distress and unhappiness. Sorrow needs its time and its tears. This point helps the sorrow to pass and places us in the caring arms of mother earth. When sorrow is given this caress, then like the weather it passes and our hearts are lightened and brightened and allowed to flow again with other emotions. Here we can regain the harmony of our heart's affections.

LIV14, *Qi Men*, means the gateway of expectation and the hope of one hundred years. It is with hope that we can see our goals and feel in our hearts what we need to strive for. When we find this hope we should share it with others so there is more hope in the world. This point gives us the energy to see how life can blossom forth. Here we are able to see and move into a new place in life that is full of greater possibilities with the hope of one hundred years guiding and fueling that vision.

REN MAI 22, *Tian Tu*, is a sudden opening of the heavens. This point is a chimney or window to the heavens point. Each of the elements has a window point that opens our vision. This point is like walking out of winter into a bright spring day of wild flowers and new growth. It is as though the haze we have been seeing the world through is lifted and everything now delights us with its vibrance and beauty. These heavenly heights can be frightening or unuseful unless we have the balance, courage and stability to move ourselves into new dimensions. We can use this point when we want to see further or experience more. This point can also give us a more balanced vision through all cycles of life.

REN MAI 23, *Lian Quan*, is correctly angled spring waters. When we want our vision to flow, widen and develop then this point can give us the vitality of a gushing spring pouring out of a mountain rock. Here we are given the ability to craft our vision through skill and experience. We feel vibrant, alive and flow with the skilled understanding of why we are here and what we may achieve. This point gives us the flowing stream to move our visions into action.

These points on the extraordinary meridians are able to touch the spirit in a profound way and can be used on anyone. For example LIV14, *Qi Men*, the gateway of expectation and hope, on the Yin Wei Mai, brings a vast network of hopeful vision to the person. GB20, *Feng Chi*, the reserves of the wind, on the Yang Wei Mai, brings the dynamic and changeable force of wind power so we can adjust to life with speed and flexibility. Here we have a clarity of vision to move our lives in a dynamic way. Also on the Yang Wei Mai, is SI10, *Nao Shu*, the vital strength of the shoulder which bring great vitality to our upper structure and particularly to the arms. Here we can reach out to the world with clarity. GB29, *Ju Liao*, means to dwell in the strength and protection of bone. It also lies on the Yang Wei Mai and brings strength and vitality to our lower structure so we walk life with stamina.

SUPPORTING SPIRIT

The Yin and Yang Qiao Mai bring us dynamic movement and help us maintain the rhythms of life. On the Yang Qiao Mai we have ST4, *Di Cang*, the gathering of the earthly harvest. Here is a great granary to nourish us when life has been hard. It is where we can experience the care, comfort and secrity of whatever hunger or loss we have suffered. Another point on this meridian is BL59, *Fu Yang*, meaning to access the movement of yang. When our structure and energy is deeply affected, this point can bring a dynamic movement of vital, warm, yang energy to where it is needed. It revitalize the energy and gets it moving again. On the Yin Qiao Mai is KI6, *Zhao Hai* which is a sea of illumination. This point reveals our beautiful inner essence and bathes it with wonder and insight. On this meridian is also the point BL1, *Jing Ming*, the eyes full of illumination. Here our vision opens to a more expanded level.

On the Dai Mai is LIV13, *Zhang Men*, the opening of a beautiful composition. This point can help us to open a new chapter in our lives. On the Chong Mai we have KI12, *Da He*, meaning the full glorious brightness. Here we bathe in the vitality of the kidneys. On the Du Mai is Du Mai 4, *Ming Men*, the gateway of life returning us to life's destiny. On the Ren Mai is Ren Mai 21, *Xuan Ji*, the jade within the pearl where we can touch the delicate pearl of our inner essence. Using these points we bring vitality to the spirit of our patients and enrich their lives with dynamic connections. Life then grows and develops with creativity and harmony.

GU SHEN - VALLEY SPIRIT

SERVING THE RULER IN THE CAPITAL
COVERED BY WORLDLY DUST, I FOUND NO PEACE.
I FOLLOW THE RIVER
HOW FRESH THE SIGHT OF GULLS ACROSS THE SAND.
KODO

OPENING OUR SENSES

The valley spirit does not die, it is eternal
It is called woman, the mysterious female
The gateway of this inner primal mother
It is the root of life of heaven and earth
It is like a veil, continuous
And at the edge of existence
Barely seen
Use it, don't force it, it will never fail
LAO TZU

When we work with acupuncture we open our senses to energy. Energy expresses itself in touch, sound, odour, colour and emotion. Each of the five elements has an energetic feel to it, a colour, an odour, a sound and an emotion. In past centuries healer and physicians would use their sense of smell to diagnose fevers, and other illnesses. One of most well known odours today is that of cancer which is a fermenting sweet odour indicating the decay in the body. When we open our senses to these energetic indications we are able to see, hear, smell, and feel the elemental imbalance in a person. If I see an ashen colour on person's face, hear in the voice a pattern of the sound going up but not quite making a laugh, smell a scorched odour and hear an anxious laugh when the person talks about difficult things, then I know that the element of fire is out of balance. I also have an energetic sense of fire that has no substance but flames up and cools down. If I see a yellow tint on the person's face, hear in the voice a pattern of sing, going up and down and around, smell a lily sweet odour and the person seems to need the care of a mother when talking about difficult things, then I know the element of earth is out of balance. I also have an energetic sense of earth that is solid. If I see a white colour on the person's face, hear in the voice a pattern of sighing at the end of each phrase and smell a rotten odour and the person feels grief when talking, then I know the element of metal is out of balance. I also have an energetic sense of the cutting blade of metal. If I see a blue colour on the person's face, hear in the voice a pattern of groan that goes on and on without stopping, smell a putrid odour and the person has exaggerated fears, then I know the element of water is out of balance. I also have an energetic sense of the unstoppable flow of water. If I see a green tint on the face, hear in the voice a pattern of sharp punctuation like the vibrant thrust of growth in spring, smell a rancid sharp odour and the person seems to express anger inappropriately, then I know the element of wood is out of balance. I also have an energetic sense of the push forward of wood in spring. What I am looking for with my senses is the imbalance so I can bring the energy of the person back into harmony again.

When I was a student I greatly enjoyed exploring my senses. To open my sense of seeing colours, I went out into nature and looked at all the wonderful colours around me each season. I could see twenty different browns on a single tree. In spring there were hundreds of greens. But then I began to see something more. In spring as I watched the new leaves form or the buds grow large, I could also see the energy pour out of the life that was creating the leaf or the bud. It was a vibrant energy full of colour. I then began to see this energy and colour just off the skin. I would sit in a café and watch people go by and see the colour on their faces. I could also see it on young children's faces. The colour on children was much brighter than on most adult faces because it was still vibrant.

I would smell at least ten odours a day. Dead mice, young flowers, people with colds, fires, wet clothes, dry earth, wet earth, cut grass, molds, sheep, cows, rotten meat, blood, stale water, compost, and anything else. Slowly my nose was able to distinguish the energetic odour from the sweat odour. I then began to distinguish types of fevers and illnesses. My nose was open to a world full of interesting smells. I even began to smell the different layers of odours in perfumes.

As a musician, I would listen to the details of the music in the voice. Slowly I began to hear the songs of the elements in each individual voice. A wood imbalance would have a voice that moved forward with a punctuation or it would have no strength at all. A fire imbalance would try to go up to a happy laugh but would just not make it. An earth imbalance would sing up and down and all around. A metal imbalance would go along and then drop down to a sigh. A water imbalance would simply go on and on and on at about the same level just like water. Sometimes the accent would be difficult and then I would close my eyes and just listen to the rhythm and song of the voice until the pattern emerged.

RECEIVING SPIRIT

Energetically I began to be able to sense the imbalance. Wood would push forward or be limp. There would be some anger or a lack of anger that did not hit right. I could see this in nature with all the buds, leaves and plants bursting forth in spring. If the conditions were not right then these plants would be frustrated and angry they could not develop. Fire would not have substance and would be over anxious or burnt out. There would be hysterical joy that would jar or a lack of joy. I could see this in summer when there was an ease to life and the sun made everything blossom forth with joy. If this sunshine was not there, the flowers would not bloom and there would be no joy and laughter. Earth would be solid and unmoving. It would demand care and attention. In late summer there would be the full harvest. If there was not the harvest then there would be worries about surviving the winter and people and animals would feel needy and uncared for. Metal would go and then cut off. It would be holding on and not able to let go or grieving for something inappropriate. If nature can not let go in autumn it is filled with rubbish and can not take in the inspirations of the heavens and loses its connection with its essence. Water would simply flow and flow. There would be fear or a lack of fear. When water flows well it cleanses the entire system. When it can't flow or if there is not enough water we fear we will not be able to live. In the same way when water overflows there is no way to stop it and we fear of being overwhelmed. In this way the seasons themselves opened my senses to the imbalances that could occur within a person's five elements. The more I used my

OPENING OUR SENSES

senses the more I could feel, see, hear and smell what needed support to be brought back into harmony again.

In addition I would work at understanding each of the spirits of the organs of the body. I would talk to my heart and ask it how it was and did it have the love it needed to help all the other organs function well giving them the love they needed. I would ask my small intestine if it was able to sort the pure from the impure. If it had the clarity to understand what was good and what was not good. I would ask my heart protector if it was strained from the rejections and batterings of life and if it could protect the heart well. I would ask the triple burner if it was able to keep all the body in harmony and at just the right temperature. I would ask the liver if it had the plan of life well in its vision. I would then ask the gallbladder how it was doing with all the decisions it had to make. I would ask the stomach if it was digesting well and able to take in all the information and understand it. I would ask the spleen if it was able to distribute all the nourishment from the stomach everywhere in the body. I would ask the lungs if they were able to take in the heavenly inspirations with each breath. I would then ask the large intestine if it was able to let go of what was no longer needed. I would ask the bladder if it had the resources to reach every cell in the body. I would ask the kidneys if they could energetically move this energy where it was needed.

For the wood element I would ask myself how good was my vision, could I see where I needed to go and how to get there. For the fire element I would ask about relationships, where they open and loving and close and full of compassion or was I protecting myself too much or not enough. I would feel my heart and calmly meditate there finding the wisdom within. For the earth element I would ask myself if I felt nourished and well cared for like being in the lap of mother earth herself or if I felt worried and unable to take things in. For my metal element I would ask if I was letting go of the old and taking in the new or was I holding on to things that I no longer needed. For the water element I would look at my reserves and my inherited gifts and see if I was using them well.

I would make an effort in each season to honour these elements and make sure I was allowing the season itself to resource me. I would renew my vision in spring for the next year. I would enjoy the long days of the summer and spend more time with friends. I would enjoy the feasts of late summer and the markets. I would let go in the autumn and take in the fresh crisp air. I would feed my reserves in winter and rest in the longer nights. All of these things help keep our elements within in balance and harmony. They also help us understand when there is imbalance and how to work at bringing it back into harmony. Let us now look at the elements and treatment.

Become totally empty
Quiet the restlessness of the mind
Only then will you witness everything
Unfolding from emptiness
See all things flourish and dance in the endless variation
And merge again back into perfect emptiness
Their true state, their true mature
Emerging, flourishing, dissolving back again
This is the eternal process of return
To know this process brings enlightenment
To miss this process brings disaster.
Be still, stillness reveals the secrets of eternity
Eternity embraces all that is possible
And this leads to a vision of oneness
A vision of oneness brings about universal love
Universal love supports the great truth of nature
The great truth of nature is the Tao
Whoever knows this truth lives forever
The body may perish, deeds may be forgotten
But he who has the Tao has all eternity.

LAO TZU

CHENG LING - RECEIVING SPIRIT

KINDNESS AND OPENNESS OF MIND
WILL ACCOMPLISH ALL GOALS
YOURS AND THOSE OF OTHERS
SHABKAR –TIBETAN SAGE

TREATMENT AND THE FIVE ELEMENTS

SUMMARY OF FIVE ELEMENT TREATMENT PROTOCOL

Check pulses and determine if there is possession.
Clear possession if it is there
Clear aggressive energy on everyone in the first treatment
Clear any other blocks to energy and check pulses again.
Choose points to help the person open their lives by
 supporting the spirit using points on the eight
 extraordinary meridians, outer bladder line points
 and kidney chest points
Ground the treatment with points on the paired
 meridians of the elemental imbalance.
Remember each acupuncture point is a beautiful
 palace of spiritual energy.
For possession and aggressive energy we sedate
 leaving the needles in to clear the energy
For anything else we use moxa and tonify
 except in the rare case when energy is excessive

When people come to me I spend time listening to them. I listen to what they say, to their pulses, to their energy and to their hearts and spirit. Simply by listening and asking usually instinctive questions, I begin to understand how I can help the person in both their energy and their life with various combinations of acupuncture points. One of the remarkable things about acupuncture is how it brings people back to themselves and who they really are. It enriches their energy and helps balance them in their lives. When this happens they then have the resources to begin changing their lives.

There are many wonderful points to help with spirit along the extraordinary meridians, the kidney chest points and the outer bladder line. Personally I prefer to choose points along the extraordinary meridians rather than use the master and coupling points. For me this gives a much more individual and precise treatment and often more profound and permanent change. Using the master and coupling points can also drain the meridian which is what we would not want to do. When we use one or two points on the extraordinary meridians it can give a wonderful balancing boost to the system and enable the person to absorb the change in their energy so they are able to use it in their lives. For me, each of the points of the extraordinary meridians have such a richness, that when I use moxa and tonification needling I rarely need anything else. The person themselves feels the wonderful energetic changes as each point is used. It is a question of what points at that moment in time will take the person more into harmony and balance. For example if someone needs a lot of energy we may use REN MAI 6 *Qi Hai*, the sea of abundantly flowing Qi. If we need to nourish the spirit and feed it we may use REN MAI 8, *Shen Que*, the inner gateway tower of spirit. I may in one treatment use a kidney chest point, a point from one of the extraordinary meridians and a point along the outer bladder line and then finish the treatment with a couple of points on the meridians of the elemental imbalance. At other times I may need points on the outer bladder line. Sometimes I simply treat on points on the two meridians of the elemental imbalance.

The kidney chest points I largely use when the spirit of the person needs a rich nourishment. For example we may see the person has suffered over a long time so we may use K24, *Ling Xu*, the wild lands of spirit to deeply regenerate the spirit and bring it back to life. If we see the person has some reserves but needs a resource of support for their spirit we may use K25, *Shen Cang*, the treasure house of spirit. When someone is feeling well and are ready to open at another level we may use K26, *Yu Zhong*, the center of elegance.

The outer bladder line has a wealth of points for opening the vitality of life. BL48(53), *Bao Huang* means to contain the vital centre. It contains the nourishment of the rich womb of life forces and feels the entire mind, body and spirit with rich heartful vitality. BL47(52), *Zhi Shu* means to arrive at our inheritance and ambition. This point rekindles our drive to be who we are. BL45(50), *Wei Cang* is the rich nourishing golden granary of the stomach. BL42(47), *Hun Men* is the gateway to the core of spirit opening our inner essence and taking us to place where our inner core is filled with the essence of our spiritual potential. BL39(44), *Shen Tang* means to receive spirit in the ancestral temple. This point takes us to the inner palace chambers of the heart where we are nourished with fire which both burns away our troubles and hurts and fills us with love and compassion. Here we can find our inner love and wisdom. BL38(43), *Gao Huang Shu* means a vital transfer from the rich vital inner tissues. This point sends vitality, love and warmth to every cell in the body. BL37(42), *Po Hu* means soul door. This opens our soul gateway and we begin to see our way out of the distractions of the world into our soul purpose. Out of all these points and others, we choose the sequence of points that the person needs at that moment in life.

There are also what are called the seas of nourishment. These combinations of points can be used to profoundly regenerate energy when it is needed. They can help many chronic difficulties but are strong treatments and result better when there has already been some balance to treatment. They provide the boost to treatment that the person needs to get to a level where more ordinary treatment becomes beneficial.

The first of these is the sea of nourishment. This gives a rich nourishment to the entire system by combining ST30, *Qi Chong* with ST36, *Zu San Li*. ST30, *Qi Chong* means a great thoroughfare of Qi. It fires the entire system with Qi when cycles are out of balance and there is weariness and a lack of movement. This point is also linked to the Chong Mai meridian where there is a united vitality and fullness of all the meridians. Here we a have a whole nourishing vital thrust of Qi energy giving great vitality to all the meridians. This is combined with ST36, *Zu San Li* meaning to walk in the great strength of stillness. This is the earth point of the stomach meridian, where we have the full the resources of earth energy that gives us great stamina and a replenishment of vitality.

TREATMENT AND THE FIVE ELEMENTS

Using these two point together we give a vast, nourishing and enriching sea of energy to the person.

The next sea is the sea of energy for revitalizing energy when it has some stability but does not seem to be getting enough through other treatment. Here we use REN MAI 17, *Dan Zhong*, BL10, *Tian Zhu*, and ST9, *Ren Ying* together. The point REN MAI 17, *Dan Zhong*, means the centre of our inner storehouse of light and life. As we move upwards along the Ren Mai meridian the points contain deeper and richer experiences for our spiritual potential. This point is a place of great tenderness. It lies in between the breasts. When we moxa this point we can feel a great sensitive tender loving warmth. It is as though pure light is pouring into our spirit, nourishing it with love. When we need to grow and open with tenderness, it is this point that nourishes the peace and harmony within. It enables us to expand our love of others. Here we are nourished with the purest grains of light, love and warmth which opens our compassion for others. BL10, *Tian Zh*u is the supporting pillar of the heavens. This point contains the stable vast resource of water to fill our system with vitality and great strength. It also connects that strength with heavenly guidance. The third point is ST9, *Ren Ying* which means to receive our humanity. With this point we return to our centre and its original stamp of our path in life. When we reconnect to this inner strength and purpose we regain the vital forces that enable us to achieve the task life has given us. These three point dynamically bring us back to the inner strength of our vitality, filling our system with energy.

RECEIVING SPIRIT

The next sea is the sea of blood. This combines BL11, *Da Zhu*, ST37, *Shang Ju Xu* and ST39, *Xia Ju Xu*. BL11, *Da Zhu*, means the great important weaving of the shuttle. This point is both the vision and organization of the inner bladder line that contains the points that have a direct contact with all the vital organs of the body. This point weaves the dynamic pattern between the vital organs to keep them in harmony. ST37 *Shang Ju Xu* means the great tiger vitality of the heavens. The tiger is said to have great vitality and strength. This point gives us the vitality and strength of the energy of the heavens that is constantly nourishing our energy while we live. ST39 *Xia Ju Xu* means the great nourishing tiger vitality of earth. This point gives us the vitality and strength of the energy of the earth that constantly nourishes us while we live. So these three points give us a burst of the vital energy of heaven and earth that is constantly flowing through all our meridians and vital organs. Combining the three gives a wealth of vitality to our blood. This point I have used with people with chronic diseases or whose vitality remains low even with regular treatment. After doing one of the seas I usually find ordinary treatment then keeps the balance.

The final sea is the sea of bone marrow. The points on this sea are Du Mai 15, *Ya Men*, Du Mai 16, *Feng Fu*, Du Mai 19, *Hong Ding* and Du Mai 20, *Bai Hui*. Du Mai 15, *Ya Men* means the gateway of dumbness. This point touches the deep quiet meditative space within us. It links both the Du Mai and the Yang Wei Mai helping to direct all yang energy from the stillness within connecting it to the vast network of life.

TREATMENT AND THE FIVE ELEMENTS

This touches our inner original source and its vast dynamic connections. DU MAI 16, *Feng Fu* means the palace of the winds. This point allows us to touch the deep inner vision of where our life is going. It takes us to a higher level where the rooms of life are freshly aired and filled with light. Here our vision brightens and heightens. DU MAI 19, *Hong Ding* means the summit of earthly life. This point brings us all our earthly influences. This is a summit where we can see the full view of our potential and deeply connect to it. DU MAI 20, *Bai Hui* means the meeting of grand unity. This is a place of council where all the meridians can come together and be united to work together for the maximum harmony and balance. Here is held the balance between yin and yang, the light and dark, and heaven and earth. It is where all the meridians are guided from the original source of life. These four points create a sea to nourish our bone marrow which regenerates our body cells as well as holds our emotional memories. This sea can profoundly heal this deepest core of our body when the time is right.

Once we have nourished spirit, we use points along the twelve ordinary meridians to nourish the elemental imbalance and bring it back into harmony. Each of the twelve meridians have a wealth of points, which when carefully chosen, can fully resource the person in their life. Indeed, it is these twelve meridians that work hard to balance our lives naturally each day throughout all the seasons. We use acupuncture when there is a disruption to the person's energy that is giving them ill health or dis-ease in their life. These points help to rebalance the spirit as well as the the elemental imbalance. If the elemental imbalance is in wood then the treatment should always include points on the gallbladder and the liver. If the imbalance is on earth, then the treatment should include points on the spleen and stomach meridians. If the imbalance is on metal then we use the lung and large intestine. If the imbalance is on water then we use the points on the bladder and kidneys. If the imbalance is on fire then we listen to see if the person has a problem of sorting or if it is one of the heart protector not being able to regulate the person's fire. If it is a question of sorting, we treat on the heart and small intestine meridians and if it is a question of the heart protector being to open or too closed, we treat on the heart protector meridian and the *san jiao* or the triple burner meridian.

Each of the twelve ordinary meridians have element points that help to balance the five elements and the pulses within the meridians. For example on the heart meridian we have HT3, *Shao Hui*, the inner sea which is the water point that brings fluidity and vibrant water energy to the meridian. HT4, *Ling Dao*, the true path of sprit is the metal point bringing the qualities of inspiration to our inner essense and allowing us to let go of what is no longer needed. HT7, *Shen Me*n, the gateway of spirit, is the earth point and brings great nourishment to our lives. HT8, *Shao Fu* is the fire point, and the real home of the heart where it rests in the love and warmth of the fire element. HT9, *Shao Chong* the inner rushing forward, is the wood point bringing fresh vision and a forward surge of energy as happens in the springtime.

TREATMENT AND THE FIVE ELEMENTS

We each have all of these points feeding us energy day and night. Just by meditating on these points we can contact and renew our energy resources and also learn more about the points. The creative potential of the acupuncture points knows no limits and each tradition gives us insights into the depths and potentials of each of the points. Let us now look at points on each of the twelve ordinary meridians in turn and how they might be used to bring energy into balance and help the person gain harmony in their life.

WOOD ELEMENT

In spring every plant and bud bursts forth with dynamic energy. There is the hope and vision of a new year in vibrant green growth and abundant blossoms. The wood element within ourselves gives us our vision and a picture of what the future will bring us. Our hope opens our ability to realize this vision. It is with this forward dynamic energy and hope that the wood element gives us, that we find the motivation and sense of purpose for what we do and realize in our life.

Our wood element is nourished by the meridians of the gallbladder and liver. The gallbladder is the decision maker, working hard to make all the decisions we need each day to live. When in balance it makes these decisions in a good and upright way so everything functions in harmony. When it is not in balance we may hold on to old ideas and become like old wood that is inflexible. The liver is the master planner and holds the vision of life. He is like the architect that draws up the master plan of life. When in balance we have a good vision of life and the flexibility to achieve our goals. When out of balance we lose sight of where we are going. Both of these meridians give us the upward thrust of spring energy and the vision to put life into action in the same way a small seed burst into flower in springtime with an unstoppable driving force. If the wood element within us is out of balance then we may not be able to make good decision and our vision of life maybe clouded over. We become frustrated and even angry that we can't seem to move forward. By using points on both the gallbladder and liver meridians we can rebalance the wood element within the person so they are no longer held back by old wood but spring forth like a new sapling. Let us now look at some of the points along these meridians and how they might help build and balance the element of wood within a person. I will give examples of treatments at the end to give an idea of the wealth of healing contained in these meridians.

The gallbladder has many wonderful points. Let us first look at some of the head points. The entry point GB1, *Tong Zi Liao*, means the bone of fresh innocent eyes. When we use this point it gives the person a freshness of vision and newness of perception that is the expression of springtime itself. GB9, *Tian Chong*, brings the full rushing inspirations of the heavens to the gallbladder. Here we can experience the fresh illumination and full force of sunshine that comes with the springtime, clearing the sky and bringing back the life force in all growing things. GB13, *Ben Shen*, means the very root of spirit. It also connects to the Yang Wei Mai which is like a great energetic yang network. This point contains the pure

TREATMENT AND THE FIVE ELEMENTS

life forming essence that is in every seed and reconnects us with our own essence. Each seed contains the ability to fully develop through life. *Ben Shen* is the established root of our spirit. This point touches the vast potential of our inner core that both reconnects us to the vast inner and outer network of life of the Yang Wei Mai, but also allows us to experience a fuller vision of life. This point is best used when a person is doing well in life but wants to go more deeply into what life holds for them. It takes the person to a deeper level of spirit.

GB17, *Zheng Ying*, means a correct, impartial, upright plan. It is also on the Yang Wei Mai meridian. This point is like the control centre of the gallbladder where life is governed with impartial, good, upright decisions. Here our vision is balanced and our plans are put into action in an upright, good and well regulated manner. GB18, *Cheng Ling*, means the receiving of spirit. Here we receive our heavenly gifts of insight and wisdom. In this way our calligraphy can be painted with vitality and our songs and poems are performed with illumination and beauty because heaven is flowing through us. This point fills us with this heavenly connection. GB20, *Feng Chi*, means the reserves of the winds. This point gives the person a dynamic resource of energy providing great vitality and flexibility. It is linked to both the Yang Wei Mai which puts life into dynamic graceful movement and the Yang Wei Mai which acts as a dynamic yang network of vitality. This point is a profound powerhouse of energy.

There are many beautiful body points along the gallbladder meridian that help to bring balance and harmony to its decision making. These points can deeply nourish an elemental imbalance in wood. GB21, *Jian Jing*, means the well of the shoulder. This is also on the Yang Wei Mai and its dynamic yang network of profound energy. This point can regulate life from a deep level and create a dynamic network of balanced energy. Here we can refind a deep connection with our entire structure to bring balance and harmony to our energy. GB24, *Ri Yue*, means sunlight and moonlight. This point brings peace, harmony and balance to the entire meridian and is often used to deeply heal the imbalance. Here day and night, yin and yang, strength and softness are all brought back into balance giving a sense of deep calm and harmony. GB26, *Dai Mai*, means to carry the vital circulations. This point links to the Dai Mai which guides all the meridians to work in harmony to give the maximum growth to life. This point holds the core essence of the meridian and is like a sheep dog that brings all the other meridian home to its vital centre. This point deeply resources the gallbladder and brings it back into balance at a profound level. GB29, *Ju Liao*, means to dwell in the strength and protection of bone. It is also linked to both the Yang Wei Mai which puts life into dynamic graceful movement and the Yang Wei Mai which acts as a dynamic yang network of vitality. This point can give a dynamic healing thrust of energy to the entire system. Here we can find the resources to walk more harmoniously and dynamically through life. When the element of wood is out of balance these points on the head and body can profoundly help to bring the balance back and enliven the spirit of the person.

TREATMENT AND THE FIVE ELEMENTS

To finish the treatment session we use the points on the lower leg and foot. These ground the treatment, supporting the person in walking their life with the changes in energy. Let us now look at some of these points used at the end of the treatment session. GB34, *Yang Ling Quan*, is the earth point and means a spring of nourishing refreshing energy. Here is a fresh spring of energy flowing out of the earth to feed the meridian and bring stability and growth. It is where our vitality can be regenerated, cleansed and revitalized. This gives us flexibility and a sense of a richly nourished balanced centre. GB37, *Guang Ming*, means clear illumination. This is the junction or luo point of the meridian. It gives the person a brilliant burst of inner wisdom and illumination to bring forth good decisions. We can feel ourselves being rekindled in fresh sunlight so we have the support to grow into who we are. We can then accomplish our goals with clear judgements and decisions. GB38, *Yang Fu*, means to be supported by the movement of yang. This is the fire point of the meridian. When the person needs more love, warmth and fire in their lives and needs support to make their relationships more mature, we can call on this point to bring the rich warm, fire yang energies of the sun to fire the person with love and compassion. A softness comes to the person and they are more able to mature and give and receive appropriate warmth, love, generosity and understanding.

GB40, *Qiu Xu*, means a hill mound in the wilds of nature. Here is the source point of the meridian and gives the meridian all that it needs at a certain point in time. It is a vantage point to see deeper into the magnificence of nature from a place of balance and security. It brings harmony back into our inner growth. Here we can see many ways and understand the variety in life as well as grow and flower in the sun and rain of springtime. GB41, *Zu Lin Qi*, means a foot that moves to walk out of winter's tears. This is the wood point of the meridian and is its heart and home. When used in springtime, it can give the gallbladder meridian a dynamic charge of energy and bring it back into balance and harmony. Here anger, frustration, and old woody habits are transformed into dynamic energy and the person sparkles with vibrance.

GB43, *Xia Xi*, means a generous bold valiant stream. The rains of winter nourish the seeds of spring. This is the water point of the meridian nourishing it with the vibrance and fluidity of water. As water is the mother of wood this point richly nourishes the meridian and enables us to be refreshed and move forward with flexibility. Here we can walk out of winter with a real spring in our step. GB44, *Zu Qiao Yin*, means to walk out of a still place of inner light. This is the metal point of the gallbladder meridian. Metal gives us the sense of our inner essence and gives us a quality to life. It helps us to let go of what we no longer need so we can breathe in fresh inspirations. We can feel our inner dignity, our sense of worth and find the insights to inspire our life. Here we can dwell in the specialness of our inner nature.

The liver is the master planner and visionary. He knows the blueprint of our lives and helps us to envision our world. When the liver is out of balance we may lose this vision and become stuck and unable to move forward. When in balance we have a good sense of our goals and with the help of the gallbladder accomplish what we desire. There are lovely points along this meridian.

Again we use the points on the lower leg and foot to ground and finish the treatment. LIV1, *Da Dun*, means the fullness of good esteem. This is the wood point of the meridian where it is in its essence and centre. Here we can shed our dead wood and move forward with new growth and inspired vision. We feel our self esteem grow and sense a thrust of dynamic energy to help us move forward. With our vision refreshed we spring into life like a fresh bud of spring. LIV2, *Xing Jian*, means to walk the space between. This is the fire point of the meridian giving us love, warmth and light to help us grow in a balanced way. When our hearts have this love, joy and laughter, then we can enter the relationships in our lives with compassion and enjoyment. We warm to new ideas and friendships and become flexible like new wood in spring. LIV3, *Tai Chong*, means the supreme rushing forward. This is both the source and earth point of the meridian bringing the nourishment and resources that the meridian needs. Here we can dwell in a safe secure nourishing centre out of which we can find the dynamic energy to move forward in our lives.

LIV4, *Zhong Feng*, means our middle seal. This point is the metal point of the meridian that gives us quality and brings a sense of worth to our vision in life. Here we can find our own special way of being that gives value to everything we do. When we have this stamp of specialness, we know the quality within ourselves and can see the special gifts of all things around us. LIV5, *Li Gou*, means a network of insects and is the junction or luo point. This point contains a great fullness of dynamic energy that can enable us to grow out of a place that is rigid, stuck or stale into a place of a dynamic network like the energy of a hive of bees creating their sweet vision of pure golden honey. LIV8, *Qu Quan*, means a maze of spring waters. This is the water point giving us resources and fluidity. At this point the plans of the liver can be rejuvenated and filled with strength and excitement. When we touch these deep inner springs within we find the answers to all our questions.

The following body points are used to nourish the spirit of the person. LIV12, *Ji Mai*, means a vital circulation. This point gives great vitality to our entire structure. LIV13, *Zhang Men*, means the opening of a beautiful composition. When this point is used it can help us to open an entire new chapter in our lives. LIV14, *Qi Men*, means the gate of hope. This point is linked to the Yin Wei Mai which is a dynamic network of yin. Here we can refind hope in life when the way has been long and difficult. This point used when we are well balanced, is where we can see and move into new places in life. We are able to see the richness and vast possibilities before us and stride forward into the wealth of the future.

Now let us look at three consecutive treatments used for three people with a wood elemental imbalance. Mr. B came suffering from stiff joints. He said he was having difficulties with his adolescent children. He also said he never felt he could clearly see where his life was going. The first treatment consisted of an aggressive energy drain, BL38(43), *Gao Huang Shu,* to send warmth to every cell in his body and the source points, GB40, *Qiu Xu* on the gallbladder and LIV3, *Tai Chong* on the liver.

The next week he was feeling better physically but low in spirits and was still having arguments with his boss and teenage son. I used BL42(47) *Hun Men* to support his core spirit, Du Mai 8, *Jin Suo,* to give ease to the whole system and the wood points, GB41, *Zu Lin Qi* on the gallbladder and LIV1, *Da Dun* on the liver to clear out the old wood and give him more flexibility.

The next time he said he was feeling more himself and was more able to discuss things rather than being angry. For this treatment I gave him GB26, *Dai Mai,* for vitality, and GB24, *Ri Yue,* for balance. Then I gave him LIV4, *Zhong Feng,* for his inner sense of worth and GB38, *Yang Fu,* to give love and compassion to his heart. His eyes were full of life and his body much more relaxed

Mrs. S had returned after several months feeling her energy was lower than normal. I did not need to to do an aggressive energy drain as she had come a couple of months before. She told me she had lost her father. Her pulses were low but fairly even. I began the treatment with BL38(43), *Gao Huang Shu,* or rich for the vitals, to send energy through her system and warm every cell in her body with love. I then went to KI25, *Shen Cang,* or the treasury of spirit to give her spirit support. She was deeply relaxed at this point and the pulses had come up. I finished this session with the source points of the gallbladder and liver, GB40, *Qiu Xu*, wilderness mound, and LIV3, *Tai Chong*, the supreme rushing forward.

The next time she came she was still tired but felt better in her spirits. Her pulses were better than the last time so I began with the vitality of GB26, *Dai Mai*, or the vital circulations of the gallbladder. The pulses came up. I did REN MAI 16, *Zhong Ting*, or the middle palace courtyard which nourished her heart in this courtyard of love and warmth. To give more strength to the meridians I did GB39, *Xuan Zhong*, the gathering goblet where the gallbladder is united with the stomach and bladder. I then did GB43, *Xia Xi*, to bring the resources of water to her energy and LIV5, *Li Gou*, the network of insects or the junction or lou point. She looked bright and full.

She came a couple of weeks later. Her pulses were balanced and had not dropped very much. I began the treatment with the beautiful point GB24, *Ri Yue*, called sun and moon. This point brings the balance of the sun and moon to the meridian and helps the patient to feel stable and strong. Because she was so much better, I then went to KI26, *Yu Zhong*, which brings great elegance to the person. She commented she felt a deep harmony within her heart at this point. To finish the treatment I did GB41, *Zu Lin Qi*, the wood point to bring fresh growth and inspiration and LIV1, *Da Dun*, the fullness of good esteem. She looked radiant and well

Mrs E comes regularly for several session in the summer to maintain her energy. Her pulses were low but even. I began the treatment with GB26, *Dai Mai*, which gives great energy

TREATMENT AND THE FIVE ELEMENTS

to the vital circulations of the body and particularly the wood element. The pulses were still a bit low so I then went to REN MAI 6, *Qi Hai*, or the sea of Qi. The pulses came up and she breathed a sigh of contentment. To help with the confusion she sometimes feels with her job I then gave her GB37, *Guang Ming*, which means clear illumination. I finished the treatment with LIV3, *Tai Chong*, the supreme rushing forward and GB40, *Qiu Xu*, the wilderness mound. Both of these source points gave strength to the pulses.

When she came the next time she was feeling better but felt she could use a resource of energy for the next few weeks. Her pulses were fairly even but straining somewhat. To even out the whole system I went to GB24, *Ri Yue*, the sun and moon. She brightened and said she felt much more calm and fortified. I then went to DU MAI 9, *Zhi Yang*, the peak fullness of yang, to feed her system with the fires of summer. The pulses were full and vibrant. I finished with the wood points on the two meridians, GB41, *Zu Lin Qi*, foot above the winter waters, to bring fresh growth and inspiration and LIV1, *Da Dun*, the fullness of good esteem. She said she felt really well.

She came again just before the end of the season and said she was expecting to adopt three children in the next months. To help prepare her for this joy I began the treatment with LIV14, *Qi Men*, or the gateway of hope and expectation. I then went to KI13, *Qi Xue*, called the opening of Qi or the door of infants. Her pulses were sparkling. I then gave her the fire points of the two meridians to bring love, warmth and compassion to her energy. These were GB38, *Yang Fu*,

RECEIVING SPIRIT

the supporting movement of yang and LIV2, *Xing Jian*, the illuminated space. She said her heart felt expanded and full.

FIRE ELEMENT

The fire element fills us with love, laughter, warmth and joy. When there are imbalances in our fire element we may lack warmth, our spirit may not be able to find the joys in life and our laughter maybe strained or anxious. Our relationships become difficult. We may over heat and become anxious and overwhelm others. If fire is out of control a person may overload their feelings and emotions. When the fire inside us is low we lack sparkle and become dull. Without enough fire people cover and protect themselves and shut off from others. When the fire element within us is full of joy and love, then we are open and honest and we enjoy meeting people with kindness and generosity. The fire element helps us to engage with others with love and a deeply mature sharing of our lives.

There are four meridians of the fire element. The heart meridian gives all the other meridians the love, warmth and joy that they need. It is the heart that deeply knows our way in life. When we move into life with the wisdom, love and understanding of the heart, we are honest and mature in our relationships. Our heart is where we feel deep passion, love and profound feelings of inner truth and wisdom. When the heart is out of balance, we become anxious, and lack feelings of love, warmth and joy. We can not find our inner calm and understanding. We do not have our spark to life and become dull. When the heart is well our spirit is filled with light, warmth and love and our life is meaningful and joyful.

The small intestine sorts the pure from the impure allowing only pure energy into the heart. It helps our body sort out the impurities and additives in our food. It helps us to realize what is good and valuable in the information we receive each day and what needs to be discarded. In this way we know what is right and proper and what we need to avoid. The small intestine sifts through and sort out our ideas, thoughts and beliefs enabling us to simply retain the pure and vital. When the small intestine is out of balance we lack this ability and our body is left with impurities in food, our minds are confused and muddled with the vast information coming in and our spirit does not have the strength to flourish. When the small intestine is in balance our body is able to sort the rubbish from the good, our minds are able to distinguish what is appropriate and what is not and our spirit is filled with the love, light and goodness of nature.

The pericardium or heart protector protects the heart from the bumps and hurts of life. Life places great stresses and strains on the heart and it is the heart protector that protects the heart from these shocks and traumas. When we have a blow to the heart, it is the heart protector that takes the impact so the heart can continue to give the love and warmth to the entire mind, body and spirit. It is the heart protector that allows the goodness of the heart to flow outward and also allows the goodness of the spirit of nature to flow inward. When the heart protector is out of balance we may over protect ourselves and others or become so open that our barriers to hurts and upsets has no protection. When the heart protector closes its barriers no love can get out nor can love come in and we become cold and unloving. Sometimes after too much battering the heart protector just gives up and allows anything in which injures the heart. We become joyless and have no inner warmth. When the heart protector is in balance then love flows freely. Our hearts are protected and able to receive and give love appropriately and our relationships are filled with laughter and joy.

The triple burner or *san jia*o gives the heart the exact temperature it needs. It gives the other meridians the warmth and love that they need to function well. It keeps all the meridians in balance and harmony so our entire body, mind and spirit functions well and fluidly. If this meridian is out of balance we can become hot and cold in our relationships. If we do not have the ability to adjust to different relationships, to give and take and to share what is needed, then we may have mood swings, give the wrong response and give inappropriate responses. When the triple burner is in balance then we easily give the warmth, love and understanding to our relationships and adjust to what life brings us. Let us now look at some of the wonderful points on these meridians beginning with the heart.

The heart meridian begins with the point HT1 *Ji Quan*, which means the utmost source. This point goes to the very source of the heart where we can find its inner calm and wisdom again, when life has been hard and difficult. We can experience the fullness of the love and fire of the heart. Here is the heart source feeding all the other meridians with love, compassion and fire energy. HT2, *Qing Ling*, means the vibrant alchemical transforming power of blue green spirit. Here are the transformations of love of the heart. HT3, *Shao Hai*, means our inner sea of loving fire and is the water point of the meridian. It keeps our heat fires in balance and harmony and gives them the fluidity to flow with strength and vitality. HT4, *Ling Dao*, means the true path of spirit and is the metal point of the meridian. Here our inner nature and core essence shines with love and compassion. We feel in our hearts who we are. We leave behind the old and have the confidence to move forward and to sparkle in our own special way. This point is like a quiet calm meditation where we feel an inner glimmering of who we can be and have the courage to then move forward.

HT5, *Tong Li*, means the flowering of our inner nature. This is the junction or luo point of the meridian. It opens our deep inner warmth and fills us with the vital love we need so we can flower into the precious being we are. Here our tender feelings and individual spirit flourishes in life. HT6, *Yin Xi*, means the view from the inner mountain. Here we stand on the mountain of the heart where we can see the wider horizons. We are filled with awe inspiring views. We can find new insights and see further into the deeper meanings in life. HT7, *Shen Men*, means the gateway of spirit. This is both the source point as well as the earth point. It gives the meridian of the heart the nourishment it needs filling it with joy, laughter, fire and love. Through this gateway we can feel the spirit of love that constantly surrounds us in nature.

HT8, *Shao Fu*, means the inner treasury of the palace. This is the fire point and when used in summer in its horary time between 11H-13H, this point can give the meridian the healing riches it needs. Here it gathers the summer fires of the natural world to bring itself back into balance and harmony. This is the residence of the heart where we can find the treasures of the inner palace chambers of the heart. Here we find all the love, compassion and wisdom we need. HT9, *Shao Chong*, means an important inner surge of warmth. This is the wood point of the meridian of the heart. Wood feeds the fire, building it up and giving it the upward surge of springtime. This burst of wood energy can give strength and fresh insights so we open to life with the freshness of a spring day.

The small intestine sorts the pure from the impure enabling us to discern the values in life. The first point on this meridian, SI1, *Shao Ze*, means an inner marshland. Marshes are places of both separation as well as mineral wealth. They are a place of stillness where we can meditate and see with more clarity, depth and wisdom. *Shao Ze* is the metal point of the meridian allowing what is no longer needed to sink down and be transformed into rich minerals while the pure water above reflects a clarity of vision. This point brings back the qualities of life and is where the person can feel their own special essence. SI2, *Qian Gu*, means a forward valley and is the water point of the meridian. At this point we can receive the reserves of water, be refreshed and flow with life again.

TREATMENT AND THE FIVE ELEMENTS

Here we have fresh vitality and the courage to move forward. SI3, *Hou Xi*, means the energetic movement of a mountain stream. This is the wood point of the meridian giving it the fresh burst of springtime. It puts a sparkle of excitement and dynamic thrust into the energy. It is wood that feeds the fire and gives it the potential to fire new ideas and growth. SI4, *Wang Ku*, mean the flexibility of the wrist bone. This is the source point of the meridian that gives it the flexibility to sort well. This point gives us great stability, nourishment and harmony and feeds the meridian with what it needs.

SI5 *Yang Gu*, means a valley filled with yang warmth. It is the fire point of the meridian where the rubbish can be burned away and we can be filled with love, warmth and tenderness. When used in the season of summer and in its horary time of 13H-15H, it receives the wealth of warm yang energy of the summer to heal at a profound level. This point can calm the blazing anxiety of a fire out of control and give warmth to a fire that is cold and bring us back into harmony. SI6, *Yang Lao*, means the nourishment and cultivation of the elders. This point brings tremendous nourishment to our energy. It connects us to the understanding and guidance of the wisdom of our inner elders and ancestors. Old problems can be seen in a more mature light and life can be viewed in greater depth from a more ancient source of wisdom. SI7, *Zhi Zhong*, means a correct, impartial, upright branch. This point is the junction or luo point where we have the support for understanding all that is exact, regular and correct.. This point bring a fullness of energy to the small intestine and brings it back into balance so it can sort the pure from the impure well by either giving more structure or relaxing too much rigidity. SI8, *Xiao Hai*, means the inner mother sea. This is the earth point of the meridian which brings stability, nourishment and centering to the person. Here the fire is nourished by an inner sea of energy, where the person can feel cared for in the joyful comforts and stability of the mother earth herself. These points we use at the end of treatment to ground the person's energy.

These next points on the small intestine are used in the middle of treatment to deeply support the meridian. SI10, *Nao Shu*, which means the vital transfer of energy to the shoulder, is a point that has a tremendous reserve of energy for regulating our core structure from the very marrow of our bones. It links to both Yang Qiao Mai and the Yang Wei Mai. It is a point that can bring a profound balance to our entire structure. Here we can also shed the burdens of our shoulders and reach out to new experiences. SI11, *Tian Zong*, means the heavenly assembly of ancestors. When we use this point the person is taken to their ancestral depths. This point can give deep spiritual support and open insights into life when the time is right for the person. SI12, *Bing Feng*, means to seize the power of the winds. Wind is spirit and the movement of the breath of the world. Here we are filled with an abundance of energy to give us the movement and inspiration to move forward and open our horizons.

SI16, *Tian Chuang*, means a window to the brightness of heaven. We use this point when the person wants to see beyond the ordinary. When used in the right time it can

TREATMENT AND THE FIVE ELEMENTS

open the person to the beauty within themselves and the world. Here we find the things that fill life with purpose and inspiration. We see the wonders in the world around us and our eyes sparkle. SI19, *Ting Gong*, means the true listening in the palace of treasures. Here is a temple where we can listen, understand and allow clarity to come to us from the depths of our hearts. As we listen deeply within, we become a palace of virtuous thoughts and knowledge that gives us clarity and refinement.

Here are three examples of treating someone with a small intestine and heart elemental imbalance. Mrs. P made an appointment saying she was finding life full of confusion. Although I gave her clear directions, she was lost several times on route. Fortunately she had a mobile phone and only arrived an hour late after several calls. When she arrived she said this was always happening to her. In the first treatment I did an aggressive energy drain. After taking pulses I did a Ren Mai/Du Mai block. It was remarkable the colour change on her face. I then did SI6, *Yang Lao* to deeply nourish the system. I finished with the source points, HT7, *Shen Men*, spirit gate, and SI4, *Wang Ku*, the flexibility of the wrist.

The next treatment she arrived on time and she said she had been much clearer all week, like a cloud had lifted. Her pulses were even but had dropped. I began with SI10, *Nao Shu* to give the meridian the reserves it needed with a good pulse result. Next I did the shu points of BL15, *Xin Shu* and BL27, *Xiao Chang Shu* to give the heart and small intestine the vitality they needed. The pulses felt even and stable. I finished the treatment with SI8, *Xiao Hai*, the earth point, to well nourish the meridian, and HT5, *Tong Li*, to bring her that inner flowering of her nature.

The next time she came she was looking well and confessed that she had a new boyfriend. Her pulses felt even so it was a question to support her joy. I gave her SI11, *Tian Zong*, to support her with the family ancestors and their approval. Then I did HT8, *Shao Fu*, giving her the joy of the inner treasures of the palace and SI5, *Yang Gu*, to fill her full of yang warmth.

Mr. C came and told me he had high blood pressure and a large amount of anxiety. After the aggressive energy drain, I took his pulses and found a Ren Mai/Du Mai block on the pulses. I very carefully explained to him that he had serious block in energy and I needed to do four points. I explained where they were. He simply said that if it would help he was all for it. When I finished the last point he looked at me and said he could feel a flow of warmth throughout his body. I told him we could even do better as I took the pulses which were low but even. I went to Ren Mai 6, *Qi Hai*, the sea of Qi. I then did SI6, *Yang Lao*, the nourishment of the elders to feed the meridian. I finished with HT7, *Shen Men*, the gateway of spirit to nourish his heart and SI4, *Wang Ku*, the flexibility of the wrist to help him remain flexible in sorting the pure from the impure. I did not use any moxa as his blood pressure was high. However at the end the blood pressure had reduced and he looked much better.

When he came the next time he said he felt less anxious. The blood pressure was lower so I used moxa on the first point.

TREATMENT AND THE FIVE ELEMENTS

The blood pressure actually reduced and I continued to use moxa with the points after that. If it hadn't reduced I would only have needled. I began this treatment by going to the shu points of the heart and small intestine. I began with BL27, *Xiao Chang Shu*, the small intestine shu point and BL15, *Xin Shu*, the heart shu point. The pulses were stronger and more even. For vitality I did BL46(51), *Huang Men*, or the gate of the vital centre. To give the pulses more strength I went to SI7, *Zhi Zheng*, the correct impartial branch of sorting power and the junction or luo point. I then gave him HT5, *Tong Li*, which is the flowering of our inner nature. He sighed and said he could feel the warmth in his heart. I finished with SI8, *Xiao Hai*, the inner mother sea and earth point to nourish him.

He came several weeks later and said he was starting a new job. His pulses were even. I gave him SI11, *Tian Zong*, the heavenly assembly of ancestors to help guide him on this new pathway. I then went to HT4, *Ling Dao*, the true path of spirit. For his vision I went to SI3, *Hou Xi*, which is the force of a mountain stream and the wood point. I finished with HT6, *Yin Xi*, or the view from the inner mountain to give him an expanded viewpoint.

Mrs. T came because she was suffering from heat flashes from the menopause. She also said her heart sometimes had palpitations. After the aggressive energy drain, I found a block in energy between the small intestine meridian and the bladder meridian which I cleared. Her heart and small intestine pulses were still low and she looked as if she needed nourishing. To send warmth and love through out the entire mind, body and spirit I did BL38(43), *Gao Huang Shu*, rich for the vitals. The pulses came up. I then went to BL39(44), *Shen Tang*, the ancestral temple of the heart. This point calmed the heart pulse and seemed to open the other pulses. I then gave her SI4, *Wang Ku*, the flexibility of the wrist to help her small intestine sort well. She was deeply relaxed at this point. I did HT7, *Shen Men*, the gateway of spirit and watched as her colour brightened. The pulses still needed a bit more so I finished the treatment with HT5, *Tong Li*, the junction point taking her to the flowering of her inner nature.

In the next treatment the heart pulses felt slightly agitated. She said she still felt tired but her spirits were better and the hot flashes less. To help the heart and small intestine I began the treatment with the shu points, BL27, *Xiao Chang Shu*, the small intestine shu point and BL15, *Xin Shu*, or the heart shu point. The pulses were more even and solid. To help build up her reserves I then went to HT3, *Shao Hai*, the small inner sea and water point. I then did the junction or luo point of the small intestine, SI7, *Zhi Zheng*, a correct impartial branch to help with the sorting. I finished with SI6, *Yang Lao*, the nourishment of the elders to help the energy recover. When she stood up she said she felt lighter and clearer.

She came a couple of weeks later when she felt her energy falling again. Her pulses were fairly even but felt they needed warmth and sunshine. I began the treatment with Du Mai 9, *Zhi Yang*, or the fullness of yang warmth. It was like giving the heart the wealth of the summer. Because it was in the horary time of the heart and small intestine I decided to do the fire points, SI5, *Yang Gu*, a valley filled with yang warmth and HT8, *Shao Fu*, the inner treasures of the palace. Her pulses were full and sparkling and her eyes bright and lively. She said she felt deeply nourished.

The heart protector or pericardium is the gatekeeper for the heart only allowing in the goodness and love. When the heart protector is out of balance our relationships maybe too cold, allowing nothing in or they maybe too warm, overwhelming others. We maybe too open and unable to protect ourselves from the hurts that come. By using the points on this meridian we bring the heart protector back into balance again.

PC1, *Tian Chi*, means the reservoir of the heavens and PC2, *Tian Quan*, means the source of a heavenly spring. Both of these points give us a drop of the vastness of the heavens so we can see with a deeper vision into the spirit of life. Here we open to the spirit within and find our inner gifts that bring joy and richness to our lives and others. PC3, *Qu Ze*, means an accommodating marshland. This is the water point of the meridian giving vitality and fluidity to the gateways to our hearts. Here our lives flow more fully and easily. PC4, *Xi Men*, means the gateway of reserves. This point can bring reserves of Qi to the person when they are needed. It also balances the reserves of energy. In this way we have the resources of love that we need no matter what the seasonal changes bring.

PC5, *Jian Shi*, means the quiet light of the messenger. This point is the metal point of the meridian that helps us to let go of what is no longer needed and opens the inspirations of new experiences. It is also the meeting point of the meridians of the heart protector, heart and lungs. In this way it brings great harmony, balance, strength and quality to the person as well as reserves of vitality. Here our interactions and relationships are filled with quality, warmth and confidence. PC6, *Nei Guan*, means the connecting net of the inner chambers. This is the junction or luo point of the heart protector. It regulates the fire within by giving it warmth when it is cold or taking a log off when it is raging out of control with anxiety or hysteria. It is like putting a warm caring hand on the heart giving it the love it needs to feel secure.

PC7, *Da Ling*, means a great ancient tumulus. This is both the earth point as well as the source point giving the meridian exactly what it needs to nourish it well. Here are the inner source fires where we feel nurtured and comfortable. Here our hearts are well protected and we have the strength and balance to move forward with love and compassion. PC8, *Lao Gong*, means the ancient palace for weariness. This is the fire point of the meridian giving it the love, joy and laughter that it needs. In this point is contained all the love, nourishment and luxuries of the great palace where a weary heart can revive its lost trust, and let go of its hurts and be filled with joy, warmth and love. When we use this point in summer the natural fire energy fills our hearts with abundance and deep healing. PC9, *Zhong Chong*, means the impetus rushing from the centre and is the wood point. This point gives fire the right amount of wood it needs. Here we can experience a sense of new vitality and growth that comes in the spring. With this push forward life begins afresh and is filled with surprise and inspiration.

TREATMENT AND THE FIVE ELEMENTS

The triple burner or *san jiao* meridian brings just the right amount of love and warmth to all the meridians so that they can function with harmonious action and movement. The meridian begins with TB1, *Guang Chong*, meaning a network full of force. This is the metal point of the meridian that helps us refind the quality in our lives and the dignity of who we are. At this point we can feel our special inner essence blossom. Our anxieties are calmed and we have the confidence of who we are. Here we have the full force of our character to meet others with respect. TB2, *Ye Men*, means the gateway of moist rich juices. This is the water point of the meridian giving us resources and fluidity to flow with life. It can cool anxiety and warm the flow when we are stuck. TB3, *Zhong Zhu*, means an inner island. This is the wood point of the meridian feeding fire with the amount of wood it needs to burn well. Like the spring, this point brings a thrust of vital energy and refreshes us with new growth. The vitality of this point can bring new insights and fresh growth. This can give our heartful meetings a fresh newness. TB4, *Yang Chi*, means a sun filled yang pool. This is the source point of the meridian bringing it the warmth and harmony it needs. It is a pool filled with unlimited sunshine and warmth giving all the meridians joy and love. Here is the source of fire that brings harmony and love to wherever is needed.

TB5, *Wai Guan*, means the gateway of harmony. This is the junction or luo point and regulates the meridian. This point enables our love and joy to flow well. We are no longer withdrawn or overexcited but have a balanced ability to share warmth, companionship and love with others. Here our network of interactions flow in balance and harmony with good exchanges of joy and love. TB6, *Zhi Gou*, means the network of branched ditches. This is the fire point of the meridian that keeps all the gateways of the meridians well oiled. When used in the season of summer and its horary time of 21H-23H, it can balance and harmonize the meridian from the full energy of the summer giving it the warmth it needs for all the year. TB7, *Hui Zong*, means the united strength of the ancestors. Here we can feel our ancestral heritage out of which comes support, wisdom and experience. At this point we can find our ancestral roots and gain a richer more profound understanding of life. TB8, *San Yang Luo*, means the connection of the three yangs. This point connects the triple burner or *san jiao* to the large intestine and small intestine. Together they give this point a tremendous reserve of energy. TB10, *Tian Jing*, means the rich nourishing well of heaven. This is the earth point of the meridian bringing nourishment, stability and care to the person. Here we can feel a great support and be nurtured in the care of mother earth. These points we use to end the treatment and ground the energy so it continues supporting the person.

The following points help to bring harmony to the mind, body and spirit at a deeper level and are used in the middle of treatment. TB11, *Qing Leng Yuan*, means a calm quiet profound pool. This point can lift us out of a deep abyss, so we can see the light again. Here is a space where our heart can be brought back into harmony when the road has been long and

TREATMENT AND THE FIVE ELEMENTS

hard and we are weary in spirit. TB12, *Tian Liao*, means the bone of heaven. This point also connects to the Yang Wei Mai and therefore holds great reserves of energy that can go to the depth of our structure to bring great harmony. TB16, *Tian You*, means the enlightened wisdom of heaven. This point opens our vision further into the beautiful wonders of nature. Here we can open the window and see the treasures of life. We enter the magical gardens within ourselves and see its qualities and deep essence. TB22, *He Liao*, means the singing bone of harmony. This point brings our entire structure into harmony so all the meridians sing together with harmonic chords. It is a good point to use to bring a refined balance to the pulses.

Here are three examples of three consecutive treatments of a fire imbalance on the heart protector and triple burner or *san jiao* meridians. Mr. H came to me because he was not sleeping, very depressed, worried about his business and going through a divorce. His colour was very ashen. During the hour it took to drain the aggressive energy we talked in depth about all of this. I then did KI24, *Ling Xu*, to deeply touch and restore his spirit. He was calm at this point. I followed with BL38(43), *Gao Huang Shu*, to give vitality to every cell in the body. I finished with the source points, PC7, *Da Ling* on the heart and TB4, *Yang Chi*, on the triple burner or *san jiao*. He said he felt calmer and his heart was warmer.

When he came for the second treatment he was still depressed but his sleep had been better. He was more able to cope with his business but still felt torn apart by the divorce. I gave him KI25, *Shen Cang*, the treasure house of spirit,

161

RECEIVING SPIRIT

BL39(44), *Shen Tang*, the palace of the heart. He was calm. I finished the treatment with PC5, *Jian Shi*, the metal point to help him refind his inner essence, and TB10, *Tian Jing*, the rich nourishing well of heaven to bring nourishment and stability.

The next time he came he was feeling as if his heart was beginning to heal. I began the treatment with the point TB15, *Tian Liao*, which deeply harmonizes the fire energy. I then did the shu points of the heart protector, BL14, *Jue Yin Shu* and the triple burner or *san jiao*, BL22, *San Jiao Shu*. His colour was much brighter. I grounded the treatment with TB5, *Wai Guan*, the gateway to outer harmony and PC6, *Nei Guan*, the gateway of the inner chambers. He said he felt a great warmth radiating out from his heart

Mr. R was a young man doing voluntary work on one of the local ecological farms. He had hurt his knee and his back was troubling him. When we talked further I found out his girlfriend had phoned to say she was now in another relationship. As aggressive energy was draining he talked about this and shed some tears. His pulses were low but fairly even. To help with his bones I went to BL59, *Fu Yang*, which give bones the full resource and movement of yang energy. I then gave him BL38, *Gao Huang Shu*, rich for the vitals to send warmth everywhere in the body. To help support him through the difficulties with his girlfriend I gave him Du Mai 12, *Shen Zhu*, called the supporting and sustaining body pillar of life. He said at this point he felt he had come back to himself and his back had ceased to hurt. I finished with the source points, PC7, *Da Ling*, the ancient imperial tumulus, and TB4, *Yang Chi*, the sun filled pool of yang. The pulses were even and felt strong.

The next week he had a block between the small intestine and the bladder which I cleared. He was feeling depressed so I then did KI25, *Shen Cang*, the treasure house of spirit. To help ease his body I did Du Mai 8, *Jin Sao*, the ease and strength of muscles. The pulses were still down so I went to the junction or luo points, PC6, *Nei Guan*, the connecting net of the inner chambers and TB5, *Wai Guan*, the gateway of outer harmony. When he stood up he looked taller and said his heart felt strengthened.

He then came a couple of weeks later. He was going home in a couple of weeks. His pulses were down but even. I began with BL39, *Shen Tang*, the heart chambers of the ancestral temple. It was like filling him with the love and warmth he needed. I then did PC4, *Xi Men*, the gateway of reserves. The pulses were nice and even. To help him feel his own inner essence and worth I gave him PC5, *Jian Shi*, the quiet light of the friend and the metal point. I then gave him TB6, *Zhi Gou*, the network of branched ditches and the fire point of the meridian. The pulses were full so to give them nourishment and stability for his journey home I finished with TB10, *Tian Jing*, the nourishing well of heaven and earth point.

Mr. X phoned to say he was in a crisis as his ex-wife had now found another man. I had not seen Mr. X for about a year at that point. He came and looked very anxious and miserable. While aggressive energy was draining we talked about his relationship and about what he needed to let go of. I began the treatment with KI24, *Ling Xu*, the wildlands of spirit. To help him let go I went to BL40(45), *Yi Xi*, which is the cry of sadness and the joy of song. This point contains us and allows us to refind a calm warmth within to let go and allow our heart to move out of sadness into other affections. He had calmed at this point and the pulses were stronger. I did PC4, *Xi Men*, to bring more energy to the entire system. I then finished with the source points of TB4, *Yang Chi*, the sun filled pool of yang and PC7, *Da Ling*, the ancient tumulus. He was calm and said he felt stronger.

He came again a week later saying he was not sleeping well. I felt his pulses and there was a husband/wife block which I cleared. I again gave him KI24, *Ling Xu*, for his spirit. The pulses were low, but even. To help support him I then went to TB7, *Hui Zong*, or the place of the unity of the ancestors. To help nourish his energy I gave him TB10, *Tian Jing*, the rich nourishing well of heaven and the earth point. The pulses were feeling more alive and even. I finished with PC6, *Nei Guan*, the connecting net of the inner chambers and junction or luo point.

The next time he came he was feeling more solid and had spoken with his ex-wife and was now able to really leave the past and make a new friendship with her. To support this I gave him DU MAI 12, *Shen Zhu*, the supporting pillar of life. I then gave him KI25, *Shen Cang*, the treasure house of spirit. The pulses were even. To give him a sense of his inner essence and self worth I then did the metal points PC5, *Jian Shi*, the

TREATMENT AND THE FIVE ELEMENTS

quiet light of the friend and TB1, *Guan Chong*, the network full of the force of our inner essence. I finished the treatment with TB5, *Wai Guan*, the gateway of outer harmony.

EARTH ELEMENT

The earth element gives us the nourishment, care and stability we need. She connects us to our mother the earth. When we have this energy we feel stable and secure knowing we have a full pantry of reserves. When our earth element is out of balance we lose this stability of being well nourished and cared for. The stomach meridian digests and ripens our Qi energy. The stomach replenishes nourishing Qi for all the other meridians all of the time. When the stomach is out of balance our digestion and ability to take in becomes difficult. There is worry and we feel unstable. Without proper nourishment the other meridians are hungry and become tired and lonely. We lose our connection to our mother the earth and her stability and care. We may begin to crave this care, sympathy and nourishment. When the stomach meridian is in balance we are well nourished, and can feel the stability of our mother the earth holding us in her caring lap.

The spleen meridian takes this nourishment to where it is needed by the other meridians. It carries nourishing Qi all day and night wherever it is needed. When the spleen is out of balance there is poor movement and we lack concentration and have a sense of being stuck. Some meridians become better cared for than others and there is a general lack of love, compassion and care in the spirit. We may feel unstable, isolated and depressed. When the spleen is balanced and functioning well we are connected to the wealth of the harvest and the bounty of mother earth. This abundance flows smoothly to everywhere in the mind, body and spirit and we feel well cared for, nourished, stable and well grounded.

The stomach meridian begins with ST1, *Cheng Qi*, which means to receive tears. Autumn enriches the earth with falling leaves. At this point, earth is nourished so it can become fertile for the next year. This point is also linked to the Yang Qiao Mai which gives movement to life with a dynamic and graceful thrust forward. ST4, *Di Cang*, means the gathering of the earthly harvest. This point also connects to the Yang Qiao Mai giving the point a deep resource of energy. When we have suffered and need this bounty, we can go to this point and find the vitality we need. ST5, *Da Ying*, means to receive with greatness. Here our inner essence is nourished in the wisdom of heaven and the bounty of the earth. This point can take us to a higher level of spiritual awareness when the time is right.

ST8, *Tou Wei*, means the place of tied thoughts. Here we can untie our worries and find the connections, relationships and inspirations we need to come out of the confusions. This point can clear the cobwebs and bring us back to our inner calm centre. ST9, *Ren Ying*, means to receive our humanity. This point opens our perception to the world around. When used in the right time it can open our vision further and deeper into the mysteries of life. In such a way we may begin to see the poetry in a falling leaf, wholeness in a drop of water and the hand of the creator in the magic of the world.

TREATMENT AND THE FIVE ELEMENTS

The following body points are used to nourish spirit. ST11, *Qi She*, means the home of nourishing Qi. This point is like being given a full five seasons meal. ST12, *Que Pen*, means a broken earthenware bowl. This point connects to the Yin Qiao Mai which brings it energy for dynamic and gracefully balanced movement. This point repairs our inner broken bowl when life has been difficult. When we have struggled and feel isolated and disconnected this point can bring us back to our centre where we can feel the warmth, nourishment and care within. ST13, *Qi Hu*, means a door of vital nourishing Qi. This opens a door to the pantry giving us a bounty of vibrant Qi. ST14, *Ku Fang,* is the granary storehouse. It is somewhere we can find what we need when we have not eaten well for a while. Here is a special tidbit to satisfy our hunger and bring our appetite for life back.

ST19, *Bu Rong*, means to fly away from the centre and not be at ease. When we are not at ease within ourselves and uncomfortable in life, then this point can bring us back to our inner calm where we can find the resources, to change our life. Here we can find deep wisdom and insights. ST20, *Cheng Man,* means to receive and contain a complete fullness. Here we experience a rich wonderful abundant fullness of Qi. ST23, *Tai Yi*, means the greatness of the whole. This point puts us in touch with the greatness within ourselves and all things. We rest in the Tao and out of its wonders are able to move forward with deep, mature connections to life.

ST24, *Hua Rou Men*, means a lubricating food gateway. When we can not digest things well, this point lubricates the gateway to help us take in and understand our thoughts, emotions and memories. ST25, *Tian Shu* means to pivot with the heavens. This point gives us great flexibility from a balanced place deep within. Here we have a depth of inner stability and wisdom to move and reach out in all directions. In this way life can pivot in new directions. ST27, *Da Tu*, means the great importance. This point gives us great strength and stamina to help us mature and develop. Here we are filled with a great strength and the fullness of our inner qualities to meet what comes. ST30, *Qi Chong*, means a great thoroughfare of Qi. This point connects with the Chong Mai which is a guiding vessel of great crossings responsible for the pattern of the development of life. This point is charged with a deep dynamic reserve of Qi energy and can be used when we need this vast reservoir of nourishing energy. All of the above points are used in the middle of a treatment to deeply nourish the mind, body and spirit.

The following points on the lower leg and foot are used at the end of treatment to ground the treatment to help the changes integrate into life. ST36, *Zu San Li*, means to walk in great stillness. This is the earth point of the meridian where we can find all the resources we need to feed our earth element. Here is the rich earth energy giving us the stamina to walk our path well nourished and from a deep centre of stability.

ST37 *Shang Ju Xu* means the great tiger vitality of the heavens. The tiger is said to have great vitality and strength. This point gives us the vitality and strength of the energy of the heavens that is constantly nourishing our energy while we

TREATMENT AND THE FIVE ELEMENTS

live. ST38, *Tiao Kou*, means a budding branch. This point opens a new direction in life and supports its development. Suddenly we are able to see the full flowering of our life and have the confidence to take the first step forward. ST39 *Xia Ju Xu* means the great nourishing tiger vitality of earth. This point gives us the vitality and strength of the energy of the earth that constantly nourishes us while we live.

ST40, *Feng Long*, means the splendour of abundant prosperity. This is the junction or luo point of the meridian filling us with full pantries of delicacies. Here we can be fully revitalized in our inner prosperity and riches. ST41, *Jie Xi*, means to untie the flowing force of a mountain stream. This is the fire point of the meridian which feeds earth with its love and warmth. Here we have the fire energy to mature in our relationships. It is where we can be replenished with the love that ripens our thoughts, ideas and feelings. ST42, *Chong Yang*, means the rush of sunshine, warmth and movement. This is the source point of the meridian giving it what it needs. Here we are nourished with the full dynamic rushing warmth of the yang energy of sunshine. It is where we can find the comfort and care we need.

ST43, *Nei Gu*, means to be in the fullness of the valley. This is the wood point of the meridian that gives us a fresh burst of energy. This also gives our vision the fresh newness of spring and its vitality. ST44, *Nei Ting*, means the inner palace courtyard. This is the water point of the meridian that brings courage, strength, fluidity and vitality to our energy. Here are the refreshing inner palace gardens full of canals, fountains and springs making our inner earth luscious. ST45, *Li Dui*, means a sharp disciplined exchange. This is the metal point of the meridian that allows us to let go of what we no longer need so we can be inspired by the new. Here we can find and feel our inner worth and see life from many sides without judgement. In this way we gain respect for ourselves and others and find our inner qualities and essence.

The spleen distributes rich vital Qi to nourish all the meridians with what they need. When it is in balance all is resourced, but when it is out of balance there are shortages and we lose our security and faith in the future. The first point on the meridian is SP1, *Yin Bai*, which means to easily work with pure clear energy. This is the wood point of the meridian that gives us a fresh burst of energy to move things forward. It can open up new ideas and give us a thrust of energy to put those fresh visions into action. SP2, *Da Du*, means a great noble elegant walled city. This is the fire point of the meridian that warms our hearts with love and joy giving it the cultured resources of the great city. This point can help us to become more harmonious and mature in our interactions with others and can deepen our heartful understandings and wisdoms. SP3, *Tai Bai*, means the great movement of pure clear Qi energy. This is both the earth point as well as the source point of the meridian. It is the home and centre of the spleen, where we can find the nourishment and energy we need to replenish our inner earth element. Here is the great energy of harvested Qi, giving us great force and vitality. SP4, *Gong Sun*, means the royal grandson's inherited riches. It is the junction or luo point on the meridian. Here are the great riches of the palace granaries giving our earth element the dynamic resources it needs.

SP5, *Shang Qiu*, means merchant mound as well as the culmination point of deliberation. This is the metal point of the meridian which brings us a sense of our own inner qualities and worth as well as allowing us to let go of what is no longer needed. SP6, *San Yin Jiao*, means the united crossing of the three yins. This point unites the spleen with the liver and the kidneys. It is a point full of dynamic energy to reboost the system when it needs this full resource. SP8, *Di Ji*, means the moving power of earth. Here is the power to move the earth and cultivate new crops. This point helps us to turn over the soil so we can plant new crops and move out of the old patterns of life into a fresh direction. SP9, *Yin Ling Quan*, means a fresh inner mountain spring. This is the water point of the meridian that brings us vitality, courage, and fluidity to flow with life. This point revitalizes our energy giving it refreshing spring waters to send us flowing into life. These points are used at the end of treatment to ground our energy and help the changes integrate into life.

The following points on the body help revitalize our spirit at a deep level. SP12, *Chong Men*, means the gateway of surging fullness. This point holds a full force of dynamically moving Qi that is able to resource the meridian when it has been depleted. It also gives a dynamic fullness to the plans of life when the person is ready to move forward. SP13, *Fu She*, means to dwell in the inner palace. This point is the inner palace of the meridian where we can find care and nourishment and feel a real sense of inner stability. It also connects to the Yin Wei Mai that resources and unites all the yin energy in a dynamic network. Here is a profound depth of energy able to rejuvenate the meridian at a deep level.

SP15, *Da Heng*, means a great balance beam and is also connected to the dynamic network of the Yin Wei Mai. This point brings us balance and harmony and gives us a great resource of profound energy to move forward. SP20, *Zhou Ying*, means to be surrounded with splendour and glory. This is exactly what this point does for the person. It takes them to a place of spirit, of elegance and beauty. SP21, *Da Bao*, means the great enveloping. This point is like a spiritual hug from the heavenly father and our earthly mother. Here we can find the wonders within ourselves and the natural world. This point also brings all the other junction points into harmony and balance.

Now for three case examples of someone with an earth elemental imbalance. Miss C came to me and burst into tears. I gently moved closer and simply held her hand until the tears paused. She said she was just falling apart and could not seem to get above the tears. Between the tears she managed to tell me she was in an accident a year ago and lost the baby she had just become pregnant with. Her boyfriend had then left her and she was finding it difficult to hold down her job. When she laid down on the couch I looked in her eye and saw the possession which I cleared. The sparkle came back to her eyes and she was calmer After the aggressive energy drain she was

TREATMENT AND THE FIVE ELEMENTS

feeling tired. On her pulses I felt a husband/wife imbalance and cleared that. I gave her KI 24, *Ling Xu*, the wild lands of spirit to bring her spirit back to life. I then did the source points on the stomach and spleen, ST42, *Chang Yang*, the rush of sunshine warmth and movement and SP3, *Tai Bai*, the great movement of pure clear energy.

I saw her a few days afterwards. She was like a different person and said she was sleeping much better and was calmer but still had weepy moments. I did KI23, *Shen Feng*, the soul seal of spirit to nourish her inner essence, as well as ST24, *Hua Rou Men*, to help her digest and clear her sorrow. At this point she was deeply calm and the pulses were balanced but still low. I did SP6, *San Yin Jiao*, the united crossing of the three yins to boost the energy. I then went to ST41, *Jie Xi*, and gave her the love and warmth of the fire point. The pulses were nicely balanced and I finished with SP1, *Yin Bai*, the wood point to bring a spark of new vision to her.

When she came the next time she was much brighter and said the weeping was over and she was finding life coming back to her. She also said that she had been promoted at work. The pulses had dropped but were even. I did REN MAI 8, *Shen Que*, the inner tower gateway of spirit to gently nourish her spirit. I then did SP13, *Fu She*, to give her the nourishment of the inner residence of earth. I finished with ST44, *Nei Ting*, the inner palace courtyard to bring refreshment and courage to her energy and SP4, *Gong Sun*, to bring the inheritance of the royal grandson to her. She said she felt calm and full. As she left she looked full, blossoming and bright.

RECEIVING SPIRIT

Mrs. F came to me in a state of severe depression and was on a certain amount of medication. I find that when people are on a certain amount of medication the pulses do not come up as well. However the support they receive in their spirits is wonderful. Mrs. F had aggressive energy on all her yin organs which I cleared. Because she is on long term medication I check aggressive energy regularly so the system can stay as clear as possible. She also had a husband/wife block which I cleared. The pulses were still very low. I then gave her KI24, *Ling Xu*, the wild lands of spirit. The pulses were now settled and softer. To further support the spirit and bring balance to the system I gave her REN MAI 12, *Zhong Wan*, which is the centre of nourishment that brings vitality, stability and security. The pulses now had energy flowing through them. I went to ST36, *Zu San Li*, with the vitality to walk with great strength and stamina. It is the earth point of the stomach and helps to build up the reserves. The pulses were much fuller. I finished with the source points of stomach and spleen, ST42, *Chong Yang*, the rushing energy and movement of the yang sun vitality, and SP3, *Tai Bai*, the great movement of pure clear energy. The pulses were full and had some strength to them.

She came the next time and was very agitated and not at ease with life. She said her worries kept going around in her head. She had a block between the spleen and heart which I cleared. I then gave her ST19, *Bu Rong*, which means not at ease and helps to bring stability and understanding to the trials of life. She sunk into the couch. To help clear the system

TREATMENT AND THE FIVE ELEMENTS

I then did ST24, *Hua Rou Men*, or stomach lubrication gate. It enabled the pulses to flow again. I then went to SP16, *Fu Ai*, which helps to let go of the sorrows of life. The pulses were lighter and flowing better. She said she was feeling different. To build the energy in the pulses I gave her SP6, *San Yin Jiao*, the crossing of the three yins which unites the energy of the spleen with that of the kidneys and liver. The pulses were fuller and moving. I finished with ST41, *Jie Xi*, the release of the full force of a mountain stream and fire point, and SP9, *Yin Ling* Quan, the fresh inner mountain spring waters and water point. The pulses were even and full.

The next time she came she was calmer and smiled as she came in. She then began telling me about the difficulties she had with her family. It was as though she was tied up with old thoughts and worries. The pulses were low but even. I began with ST8, *Tou Wei*, the place of tied thoughts. I then went to KI25, *Shen Cang*, the storehouse of spirit. The pulses were coming up. To give her nourishment I did ST4, *Di Cang*, the gathering of the great harvest. I built up the energy more with the point ST39, *Xia Ju Xu*, the great nourishment of earth. The pulses were even and full. I did SP2, *Da Du*, the energy of a noble city and fire point and ST42, *Chang Yang*, the rush of sunshine, warmth and movement, and source point. The pulses were full and solid. She was smiling and radiant.

Miss O came back after several months to have a few treatment to build up her energy and to help her move into a new job. Her pulses were low but even. I began the session by giving her the rich nourishment of REN MAI 8, *Shen Que*, meaning the inner gateway tower of spirit. To build the pulses and spirit further I gave her ST20, *Cheng Man*, which means receiving fullness and is like being given a full harvest. The pulses needed more energy so I did SP6, *San Yin Jiao*, the crossing of the energies of the spleen, kidneys and liver. I finished with the source points, SP3, *Tai Bai*, the great movement of pure clear energy and ST42, *Chong Yang*, the rushing warmth and movement of the sun, to give her energy nourishment and centering. She looked bright and the pulses felt full and solid.

The next time she came she was going for an interview the next day. In preparation I began the treatment with KI26, *Yu Zhong*, the centre of elegance. The pulses filled and sparkled. I then gave her ST25, *Tian Shu*, meaning to pivot with the heavens. To help her see further in life, I gave her SP15, *Da Heng*, the beam of the great horizon. To finish the treatment I did the junction or luo points, ST40, *Feng Long*, abundant splendour and SP4, *Gong Sun*, the prince's inherited riches. She said she had never felt so good.

The next time she came she said she had gone for the job but they had given her an even better job as they were so impressed with her. To support her in this new venture I began the treatment with ST38, *Tiao Kou*, a new budding branch and ST23, *Tai Yi*, the greatness of the whole. To help her flow in her relationships I then did the fire points, ST41, *Jie Xi*, the untied force of a mountain stream and SP2, *Da Du*, the resources of the great empire. She said she felt as though she could conquer the world. The pulses were shining.

TREATMENT AND THE FIVE ELEMENTS

METAL ELEMENT

The metal element allows us to let go of the old and take in the new. It represents our special essence and the divine spark that inspires our lives. It is this divine fire that lightens our spirit even in our darkest moments. The metal element give us our connection with our heavenly father. When we feel this connection we feel a sense of value and worth in ourselves. Our self esteem helps us to take care of ourselves, to nourish ourselves and to become the best we can become. The metal element also allows us to let go of what we no longer need, just as the leaves fall in autumn. When the metal element is imbalanced we cannot let go. We become stuck in ideas and thoughts, and cannot find our way out of the rubbish and are unable to take in fresh inspiration. We become empty, cold and detached and we loose the deep sense of the quality of our life. When the metal element within us is in balance then we find our sense of self worth, are able to let go of old unuseful ideas and beliefs and feel inspired by the heavens each day.

The large intestine meridian allows us to let go of what we no longer need. It has the responsibility of removing all the rubbish. When it is out of balance this rubbish accumulates and we can not let go. Our lives fill up with the mess. We may begin to rubbish things. When the large intestine is working well, then all the rubbish is cleared out of the system and we see clearly again and our spirit can take in the new.

The lung meridian helps us to take in the fresh air and inspirations of the heavens. This gives our energy both vitality and quality, bringing guidance and authority to our lives.

When it is out of balance we do not have a sense of our inner essence and feel isolated and alone and deeply grieved. When the lung meridian is in balance then we feel our connection with the heavens and have a sense of the true quality of who we are. It brings inspiration and a special quality to each day.

The following body points on the lung meridian revitalize our energy and spirit at a profound level. The first point on the meridian is LU1, *Zhong Fu*, meaning the centre of the palace riches. In this palace of elegance we can meet with our heavenly father who deeply listens to who we are with respect. In this way we find our own unique qualities and insights. LU2, *Yu Men*, means the gateway of clouds. We can go to this point to lift the clouds of depression when life has been hard as well as find the clouds of our dreams when we are wanting inspiration.

LU3, *Tian Fu*, means the great celestial palace. This point takes us to another level, opening our vision and soul to the beauties within ourselves and nature around us. We use this point when the person is well and able to change. LU4, *Xia Bai*, means a generous valiant pure white energy. This point gives us courage and strength to walk our true path.

The following points on the lower arm and hand are used at the end of treatment to ground the treatment and support the changes. LU5, *Chi Ze*, means an expansive marshland. This is the water point of the meridian giving us vitality and fluidity to enrich our inner qualities. LU6, *Kong Zui*, means to penetrate the opening of the void. When we are low in energy or spirit, then this point can deeply move and resource our energy with vitality, respect, courage and love. LU7, *Lie Que*, means to place in order and partake. This is the junction or luo point of the meridian and contains a great concentrated vibrant energy that helps us leave behind what we no longer need and gives a vitality to help us move forward and become who we are.

LU8, *Jing Qu*, means to arrange and regulate the gutters. This is the metal point and home of the meridian. Here the gutters are cleaned out and the inspirations of heaven flow clearly like vibrant rain. Here we can weave the pattern of our life from our own special inner gifts and qualities. When this point is used in the season of autumn it brings the vitality of the season to meridian giving it vitality, freshness and profound healing and rebalancing. LU9, *Tai Yuan*, means a supremely profound pool. This is the source point as well as the earth point of the meridian where it can be given what it needs to be brought back into balance and harmony again. Here is the nourishment and stability that give us the energy and spirit to move forward no matter what the Tao brings to our daily journey.

LU10, *Yu Ji*, means the palace of the great fire fish spirit. This point bathes us in warmth and love. We can relax and feel the respect within us grow stronger and become more open. Here we also find a deep spiritual place of connection. LU11, *Shao Shang*, means our inner quality of values. This is the wood point of the meridian that gives us a fresh burst of energy. Our eyes are washed in fresh spring waters and we let go of the old year and recreate our world with the brightness of springtime. Here we can move forward with new growth, insights and inspirations.

The large intestine sends the rubbish out of the system keeping the meridians clean and flowing well. The following points on the arm and hand are used to finish the treatment and ground it. LI1, *Shang Yang*, means to trade with warmth and great movement. This is the metal point of the meridian where it is in its home. When used in the season of autumn, this point gives the meridian what it needs at a profound level. We can let go of what we no longer need and find the respect and qualities of goodness within. Here we have the bright, warm and expansively full energy of yang. LI2, *Er Jian*, means the space of light between heaven and earth. This describes the constant fertile interaction between heaven and earth. At this point we feel this fertile flow. It is the water point of the meridian enabling us to be revitalized and flow with life.

LI3, *San Jian*, means the space of light between heaven, earth and man. This is the wood point of the meridian. Here is a full burst of energy that brings forth new growth. LI4, *He Gu*, means the joining of the forces of the valleys. This is the source point of the meridian giving it the force it needs to clear out the rubbish. Here the rivers of the valleys give great vibrant vitality to the meridian leaving us clear and refreshed.

LI5, *Yang Xi*, means the warm vibrant movement of a mountain stream. This is the fire point of the meridian that fills us with dynamic, loving warm, joyful energy. With this warmth and love our relationships mature, strengthen and grow in quality. LI6, *Pian Li*, means to lean towards an end of a cycle. This point is the junction or luo point. Here we can let go and finish the cycle so we can move on to the next. This point allows us to let go so the freshness and vitality can come in and we can move forward into the richness of life.

LI7, *Wen Liu,* means a stream of warm kind benevolence. This point give us great warmth and enables us to feel close to others and softer in ourselves. LI10, *Shou San Li,* means the strength of three miles. This point holds a great resource of Qi and can be used when we need stamina and a resource of energy. LI11, *Qu Chi,* means a pool of accumulated Qi. This is the earth point of the meridian that brings nourishment, care and stability to our lives.

The following points on the body are used in the middle of treatment to bring vitality and refreshment to the mind, body and spirit at a deep level. LI15, *Jian Yu,* means the monkey bone that shoulders life. This point gives us the resources to shoulder our work with strength and good authority bringing a sense of self esteem and pride. Here we can let go of the rubbish of years and move into life with a strength of character, pride, quality and competence. This point also links to the Yang Qiao Mai giving our movement grace and power. LI16, *Ju Qu,* means a very great bone. This point is linked to the Yang Qiao Mai giving our energy power and graceful movement. Here is an abundance of dynamic and profound energy able to resource our entire structure and take us to the depth of our inner core.

LI18, *Fu Tu,* means a supported rushing forward. This point takes us to another level where our perceptions open

RECEIVING SPIRIT

and our inner gifts and qualities reveal themselves. Here the window opens and we see vitality, inspiration and beauty everywhere. LI20, *Ying Xiang*, means to desire fragrances. This point brings freshness to our lives and we find pleasures and delights. Here our appetite for life and its inspirations can be re-awakened.

Here is an example of three treatments of three people with a metal imbalance. The first thing Mrs. P said to me was that she had a great sadness that deep down had always been there. She was also having a lot of stress at work and was not sleeping well and had digestive problems. I very respectfully listened to what she said feeling this was what her metal element needed. When I took the pulses she had an entry/exit block between the small intestine and the bladder. I also felt her spirit needed support. She needed to be taken to the heart of the metal element with LU1, *Zhong Fu*, the middle palace, but not perhaps in the first treatment. I cleared aggressive energy. I then cleared the energy block with SI19, *Ting Gong* and BL1, *Jing Ming*. I then did KI24, *Ling Xu*. At this point she had brightened enormously. I then went to the source points of lung, LU9, *Yai Yuan*, and the large intestine, LI4, *He Gu*. She looked much brighter.

The next time she came in she said she had been promoted but laughed and said it would bring even more stress. Her pulses were low but even. I did LU1, *Zhong Fu* and felt the pulses respond well. I then did LI7, *Wen Liu*, to bring her warmth to help ease the stress in her relationships. I then went to LU8, *Jing Qu* the metal point to really enrich the meridian

182

TREATMENT AND THE FIVE ELEMENTS

and give it what it needed. I finished with the point, LI11, *Qu Chi*, the earth point to nourish the entire system.

The next time she came she said she was tired but work seemed to be flowing better. I began the treatment with the bladder shu points of lung and large intestine, BL13, *Fei Shu* and BL28, *Pang Guang Shu*, to give the meridians a clearing out and new strength. I then did LU4, *Xia Bai*, to give her courage and great harmony. I then went to LI5, *Yang Xi*, meaning the warm vibrant movement of a mountain stream. I finished with the point of LU9, *Tian Yuan*, to nourish and bring the meridian to its source and strength. The pulses were full and she looked vibrant.

Mr. A was suffering from a lack of energy. He had contacted tick fever several years ago and had never recovered. His pulses were very low. I did an aggressive energy drain which lasted for over an hour. I then felt a block between the spleen and the heart which I cleared. The pulses were still straining, so I went to BL38(43), *Gao Huang Shu*, or rich for the vitals and did eleven moxas each side before needling. The pulses now had energy running through. I then did REN MAI 6, *Qi Hai*, or the sea of Qi which built up the energy. To support his energy I then did DU MAI 12, *Shen Zu*, or the supporting pillar of life. The pulses were now calm and filling nicely. To finish I did the source points to give his metal element exactly what it needed. These are LI4, *He Gu*, a valley of united harmony and LU9, *Tai Yuan*, a supremely profound pool. He said he felt lighter.

He came back the next time saying he had felt better for several days and then the energy sagged. I checked pulses and they had dropped but were even. To give the energy what it needed I went to the shu points of BL13, *Fei Shu,* the shu point of the lungs and BL25, *Da Chang Shu,* the shu point of the large intestines. Again I used a lot of moxa on the points before needling. I again used BL38(43), *Gao Huang Shu,* or rich for the vitals with fifteen moxas to send rich warm goodness to all the cells of the body. To build the vitality more I gave him BL48(53), *Bao Huang,* the rich vital centre. The pulses were full but needed strength and warmth. I gave him LI7, *Wen Liu,* a stream of benevolent warmth, then LI3, *San Jian,* the growth between heaven and earth that gives energy to man, and is the wood point for fresh growth. To bring stability and nourishment to the pulses I finished with LU9, *Tai Yuan,* a supremely profound pool, the earth and source point of the lung meridian. The pulses were full and strong

When he came the next time the pulses had again dropped but not as much. He said he was feeling much brighter but still had times of weariness. I felt the weariness was weighing on his spirit. I began the treatment with LU2, *Yu Men,* or the gateway of clouds to help clear the clouds away and bring the sunshine through. I then did KI25, *Shen Cang,* the treasury of spirit. The pulses were much calmer and more open. I did BL48(53), *Bao Huang,* the rich vital centre with seventeen moxas. The pulses were fuller than I had ever felt them. To further feed the system I gave him LI19, *He Liao,* the bone of harvested grains. I then went to the metal point, LU8, *Jing Qu,* meaning to arrange and regulate the gutters. The pulses were wide, even and full. To bring joy and warmth back I

TREATMENT AND THE FIVE ELEMENTS

finished with LI5, *Yang Xi*, the warm vibrant movement of a mountain stream. His eyes were sparkling. He said everything seemed brighter as if the clouds had parted.

Miss Q had half her skull crushed when she was small but had managed to overcome most of her handicap with skill. She came because she had fallen badly and could not seem to build up her energy again which was causing her to fall behind in her college studies. It was obvious that she was possessed and I did both the internal and external dragons. I then did aggressive energy. To bring her spirit back to life I gave her KI24, *Ling Xu*, the wild lands of spirit. Her eyes had come back to life. For protection I gave her REN MAI 15, *Jui Wei*, the loving protection of the dove. The pulses were even and calm and I finished with the source points of LI4, *He Gu*, a valley of united harmony and LU9, *Tai Yian*, a supremely profound pool. The pulses felt stronger and more solid.

The next time she came she said she was feeling much clearer and her studies were easier but she still felt tired. She had a block between the small intestine and the bladder which I cleared. The pulses were even but low. I gave her KI25, *Shen Cang*, the treasury of spirit. The pulses widened but were still low. I went to the junction or luo points, LI6, *Pian Li*, which allows a letting go so we are filled with a great vitality of moving forward, and LU7, *Lie Que*, which is like the force of a narrow mountain ravine where we receive a penetration of heavenly light. The pulses were full.

The following session she said she could feel her old self returning. She was looking much brighter and more mature.

RECEIVING SPIRIT

Her pulses had held. I went to LU1, *Zhong Fu*, the centre of the palace riches. I then gave her LI7, *Wen Liu*, a stream of warm, benevolent kindness. The pulses were full and open. To enrich and feed the meridians I gave her LI11, *Qu Chi*, a pool of gathered nourishment and the earth point. I finished with the fire point on the lungs to give her spirit the love it needed. This point is LU10, *Yu Ji*, the great fiery fish spirit of life. She was looking vibrant and said she felt sparkling inside.

WATER ELEMENT

The water element gives us resources, vitality and our ancestral fertility and reserves. It washes away the pollutions that can affect the very core of our being. Water enables all the vital substances in the body to flow well. When the water element is out of balance there are disturbances in the flow of our secretions, and we become fearful that we will be overwhelmed or our resources will entirely dry up. We freeze up or try and flee from our fear. We have a deep need for reassurance. When the water element is in balance we feel the security of our inner resources and feel our lives flowing well.

The bladder is our reservoir of the vitality of water. It gives all the meridians the fluidity they need to function well. When we have fluidity of mind and spirit and are properly irrigated then we are able to let ideas and thoughts flow. When the bladder is out of balance the well may run dry and we fear there will be no reserves for the next year. We may begin to imagine the worse possible outcomes happening. When we are flooded we may feel ourselves drowning and being beyond

TREATMENT AND THE FIVE ELEMENTS

help. When the bladder is in balance then we have the reserves we need and feel a fluidity with the changes of life.

The kidneys are the energetic movers of this life giving force. Within the kidneys are our ancestral inherited reserves that can deeply heal the mind, body and spirit when life has been hard. The kidney chest points nourish the spirit with a deep vitality. When the kidney meridian is out of balance we can no longer cleanse our blood and body fluids. We do not have our resources and our spirit can not find its inheritance. We become old and feel we are only just about surviving. The kidneys contain our energetic ancestral inheritance. These reserves are what serves us when we need energy to go beyond our normal endurance. They give us the strength and stamina to survive and reach our goals When the kidney meridian is in balance then we have these reserves and our spirit is deeply and profoundly nourished. When we touch this meridian we contact our deepest reserves of energy.

The following are head points on the bladder used to nourish the spirit. BL1, *Jing Ming*, means the eyes full of illumination. This point links to the Yang and Yin Qiao Mai and holds a depth of vitality and profound source of energy. It contains both the light of the sun and moon to bring the meridian back into harmony. BL6, *Cheng Guang*, means to receive illumination. Here when the time is right, we can connect to the illuminations of heaven and feel their guiding influences. BL10, *Tian Zhu*, means the supporting pillar of the heavens. This point takes us deeper into our spiritual awareness. Here our vision opens and we have the courage and strength to move forward with insightful purpose. These points and the outer and inner bladder line on the back are used in the middle of treatment to bring deep resources of energy to the person. We then finish the treatment with the points on the lower leg and foot.

INNER BLADDER LINE

The inner bladder line has points that directly nourish all the individual organs and are used when we need to give them a resource of energy.

BL11, *Da Zhu,* is where our way in life can be woven in harmony with the cycles and patterns of life. When a tapestry is woven a shuttle is used to weave the patterns of design. It is the shuttle that guides and creates the details that will make the overall picture of the tapestry. This point is both the vision and organization of the inner bladder line. The inner bladder line of points on the back contains points that have a direct contact with each of the meridians and their vital organs. This is the first point on this line of points that is both able to rejuvenate and revitalize each meridian. This movement and force of a shuttle is able to weave dynamic patterns that enrich the working cycles and patterns of our organs so their efforts work in harmony. This point is also one of the points of the sea of blood enriching our vitality. *Da Zhu* is a shuttle receiving the influences of heaven and feeding them into the vital organs influencing and enriching their energetic cycles.

BL12, *Feng Men* is the gateway of the winds. The I Ching is made of sixty-four hexagrams that describe the movements and changes of the yearly cycles. At *Feng Men* our meridians are feed and influenced by these changes and indulge in the wonders and movements of the seasons as they go through their cycles. In nature there are eight winds that move all the seasons with strength, abruptness, softness and calm. The wind is said to create spirit. The Chinese say that when our hearts are calm and tranquil, we can harness and move with these winds of change. When the wind blows we are able to feel this movement and the power of the Tao moves through us. When we keep tranquility in our own hearts, we can ride on the winds and flow with the changes of each seasons. Feng Men gives us exactly the right energetic wind to adjust and profit from each season.

At BL13, *Fei Shu,* the lung shu point, we touch the heavens above that are a vast space of constant wonder. The lungs are said to be the receivers of this vast wealth of inspiration for they receive this vital Qi through each the breath. With each inhalation we not only receive the vital force of life but the inspiration that comes with contact with the heavenly father. It gives inspiration to each breath and with its penetration of vital energy, It provides guidance for life filling us with vitality. The lungs are said to hold the office of minister and chancellor. They spread the wisdom of the heart throughout the body. It is no wonder in meditation by focusing on the breath we can find this deep inner wisdom within ourselves. *Fei Shu* is the vital transfer to and from the lungs. It is a place of direct communication with the lungs giving inspiration from the heavenly father. It is a vital, rich heavenly transfer of vital Qi that flows directly into the lungs. This vital energy nourishes our special unique essence and puts us in direct contact with the greatness of the heavens.

BL14, *Jue Yin Shu* is a place of direct communication with the heart protector that gives warmth and vitality to every cell in the body. In Chinese medicine the heart is protected by the heart protector. It is both a secretary that allows in what is necessary and a knight that bears any difficulties. In this way the heart or the Emperor within each of us can give loving guidance to all the kingdom without hardship. The heart protector surrounds the circulation of the inner chambers with protection and circulates the blood and the Emperor's warmth and love throughout the body In the ancient Imperial palace there was an inner courtyard where the temple of heaven stood. At the times of the solstice the Emperor would go to this temple to pray for the fertility of the harvests and ask for blessings for the next year. Here with complete calm in his heart, he would receive these blessings and words of wisdom from the heavenly ancients. *Jue Yin Shu* means the vital transfer to the mysterious inner place of protected circulation.

BL15, *Xin Shu,* is a direct transfer to the heart. The heart is said to be the lord and sovereign of all the mind, body and spirit. It is said that from the heart comes the radiance of the spirits. The heart is the place of virtue, truth, and understanding where love radiates and the emotions guide thought to truth. It is where intuition creates logic, action brings forth ideas and thinking comes from the emotions and inner feelings. The heart is an open void where there is uninhibited communication with the spirit. This radiates love and warmth where it is needed. When the heart is full of tranquility and peace, then it can receive the *shen* spirits of heaven and spread its virtues. *Xin Shu* is the heart of the kingdom, the forbidden city and the inner chambers from where loving commands are radiated. Here is a place of direct contact with the love and wisdom contained in the heart. *Xin Shu* holds this distribution of love and warmth. *Xin Shu* is a place of direct communication with the heart revitalizing its fire, warmth and love.

BL16, *Du Shu* is a direct transfer to the Du Mai or governor vessel. The governor is like the uncle of the heart overseeing the kingdom from an older more ancient generation. Here are these governing regulations coming from the governor vessel or the Du Mai which helps all the twelve meridians to function in harmony with each other. It is this governor who oversees the generation and development of our twelve ordinary meridians from conception and continuing throughout life. He is like the ridge pole of the roof holding up the entire structure. The governor gathers together information to unify the purpose of life and to direct good communication to the twelve meridians with purposeful harmony. He oversees the emperor's will with skill, authority, understanding and guidance. *Du Shu* is in direct contact with the more ancient strength and direction of the governing vessel. It is a place of direct communication with the Du Mai that guides and directs the other twelve ordinary meridians.

BL18, *Gan Shu* is the direct transfer to the liver. When spring comes the great plan of nature gives everything direction and enables the seeds to penetrate the ground and burst into flower. The liver contains this same force to put the plan of our life into action in the same way that a seed bursts forth in the warmer weather. The liver is said to be the master planner of the meridians. Like an architect it directs life from a blue print of our own individual uniqueness. Out of this plan of our inner essence comes the force and the ability to consider, reflect and to move forward with a striding pace. When we have a plan and a design of our life, then we know which direction to go in and can go there with directness. *Gan Shu* is a direct connection with the liver and its inherited idea of what inner plan directs our life. Here is the essence of the blueprint we have been given to fulfill life in a special way. It is a place of direct communication with the liver where our own unique master plan of life can be envisioned and put into action.

BL19, *Dan Shu* is the direct transfer to the gallbladder. It is the gallbladder that takes the plans of the liver and puts them into action making hundreds of decisions every minute of the day. Here plans are put into action with precision and direction using imaginative power and strength to make good decisions. These upright decisions give shape to the vital growth of each individual being. The gallbladder sees that these fine, correct, proper and upright decisions are applied without obstruction. This is the courage of the gallbladder. *Dan Shu* is the direct communication with the gallbladder. At

TREATMENT AND THE FIVE ELEMENTS

Dan Shu there is a direct transfer of energy to the gallbladder who can then put the plan of who we are into action in an upright and dynamic way.

BL20, *Pi Shu* is the direct transfer to the spleen. The spleen serves all of the meridians by distributing Qi and nourishment throughout our mind, body and spirit. It is the meridian of transportation and distribution of Qi from the great granaries of the stomach. *Pi Shu* is the direct contact with this supreme transporter. *Pi* is drawn as flesh and an ancient drinking vessel with a handle. This ordinary everyday drinking vessel is said to be like a serving girl who no one really notices but who serves and works all the time transporting and giving nourishment. It is a serving girl who does very unnoticeable work that enables everyone else to feel nourished, full, centered and satisfied. It is the spleen that distributes the food and drink of blood and Qi to all the other meridians. *Pi Shu* is a place of direct communication with the spleen giving us nourishing energy. It sends and distributes nourishment from its great granaries and storehouses full of golden Qi to wherever it is needed in the mind, body and spirit.

BL21, *Wei Shu* is the direct transfer to the stomach. The stomach is the container responsible for the rottening and ripening of food. When we are well fed we feel comfortable and balanced and have harmony in our centre. When the granaries of the kingdom are full of good harvest grains there is a sense that there is security and stability to survive the winter hardships. It is this harvested wealth that brings security in knowing everyone will be well fed. Here we are truly nourished with the great riches of our mother earth. When we harvest our experiences in life then we are nourished with wisdom and the wealth of contemplation. The stomach brings this wealth of stability out of a great sea of grains and cereals that nourish life. *Wei Shu* is the direct connection to this wealth of nourishment. *Wei* is made of flesh and a container of the five grains or cereals, each one for one of the five seasons. It is also a centre out of which comes all the nourishment of our great mother, the earth. *Wei Shu* is a place of direct communication with the stomach that brings us a well fed feeling of balance and stability.

BL22 *San Jiao Shu* is the direct transfer to the triple burner or *san jiao*. The triple burner is responsible for creating harmony between the three *jiaos*. The upper *jiao* in the chest contains the heart, the heart protector and the lungs, the middle *jiao* contains the stomach, spleen, gallbladder and liver, and the lower *jiao* contains the small and large intestine, bladder and kidneys. The triple burner is responsible for keeping our entire system in balanced harmony with warmth, love and goodness. It works to keep all the other meridians at the best temperature possible so they can work in the best conditions and atmosphere. Here is the ability to regulate the cooking fires for each meal and the right warmth for each activity in the royal palace. Here is a warm, loving environment for each of the meridians. *San Jiao Shu* is a place of direct communication and energetic transfer to the triple burner. It brings just the right amount of warmth, goodness and love to give balance and harmony to all the meridians.

TREATMENT AND THE FIVE ELEMENTS

BL23, *Shen Shu* is the direct transfer to the kidneys. The kidneys are the controller of water. They are the energetic mover of the vitality of water that is needed in every cell of life. Here is the inner powerhouse, out of which comes will, purpose, vitality and strength. It is the kidneys that have the store of our ancestral inheritance that can be drawn on in times of endurance. *Shen Shu* is where direct contact can be made with this vitality to rejuvenate our mind, body and spirit. Our inheritance is a gift we receive from heaven, our parents and our ancestors. It is these abilities that enrich our lives. The kidneys hold this treasure chest where we can find our inheritance and serve life with the wholeness of our goodness and abilities. Here we are filled with virtue, experience and knowledge. This is where our deepest reserves are found, directing life and revitalizing the spirit. *Shen Shu* is a place of direct communication with the kidneys who bring the vitality of inherited energy and energetic movement to the other meridians.

BL24, *Qi Hai Shu* is the direct transfer to our sea of Qi. It is said that the eight grains of life are mixed with the eight breaths of the winds of heaven to form the life force called Qi. Rice or seeds are drawn as a growing plant with seeds around it. In studying the Tao the ancients would show their student a grain of rice and explain that the cycle of life was in the seed. First it has to be planted by bending down and being humble. Then it needs to be tended with patience. Finally we have to wait for the harvesting. We then have to follow the seasons in order to plant when the rains will come and harvest before the rains come again. In this way the students learned humble diligence that would enable them to ripen their lives. Qi is this rice being cooked and transformed into the energy of life. We are given this Qi as an inheritance. It is renewed with each breath we take throughout life and with each morsel of food and water we consume. *Qi Hai Shu* is where we have a vital connection to this inner sea of Qi and the conception vessel or Ren Mai. At this point we have the great vitality contained in a sea of Qi, full of life-giving vital forces.

BL25, *Da Chang Shu* is the direct transfer to the large intestine. The large intestine is in charge of the wonderful job of transforming the last of our nourishment into what can be absorbed and then sending the rest out of the body as compost. It is in charge of the drainage and dregs, clearing all the rubbish from the other meridians so that they can do their jobs well. When this manure is composted well it puts vital nutrients back into the soil. It is a well known fact animal manure provides the best nourishment for the soil. It is the earth in her wisdom that knows how to absorb and transform these nutrients. *Da Chang Shu* is the direct vital connection with the large intestine allowing it to open its great collecting ability to clean the entire system. When everything that can be digested is absorbed, then the large intestine takes the rest and eliminates it from the body. It is a place of direct communication with the large intestine where we can let go of all that is no longer needed.

BL26, *Guan Yuan Shu* is the direct vital connection to the primary gate or the gate of origin. It is like the gateway of all

TREATMENT AND THE FIVE ELEMENTS

gateways with connections to the other shu points. It is also where the pure vital energy goes one direction and what is not needed the other way. Here is a gateway of both wholeness and goodness where there is great fluidity to revitalize and purify the system. It is a place where things can be filtered with strength and vitality coming from the original source. *Guan Yuan Shu* is the great primary gateway. *Guan Yuan Shu* is a place of direct communication with this network connecting all the other meridians to the origin. In this way everything can be brought back into great wholeness. Here we can feel the balance point between taking in and letting go, between yin and yang and other opposites.

BL27, *Xiao Chang Shu* is a direct vital link to the small intestine. Here is a smaller more intimate and refine movement along the way. It is the small intestine that separates out the pure energy from that which needs to continue along the way. By sorting the pure from the impure, the pure can then be transformed into vital Qi energy. In this way all the other meridians can thrive in an atmosphere of vital clarity and purity. It is the small intestine that has the capacity to circulate pure energy enabling the system to prosper with clarity, abundance, purity and refinement. *Xiao Chang Shu* is a vital transfer to the small intestine and its ability to circulate pure Qi energy. It is a place of direct communication with the small intestine where the pure can be sorted from the impure so our understanding has clarity, abundance, purity and refinement.

BL28, *Pang Guang Shu* is a direct transfer to the bladder. The bladder is responsible for the storage of water and its vitality. It is a reservoir that resources the body, mind and spirit. Water gives life its vitality and fluidity. The bladder contains the freshness and vital supplies of our inner lakes, river and springs. Out of its great stores, reserves and reservoirs come the qualities of fluid movement and a guarantee of vital resource. When our reservoirs are full we have the strength and force of water as well as its stillness and deep pools. We then can flow through all changes in life just as water is able to go around any obstacle. *Pang Guang Shu* is a place of direct communication with the bladder where the vital reserves of water are able to resource the entire mind, body and spirit.

BL29, *Zhong Lu Shu* is a direct transfer to the back bone. It is said that the backbone is the ladder to heaven. Our bones give the body structure as well as flexibility and protection. Within the bones is the marrow that creates new vital cells to regenerate life. In this way the bones are said to hold our deepest structure. It is said when we can feel that deep inner structure it will guide us along the way. If we walk from that centre then our path will be balanced and in harmony. *Zhong Lu Shu* is the middle of the backbone providing flexibility and movement from this vital centre to give great strength to life. It is a place of direct communication with the backbone that gives strength, flexibility, balance and movement to our entire structure and unity to our yang energy.

BL30, *Bai Huan Shu* means a white jade ring. In ancient times white was the symbol for purity and spirituality. The Chinese believe that we are born with this pure empty whiteness of spirit. When we can let go of what has covered

TREATMENT AND THE FIVE ELEMENTS

our essential essence, we will again find the richness of this inner purity. In this way no matter how hard we polished a stone it can only become itself whether it be a diamond or a piece of jade. Jade is made into beautiful objects. For the Chinese jade represents that which is pure for no matter how it is cut or polished it always remains itself and retains its faults in its cloudy colours. Here is where there is a ring of vital energy uniting all the inner yin organs in harmony. *Bai Huan Shu* means a vital transfer to this ring of pure jade energy uniting our inner yin energy.

OUTER BLADDER LINE

The points on the outer bladder line deeply resource and nourish our spirit. BL37(42), *Po Hu* is the doorway of the spirit and is on the same level as the lung shu point. When we think about soul certain phrases come to mind. 'Music stirs my very soul.' 'This place has a special soul.' 'That painting has awakened something in my soul.' Soul is a part of everyday life. It is our deep, gentle, subtle humanity. It is that place where our deepest thoughts, questions and answers lie. When our spirit is cut off or weak, this point can reconnect us to our soul within bringing back joy, sparkle and vitality. It is like watering a rose bud that then becomes a fully mature rose.

The *Po* are the guardians of the body and in particular the inspirations that come into the lungs with the breath. They are also the spirits of the autumn and the element of metal. Here with each breath our soul is filled with the beauty of nature giving us clarity, brightness, and inspiration. When we die, it is the *Po* that are sealed in the body enabling it to descend and transform itself into another life. If they are not sealed in the body they may wander about the earth and cause trouble. *Po Hu* is the doorway of our earthly spirit and our inner diamond essence.

BL38(43), *Gao Huang Shu* means a vital transfer of rich vibrant energy. The heart protector nourishes our heart with love and the richness of what is around, protecting us from anything that is not vital, enriching and full of love. It is here that this revitalizing goodness can spread to every cell in the body bringing warmth, quality and vital nourishment. *Gao Huang Shu* moves vital energy everywhere in the mind, body and spirit. It brings warmth, nourishment and quality, giving our life purpose and joy. It is a very potent point bringing vitality and opening a sea of energy for all the meridians. This point lies at the level of the heart protector shu point.

At *Gao Huang Shu* the quality of the blood is enriched and filled with warmth, love, protection and appreciation. This enriches us and enables us to find our purpose in life as well as rekindling the joy and love inside us. It is like a great warm soothing sea, bathing all the meridians and indeed every cell in the body in vitality. It is a wonderful point to use when there is great weariness in the mind, body and spirit.

BL39(44), *Shen Tang* is the ancient temple of the spirits. When our spirit is nourished in the home of our heart then it grows stronger and our love, warmth and wisdom not only nourishes our inner being but those around us. It is here that our heart strings are nourished in the royal chambers. It is where the warmth and love of life is restored to its fullness. *Shen Tang* means to receive spirit in the ancestral palace full of the riches of the heart. Here are the inner chambers of the royal palace of the heart, where our spirit can feel at home and be bathed in love and understanding. We can feel the truth of the Chinese saying that spirituality is not only all around us but also within us. Each of us is a microcosm of the universe where its wisdom is reflected in our movements and encounters. The diviner can see the entire universe in the cracks of a tortoise shell. A sage can see the Tao reflected in the weather changes of the skies. When we can see spirit in a field, flower or movement of cloud then we have embraced the whole and have a sense that there is no division between the physical and the divine.

BL40(45), *Yi Xi* is a cry of sadness or grief. When the tears are overwhelming, it is here we can find the joy contained in the calmness of spirit to help the passage of letting go and allowing the tides to pass. Then our heart can move again with all its constant changes of affections and emotions. Out of this grief, true compassion comes. *Yi Xi* means the cry of sadness and the joy of song. Sadness is a part of being human and will pass in its own time. All emotions are a part of our inner lives and ebb and flow like the tides of the ocean waves. When sadness comes it is necessary to feel its full intensity but it should not rest predominant and other emotions should follow in their own time. It is good to seek the advantages that sadness offers in its time that also help to transform its energy. As we move through the pain of loss, calmness and peace come like a small light in the dark sky that eventually fills with stars. Here, when we are lost in grief, we can find a guiding star to bring back the light of joy, peace and calm.

BL42(47), *Hun Men* is the gateway to the spiritual soul and its purpose. The *Hun* are the spirits of spring and the element of wood. They give us the vision and direction for life coming from its original source. When we die it is the *Hun* that return to heaven and to the great oneness of the Tao. When someone dies in China their relatives go out on the roof and call to the *Hun* to return to the body. If there is no reply then the *Hun* have returned to the greatness above and the person dies.

Here is the real central core of our inner essence. When we touch this inner kernel, our vision returns, guiding life on its path. This point lies at the same level as the liver shu point. When we have lost our sense of direction, or have withdrawn and can't access our spirit essence, then this point can be used to penetrate to the deepest part of our spiritual soul bringing back life, calmness, light, joy and peace. It can be used when we are easily thrown by challenges, burdened by depression or when there is no strength of spirit. When used, it brings our soul vision back, so we can see the world in all its beauty and move our lives again from our own inner vision

BL43(48), is *Yang Guang*. At *Yang Guang* the gallbladder's decisions flow in a net of vital yang movement in harmony and balance. This is where the plan of our life and our inner vision can be filled with vibrant and warm connections to move life into vibrant action. The gallbladder is the great decision maker putting the vision of the liver into action.

TREATMENT AND THE FIVE ELEMENTS

This point lies at the same level as the gallbladder shu point. *Yang Guang* is a network that can finely tune our inner and outer energy so all decisions work in perfect harmony and everything functions with the best of choices. This is a net that is made of very fine woven threads like the sensitive strands of a spider's web or a net of watercourses that run through the earth. These threads have the sensitivity of a web, feeling the most delicate changes and adjusting to them. Here are the fine threads of insight that provide the structure to weave our lives. It is a network that brings all the decisions of our life into balance and harmony. It also brings a clarity of vision

BL44(49), *Yi She* means the sentiments of our inner residence or dwelling place. The spleen is the great transporter of the vital nourishment. It gathers this abundance from the great granaries of the stomach. It then distributes vital Qi to where it is needed. This brings great balance and stability. Here is our inner home full of enrichment, nourishment and generosity. When we are nourished in the lap of mother earth we feel in sympathy with everything else that lives on her great surface. At *Yi She*, we can feel a great sense of a warm home and our inner centre out of which we are able to move with compassion and understanding. This point puts us back into sympathy and communion with life. We are no longer alone or struggling but at the very centre of life and nourished by the earth. It lies at the same level as the spleen shu point

BL45(50), *Wei Cang* is the golden granary of the stomach. It lies at the same level as the stomach shu point. When the grains are harvested, we have the security of knowing we will be warm and nourished through the cold days of winter. When we harvest the experiences of life we can find the golden grains that will last through the winters of our lives giving us richness and inspiration. Here is the bounty and fullness of our mother earth bringing the stability, warmth, nourishment and care of a full storehouse. The Chinese say that those that harvest the ordinary with care, and take in and digest the wisdom contained within, are those who ultimately gain in life. At *Wei Cang* our spirit can be fed with care, warmth and stored vitality to give us a real earth home and centre. Here we can feel whole and at one with the world. When we find these golden grains that exist in our own lives then we glean the richness of the harvest. Here we can have a fullness of a rich satisfying spiritual harvest feast.

BL46(51), *Huang Men* is the gateway to our vital centre giving a renewed flow of vitality. It opens our spirit like the burst of vibrant flowers after rain falls on the desert. The triple burner lies at the same level of *Huang Men* and it is the triple burner that warms and regulates the temperature of the entire body. Here our energy and vitality are given strength and equilibrium to spark us into life. At *Huang Men* all the meridians are strengthened with vitality and rejuvenated with a special spark of energy. They take in a deep breath of inspired mountain air and are harmonized with the vitality they need. Here is the vitality to fill our spirit with joy and love

BL47(52), *Zhi Shi* opens our gateway to our inheritance, purpose, ambition and determination to both envision and put into action our unique purpose. It is our gateway to life.

TREATMENT AND THE FIVE ELEMENTS

The Chinese say that as we pass through the gates of life and are born into this world, the angels whisper the secret of our life. We forget this at the time but it remains an invisible thread that guides our life. If we can follow this thread we will live in harmony and be enriched by the path we have been given. But in the same way if we choose not to listen, then in the way of the Tao and the whole, someone else will fulfill our purpose and we will have lost the unique opportunity we have been given. This point lies at the same level as the kidney shu point. The kidneys store our ancestral inheritance giving us the will, determination, purpose, ambition, vitality and strength to fulfill our deepest plans and desires. In this point is stored this vitality and unique purpose of life. This point stirs the fires of our soul purpose and revitalizes our ambition, will, and determination. Here we can find our path and rekindle our desires and enthusiasm for life

BL48(53), *Bao Huang* is an ocean of creative strength. The water element gives great fluidity and vitality to every cell in the body. The bladder is the reservoir of these resources. This point lies at the same level as the bladder shu point. The largest reservoir on earth is the sea. It is out of the sea that life first came. It is the sea that is a vast reservoir of the vitality, creating and supporting life. It contains the primitive sensuality and sexuality of this creative process. At *Bao Huang* is the creative force necessary to move our ambitions and visions fluidly and dynamically into life. It awakens our inner powers and we ride on the waves feeling the depths and strength of the sea beneath. Here is the great muscle of vitality of the heart nourished by the creative force of the womb, bathed in the vitality of the bladder's resources and reserves

BL50(36), *Cheng Fu* means to support an undertaking or what is received. A tree receives what it is given. If it is battered by the wind it grows to one side. It knows it will never grow straight and doesn't even try for that would be unnecessary activity. When we empty ourselves in meditation we can receive the subtle currents of life. In this way we can gain the wisdom that comes and grow more peaceful within. This point is at the place where the leg joins the body. It is where the entire body is supported with great strength like a mighty pillar but a pillar that moves with strength and flexibility. Here is the strength of being open to that which comes. Here we can rest on the great pillar of strength of our legs and learn and grow from what comes whether it be misfortune or luck.

The following points on the leg and foot are used at the end of treatment to ground the energy. BL54(40), *Wei Zhong*, means to serve and balance from the strength of the centre. This is the earth point bringing the meridian stability and nourishment. Here water is well contained. BL55, *He Yang*, means the united forces of yang. This point contains a full united force of water able to resource our Qi at a deep level and rebuilt our vitality. BL58, *Fei Yang*, means the flight of yang movement. This is the junction or luo point of the meridian giving us the strength, energy and power of water as well as its ability to fly anywhere with its dynamic fluidity. Here we receive water's force and drive, but also its flexibility and stillness. BL59, *Fu Yang*, means to access the movement of yang. This point is also connected to the Yang Qiao Mai. Here is the profound fullness of yang movement able to give our entire structure a depth of vitality.

BL60, *Kunlun*, means the mythological Kunlun mountains that support the heavens above earth. This is the fire point of the meridian bathing us in warmth and love. Here we find the maturity and warmth to build and develop our relationships in life. BL62, *Shen Mai*, means to order the vital circulations. This point connects to the Yang Qiao Mai and organizes, resources and revitalizes all the vital circulations of the body giving us a rich vitality. BL64, *Jing Gu*, means the central bone of the empire. This is the source point of the meridian that gives us what we need to harmonize our reserves of water. Here is the core of our vitality and the water element.

BL65, *Shu Gu*, means the ordering of bone. This is the wood point of the meridian giving it a forward thrust and fresh growth. Here, just like in springtime, we have a fresh vision of new life and burst forth like a young plant. BL66, *Tong Gu*, means to penetrate the open valley. This is the water point of the meridian where it has its deepest source. When used in the season of winter and its horary time of 15H-17H, this point can revitalize and rebalance a water element imbalance with deep and profound healing. BL67, *Zhi Yin*, means to arrive at our inner nature. This is the metal point of the meridian where we can let go of what is no longer needed and find the gifts and precious qualities of our inner essence. Here we can feel our true self emerge and we have the confidence to be who we are.

RECEIVING SPIRIT

The kidneys hold our inherited reserves and give vitality to our water element. The kidney chest point can profoundly nourish our spirit. The body points contain great vitality and fertility. They are linked to the Chong Mai which is responsible for the pattern of the development of life. They give great vitality and fertility to life. We use these body points to deeply resource the energy in the middle of treatment. KI12, *Da He*, means a full glorious brightness. This point is full of fire giving warmth and vitality to the inherited creativity of the kidneys. KI13, *Qi Xue*, means the opening of Qi. Its other name is the door of infants. Here is the opening to our creative life force. KI15, *Zhong Zhu*, means to flow into the centre. This point brings our entire structure into balance and harmony again. KI16, *Huang Shu*, means a direct transfer to the vital regions. This point rejuvenates, revitalizes and harmonizes the flow of water deeply and profoundly.

KI19, *Yin Du*, means our inner capital. Here are great resources giving us the force and creativity to revitalize our lives with the wealth we have inside. KI20, *Tong Gu*, means an open flowering valley. Here we are bathed in elegance and our spirit sings again. KI21, *You Men*, means a dark secret gateway. Here we can move out of the darkness into the light, out of loneliness and despair into comfort, love and joy. This point can turn things around. KI22, *Bu Lang*, means to step out into the garden courtyard. Here is a beautiful place to rest and recover when suffering has been long. At this point we sit on the veranda and refresh ourselves. It is the exit point of the kidney meridian allowing the flow of its vitality to move into

TREATMENT AND THE FIVE ELEMENTS

the heart protector and fill its pools with energy. Here are deep reserves of energy to help the heart protector protect the heart and rejuvenate the flow of that protection

The kidney chest points begin with KI23, *Shen Feng*, which opens our soul seal. This touches the deep inner essence of who we are and what we can become. *Shen Feng* opens our hearts to the wonders and special gifts within. The Emperor would place his wax seal on documents to give them his authority. In this way the seal was the Emperor's word and was to be trusted. Here is the stamp and identity of who we are. *Shen Feng* is like a place of honour where we are truly ourselves. The ancient shamans would watch the heavens for signs and omens when someone was born to help understand who the child would be. In this way their uniqueness could be encouraged and made strong. When our spirit is depleted this point can bring us back to ourselves and remind us of our identity and purpose in life. It gives us a real sense of who we are and why we are here. At *Shen Feng* our spirit is given a stamp of approval that brings back sparkle and quality to life

KI24, *Ling Xu*, is a profound source of spiritual depth that is able to fill our spirit with life, wonder and its own inner wisdom. When the struggle has been long and hard, *Ling Xu* can restore our spirits with hope and wonder. Here we can be brought back to life in its fullest. *Ling Xu* is the wild lands of spiritual power where our inner being, and our spirit can be revived. It is said that if one practices Tai Qi or calligraphy then one brings the Tao into oneself in the same way the heavenly rains fall to earth and penetrate her with heavenly nourishment. When calligraphy is done with grace and presence, it is then that it shows a vitality with unerring movement. When this happens it is said that Ling or spirit has entered the person. *Ling Xu* is this magical land of spirit. When we are resigned, low in spirits, or have suffered a long hard road, then this point re-establishes contact with our inner strength and brings back our vital reserves. Here our spirit can be resurrected and we can again experience the riches of life, joy, enthusiasm, hope and meaning. It gives us a deep connection to our soul and a great lift to our vitality

KI25, *Shen Cang,* is a storehouse of the treasures of the spirit. Here are the reserves of the spirit, the pantry of dreams, visions, secrets of the heart and the riches of destiny. The ancient shamans would watch the heavens for signs and omens when someone was born. In this way they were able to see who the child was, what their potential in life would be and ways of supporting their spiritual development. When the spirit is not flourishing or is weak or fragile, then *Shen Cang* can be used to build up our spiritual reserves. Our soul can feed on what it needs to grow and develop. Here is a spiritual storehouse that can feed our spirit what it needs to grow and mature. *Shen Cang* gives our spirit the dreams and visions we need

KI26, *Yu Xhong,* is our centre of spiritual elegance. Here is the beauty and elegance that is within our very centre. It is the place of the poetry of our special soul. The sages say that those who wish to know the Tao should cultivate the poet in themselves. They should write a poem while waking, working, bathing, loving and even in anger. Poetry is a way of great health. The Chinese say that poetry is worship with words. When we cultivate this elegance it opens our spirit to life, beauty and happiness. Here our inner gardens are filled with vision and hope. *Yu Zhong* is the centre of our brilliant accomplished elegance. This inner beauty refreshes our vision and gives hope to our dreams. This point brings our spirit to the surface and enables us to see and experience the beauty we have inside. Here we enter a place that gives us great self respect, elegance, peace, joy, and tranquility.

KI27, *Shu Fu* is a storehouse of reserves or a reservoir of spirit. Here is a pantry of vitality to boost the reserves and build up our life so it flows with a full resource of spirit. We can use this point when we need our vitality restored with abundance. Here are the vital reserves of the kidneys stored in the comforts and riches of the treasury of the inner palace. *Shu Fu* is a vital transfer to the creativity, inherited riches and vitality of our inner palace treasury of spirit. Here our spirit is bathed in the wonders of our inner being.

The points on the lower leg and foot are used at the end of the treatment to ground the treatment so the changes are supported. KI1 *Yong Quan*, means a burst of vibrant spring waters. This is the wood point and gives us the full force of a vibrant fresh spring to move forward. KI2, *Ran Gu*, means a valley full of bright warm sunshine. This is the fire point of the meridian where we receive the love and warmth we need to make mature relationships in our lives. KI3, *Tai Xi*, means a great forceful torrent. This is the source point as well as the earth point. Here we can find the nourishment and resources we need. It is where we are well fed, nurtured and filled with the vibrant forces of water.

KI4, *Da Zhong*, means a full well crafted goblet. This is the junction or luo point of the meridian. Here is a greatly concentrated refreshing vitality that is able to bring harmony and balance to our energy. It is a goblet filled to the brim with vital waters. KI6, *Zhao Hai,* means a shining sea of illumination. This point fills us with beauty and wonder like a sea in full sunlight. Here we can feel the beauty within. It is a point that makes us sparkle. KI7, *Fu Liu*, means a returning current. This is the metal point of the meridian allowing us to let go of what is no longer needed and find the inspiration in life. Here the flow of our life can be enriched with quality and specialness. KI10, *Yin Gu*, means the inner mysterious valley. This is the water point of the kidneys and its home. Here is a great pool where our reserves and resources can be renewed so our inner valley can again flow with the vitality of life.

Let us now look at three treatments each of three people with a water elemental imbalance. Miss M phoned me for an appointment. When I asked what would be a good time for her she said, that first she would have to do this, then diverted off about what she did and then talked about her family and after about ten minutes I suggested a date. When a person has a water imbalance they may flow everywhere. She was also possessed so I cleared that first. Then I drained aggressive energy. The pulses were low at this point but fairly even. I did REN MAI 15, *Jui Wei*, to help protect her as she seemed fragile and did BL38(43), *Gao Huang Shu*, to give the whole system more vitality. I finished with BL64, *Jing Gu*, and KI3, *Tai Xi*, the source points. She was looking more solid at the end of the treatment.

The next time she came she was in tears and said she had lost her boyfriend. I began the treatment with the point of KI25, *Shen Cang*, to support her spirit. I then went to BL57, *Sheng Shan*, to give her strength. She was calm at this point. Next I did BL66, *Tong Gu*, to give water its home and finished with KI3, *Tai Zi*, to nourish her and give her stability.

The next time she was seeing her boyfriend again and coping better in her job. Her pulses were even and had not dropped as much as the last time. I began the treatment with KI16, *Huang Shu*, to give her stability and vitality. I then did the point BL48, *Bao Huang*, to give vitality and containment. She had stopped talking and was deeply relaxed. I then gave her BL60, *Kunlun*, the fire point and strength of the Kunlun mountains and KI4, *Da Zhong*, a cup full of vitality. The pulses were fully resourced and she was contained

Mrs. G came to me because she and her husband had been trying to have a baby for several years and nothing had happened. Both of them had tests and were fertile according to the doctor. She seemed a healthy woman in her late twenties but was obviously distressed at not becoming pregnant. We talked about a child entering her life and I suggested she and her husband meditate on receiving a child into their world and sharing with the child how they would love it and create a loving space for it. She suddenly relaxed and said she had never thought about it that way and was excited to share the idea with her husband. In the first treatment I checked for aggressive energy but she had none. Her pulses were low but fairly even. I went to REN MAI 8, *Shen Que*, the inner gateway of spirit to nourish her spirit and her own mothering. To build up the kidney resources I gave her KI12, *Da He*, a full glorious brightness. The pulses were deep, calm and even. I ended the treatment with the source points of BL64, *Jing Gu*, the strength of the central bone of the empire, and KI3, *Tai Xi*, a great and forceful current. She was looking fuller and brighter

She returned for the next treatment and said her husband would also like to come for treatment and they had found the meditation very helpful and hopeful. Her pulses were even but had fallen a bit. I gave her KI23, *Shen Feng*, the soul seal of spirit to bring her inner essence alive. I did KI4, *Da Zhong*, meaning a full well crafted goblet and the junction or luo point of the kidneys. I finished by giving her BL58, *Fei Yang*, the dynamic flight of yang vitality and movement.

The following treatment happened a couple of weeks later. Her pulses were stable. I began the treatment by giving her KI20, *Tong Gu*, or an open flowering valley full of vitality to open her energy to receive. I then did KI13, *Qi Xue*, the door of infants and the opening of Qi. The pulses were open, even and full. To help her joy and warmth I then gave her the fire points of the two meridians, BL60, *Kunlun*, the mystical mountains of spirit and KI2, *Ran Gu*, a valley full of bright warm sunshine. I finished with KI6, *Zhao Hai*, the shining sea

TREATMENT AND THE FIVE ELEMENTS

of illumination. Several weeks later I heard she was pregnant and later had a beautiful son.

I had not seen Mrs. K for sometime when she phoned me in tears. Her boyfriend had left her for someone else. She arrived and tearfully told me the story. I checked for aggressive energy of which there was none. To help move her through the crisis I went to the shu points of BL28, *Pang Guang Shu*, the shu point of the bladder and BL23, *Shen Shu*, the shu point of the kidneys. She was calmer and the pulses were even. To support her spirit I gave her KI25, *Shen Cang*, or the treasury of spirit. Because this was a recurrent theme in her life I then gave her KI7, *Fu Liu*, returning current. It is also the metal point which I felt would help her refind her inner essence. I finished the treatment with the source points of BL64, *Jing Gu*, the central bone of the empire and KI3, *Tai Xi*, the great forceful current. She was looking much better and said she felt more stable.

She came the next time looking sad but more contained. Her pulses were even and had not dropped very much. To support her I began with KI15, *Zhong Zhu*, the gathering together of the great vitality of water to feed the centre. The pulses were fuller and stronger. To help her let go I gave her KI21, *You Men*, the dark hidden gateway that helps to bring back the light when times have been difficult. To bring back her vitality, I gave her BL46(51), *Huang Men*, the gateway of the vital centre. The pulses were even and full at this point. I finished with the following two water points to bring stability and strength to the pulse change. I gave her BL66, *Tong Gu*, meaning to penetrate and open the valley, and KI10, *Yin Gu*, the inner mysterious valley. She smiled as she sat up on the couch.

The next time she came she was still sad but said she was beginning to accept the change and go out again to meet people. I began the treatment with KI22, *Bu Lang*, where one can rest and recover in beautiful gardens. It means to sit on the veranda. I then gave her LIV14, Qi Men, the gate of hope. This is on the extraordinary meridian of the Yin Wei Mai. I then gave her BL58, *Fei Yang*, to give her the flight and movement of yang energy. Then I gave her BL54, *Wei Zhong*, the earth point to bring stability and nourishment to her life. I finished with KI2, *Ran Gu*, meaning a valley of bright warm sunshine and the fire point to feed her heart. She looked full and bright and said her heart felt full of warmth and her feet were on the ground again.

These are just a few examples of how we can use five element acupuncture to help people to regenerate and revitalize their energy and spirit, when life has become unbalanced, and they have lost their way along the path of the Tao. When a patient comes to me I sense where their energy and life is out of harmony. I then choose the points that will help both bring the pulses into balance as well as support the changes in the person's life. In this way life develops creatively and with balance.

TREATMENT AND THE FIVE ELEMENTS

Carrying body and soul, embrace them as one,
Can you keep them from separation?
Concentrating energy and become subtle
Can you be like a newborn child?
Washing and cleansing inner vision,
Can you make it flawless?
Loving everyone, ruling the nation,
Can you be uncontrived?
As the gate of Heaven opens and closes
Can you serve, be impassive?
Understanding reaches everywhere, opening to all beings
Can you be innocent, do nothing?
Birthing, nurturing, sustaining, can you remain unpossessing?
Do without taking credit,
One who holds this power brings the Tao to earth
And triumphs over a raging fire and a freezing winter.
Yet when he comes to rule the world,
It is with the gentleness of a feather.
Grow without dominating,
As your wisdom reaches the four corners of the world
Keep the innocence vision.
Know the primal power guides, serves and sustains.
This is the mysterious power.

LAO TZU

ZI - CHILD

*AS WE LISTEN IN THE WIND
WE CAN HEAR THE SOUNDS AND SONGS OF OUR ANCESTORS
AND AS WE WALK ON THE GROUND,
WE ARE WALKING ON THE FACES OF THOSE YET UNBORN.
LET US MAKE A BEAUTIFUL DREAM, FULL OF HOPE, CLEAN WATER,
GOOD LAND, AND A GOOD WAY OF LIFE FOR THEM.*
WINONA LADUKE

HEALING TOUCH
WITH CHILDREN

Children are one of the most precious parts of life. We, as adults must encourage our children's curiosity, individuality and initiative. There is story told about a thief who stole into heaven. He took the peaches of immortality from the gardens. He then came back to earth. He was just about to eat the peaches when two little boys arrived. He began asking them riddles. He went on to ask them about the deepest meaning of life. Each time they smiled and answered with ease. He then decided to share his peaches with the boys and they all became immortal together. Now if these boy had not been curious, they would not have been able to answer well. If a thief could be kind to these children then should we not be kind too? If these two boys had never had this opportunity, how could they have become immortal? So we too must make life creative and rich for all children. We must leave them as many opportunities as possible for their future.

Children are born with a dynamic energy that helps them to grow and reach out to the world with their own specialness. Most of the time their own energy enables them to adjust to the changes that come their way. But at times with illness or with the bumps and bruises that come with life, we can help support their energy, enabling it to rebalance itself, with our healing touch. Our healing touch is used to simply remind the body to return itself to a well balanced healthy place.

RECEIVING SPIRIT

With illness or emotional stress, the muscles of the body tighten. By placing our caring hands on areas of the body, we can help ease the tightness. By holding the seven main chakras of the body in turn, we can help the body regenerate its own energy. There are also certain areas of the body that can be held to activate certain acupuncture points that help with healing.

Rub your hands together and feel the Qi energy that flows through your hands. Bring your hands together and feel a cushion of energy between your two hands. This is Qi energy that gives life to all things. The body has all it needs to heal itself with this energy. When we place our hands on another person we are simply saying hello to their energy, and asking it to help them. We are also embracing that person with our loving attention. It is nature and love that heals. We simply assist nature and the body to do what it needs. In children this healing ability is very sensitive and works quickly.

Touch is very intimate. When we touch an acupuncture point, we simply touch the point gently but firmly enough so it doesn't tickle. When you feel the contact with the energy of the point you can take your finger off the point. The body's Qi energy will do the rest. Again when massaging areas of dis-ease use a gentle firm touch allowing the body to build its own energy. When I suggest to touch bone it means to again use a firm gentle touch to simply contact an area of bone and hold it a few seconds allowing the body to build its own Qi. With the chakras, by placing your hands around the areas of the chakras, the energy again naturally builds itself.

When you begin the session with a child make sure you are calm and loving. The child should be lying comfortably on its back somewhere you can easily reach both sides of the child's body. Then just enjoy expanding the healing energy of the child's body that you contact through your hands. Children on the whole like touch. Using the following sequence once a week, once a month or once a season can help keep the child's energy at a good level.

With the child lying on its back begin by holding the heels in your hands just above the table and give a gentle pull curving slightly upwards. Hold it for a few seconds and then put the heels back on the couch, bed or floor. This curve allows the energy to fully flow up the spine and the Du Mai meridian.

Next place your hands on both sides of the spine on the lower back. Lift your fingers gently upwards contacting the energy of the lower half of the inner bladder line holding it for a few seconds. This allows the energy to flow through the points in this area and brings the refreshing vitality of the water element to the child. Then move down to the sacrum and hold it in the same way for a few seconds. This makes contact with the inner sacral-cranial rhythm and allows it to rebalance itself. Hold behind the knees for a few seconds. This relaxes the entire back area. Massage down the lower legs. This opens the channels of the six meridians that run down the legs. Then go to the feet again and holding the heels slightly above the couch do another gentle curve. This integrates the energetic work of the lower back

RECEIVING SPIRIT

Then move to the upper back and hold both sides of the spine again for a few seconds. This allows the energy to flow through the points on the inner bladder line of the upper back. Gently massage the shoulders and the chest region. This relaxes the heart and lungs. Then place your hands under the child's head and gently touch the cranial bone and hold it for a few seconds. This contacts the sacral-cranial rhythm and allows it to balance itself. Then massage the child's arms beginning with the shoulder and work downwards towards the hands. This open the six channels of the meridians that run down the arms.

Now place one hand over the child's belly button at REN MAI 8, *Shen Que,* the inner gateway tower of spirit and the other hand on the spine at the same level of the body. This is like making a sandwich with one hand on top, the other underneath and the child's body in the middle. Simply hold the child's middle at this place for a few seconds. This sends energy through all the meridians giving them a gentle balancing and gives the child's spirit a gentle lift.

Now using this sandwiching we are going to balance the child's chakras. Begin by placing one hand over the child's pubic bone, around REN MAI 2, *Qu Gu,* the maze of bone structure and the other on the spine at the same level. Hold it again for a few seconds. This balances the child's wood element. It gives hope and vision and a dynamic thrust of growth and energy like at tree growing in springtime.

Next place one hand over the area between the pubic bone and the belly button, around REN MAI 6, *Qi Hai,* the sea of abundantly flowing Qi, and place the other hand on the spine at the same level. Hold this area for a few seconds. This helps to balance the child's water element. It gives vitality and reserves of energy to the body, like a fresh mountain spring.

Next place one hand over the area just above the belly button, around REN MAI 12, *Zhong Wan*, the core of our nourishment and middle duct. Place the other hand on the spine at the same level. Hold it for a few seconds. This helps to balance the child's earth element and gives nourishment to the entire body and spirit, like the earth at harvest time.

Next place one hand over the area of the heart, around REN MAI 14, *Ju Que*, the great palace gateway of the heart, and the other on the spine at the same level. Hold it for a few seconds. This gives the child the warmth and love of the fire element, like the warmth and beauty of a summer garden.

Next place one hand over the area of the upper chest and throat, around REN MAI 21, *Xuan Ji*, the jade within the pearl, and the other on the spine at the same level. Hold it for a few seconds. This gives the child the quality of its own unique essence in the form of the metal element, and is like touching the heavens.

Next place one hand under the head, around DU MAI 16, *Feng Fu*, the palace of the wind, and the other on the child's forehead. This point allows our vision to grow. Hold it for a few seconds. This opens and clears the child's vision so his eyes sparkle with wonder and inspiration.

Next still holding one hand under the head, place the other hand on the top of the head, around DU MAI 20, *Bai Hui*, the meeting of grand unity. Hold it for a few seconds. This allows the heavenly energy to flow through the entire body.

To finish gently massage down the back, sacrum, and legs. Finally hold the heels again just above the couch and give a gentle curved pull. Using this sequence keeps the body at a good, balanced energetic level. It is also something you can use on yourself or have someone give to you.

When the child is ill we can massage areas of the body and use points to help with healing. Use these points or massages before the chakra balancing. To begin, it is good to massage the area where the dis-ease lies. For example with colds the face and chest areas help. With stomachaches, the area of the stomach can be massaged. With earache the area around the ear and sinuses can be massaged. Sometimes just putting a hand over the area is sufficient as it allows the Qi to warm and help heal. With breaks hold the bone and ask it to remember how it was before the injury and allow the energy to move and change where it needs to in the bone. With a sprain gently hold the area allowing the circulation to build and heal.

To help the immune system it is good to hold the area of the arm just above the wrist for a few seconds as well as the area above the ankle for a few seconds. The meeting point of the upper yin meridians, PC5, *Jian Shi*, the light messenger, and the meeting point of the upper yang meridians, TB8, *San Yang Luo*, three yang junction is above the wrists. GB39, *Xuan Zhong*, suspended goblet, is the meeting point of the lower yang meridians and SP6, *San Yin Jiao*, crossing of three yins, is the meeting point of the lower yin meridians. These are on the leg above the ankles. Using these points helps the energy unite to heal. LIV 13, *Zhang Men*, gate of hope, is the meeting point of the five yin organs. It is on the lower ribs. Ren Mai 12, *Zhong Wan*, middle duct is the meeting point of the five yang organs. It is in the middle of the stomach between the zyphoid and belly button. Using acupressure on these points gives a boost of energy to the healing energy in the body. With fevers acupressure can be used on LI 11, *Qu Chi* curved pond. This point is in the curve of the elbow. Using moxa or acupressure on Bladder 38(43), *Gao Huang Shu*, rich for the vitals, gives gentle healing to every cell in the body. This is on the back on the inner bladder line just below the top of the scapula. Moxa or acupressure can also be used on Du Mai 14, *Da Zhui*, great vertebrae force, which unites all the yang pathways. This point is at the top of the back in the centre just under the neck. Using moxa over salt on Ren Mai 8, the palace gateway of spirit, on the belly button gives a great warmth to all the meridian and a gentle boost to spirit.

Depending on the child's odour and colour, we can use acupressure on the source points (see page 68) of the appropriate paired meridians, to give support to the elemental imbalance. We finish the session with the chakra balancing. Just simply enjoy giving the child your healing touch.

> *There is a garden in every childhood, an enchanted place where colours are brighter, the air softer, and the morning more fragrant than ever again.*
> **ELIZABETH LAWRENCE**

HEAVEN

EVERYDAY, PRIESTS MINUTELY EXAMINE THE DHARMA
AND ENDLESSLY CHANT COMPLICATED SUTRAS
BEFORE DOING THAT, THOUGH
THEY SHOULD LEARN HOW TO READ LOVE LETTERS
SENT BY THE WIND AND RAIN, THE SUN AND MOON
IKKY

PRAYERS AND HEALING

When Buddhism came to China the prayers and healing Buddhas came to be integrated in the Taoist temples. When someone can not be healed by ordinary means they are even today sent to the healers in the temples or monasteries. When I was in Tibet all the medicines at the Traditional Tibetan Hospital were blessed. In Llasa as well as other nearby monasteries, I was able to see the power of healing prayer in the ancient monasteries. One monk even wrote out prayers for relatives of those who had died on red parchment to help the souls of the dead become enlightened.

In my own work I begin with silent prayer. I also bless all the medicines that I make. At times when I am contacting a point for someone, I call on the higher beings to help that person heal. I feel this connection is what in the end brings true healing to the person. Let us begin by looking at the healing qualities of several of the Buddhas. There is a Buddha for each of the five elements that heals that element at a deep spiritual level. Following the Buddhas, there is a selection of healing prayers from all over the world. These I sometimes say silently as I am working with someone, or I give them to people after the session to help with their own healing.

THE FIVE BUDDHA FAMILIES

In the Eastern Realm of spring and the wood element is the Buddha Akshobhya. His prayer is, *om vajru akshobhya hum.*

As a simple monk he asked to become enlightened. He was told that he would have to foreswear all anger. With unshakeable faith he took the vow to never give way to anger, bear malice, do immoral acts and many other things. He become the unshakable Akshobhya. His whole body radiates the light of wisdom where we can enter the path of enlightenment where there is no going back. It is like the burst of a seed in spring when life bursts forth and goes forward. He is said to have the unshakable certainty of an elephant placing its foot on the ground. It is he who guides us in showing us that hatred and anger can be redirected by seeing the clear fault of things and using the energy to change the real enemies of suffering.

He belongs to the Vajru family who have the diamond thunderbolt. It is said that when an irresistible force met an immovable object the vajru was made. It can cut through anything but nothing can cut it. It is just like a diamond. In the centre, it is egg shaped representing the primordial unity. Then there are lotus flowers each side representing all opposites and then the tips representing the negative and positive qualities that are then retied and reunited to the centre where all opposites become one.

Here is the stamp and seal of each moment when each action once past can never be erased or undone. For Akshobhya each moment is total, lacking nothing, complete as it is. When the Buddha himself was about to receive the enlightenment, he touched the ground to symbolize he was ready to receive enlightenment because the seeds of all the positive actions he had done were now ready to come to fruition. Here is our unique seed bursting forward when the thunderbolt has smashed through all our ideas and concepts. Duality becomes a dream as the concept of you and the world disappears. Here is a mirror like wisdom seeing everything just as it is like the fresh innocent vision of spring. The mind can reflect without staining the vision like the waters of stillness reflecting the shapes above it.

In the Southern Realm of summer and the fire element, is the Buddha Ratnasambhava. He holds the wishfulling jewel in his hand. His prayer is, *om ratna ratnasambhava hum.* Here is the joy of the heart where all can be received and given. In his realm every one is given what they have wished for. A golden light emanates from his body full of an abundance of energy and creativity. Here is rich fertile soil where life grows in profusion. This is where pride is transformed into the wisdom of sameness. Ratnasambhava sees common humanity in all men and women and cares for them all equally, believing all beings to be equally precious. In his realm we develop a solidarity with all forms of life experiencing gain and loss, fame and disgrace, praise and blame and pleasure and pain as equals. As we treat them with calm impartiality they let go of their hold and each moment becomes a precious sharing with everything around us. His open palm is turned outwards showering everything with what it desires. Here our inner self opens out to others just as the lotus flowers opens in the sunshine. His hand expresses the mundra of giving. As we give we feel this expansiveness within ourselves until we can feel the ability to pour out spiritual riches without any thought of running out of reserves. Ratnasambhava promised to be a lantern for those desiring a lantern, a bed for those desiring a bed and anything else needed. In this giving we change from a poverty material mentality to a wealthy spiritual mentality.

We need to believe in our own heart potential as a human being. When we give, we are taken out of ourselves and go beyond ourselves to see the needs in others as well as appreciating their good qualities. We open ourselves to a wider world and learn to appreciate all things rather than exploiting them. This jewel is to gain enlightenment for the sake of all living beings and sharing the spiritual riches found everywhere. Indeed, no one can use or possess a sunset, but all can expand their love and wonder in its beauty. Here we give ourselves completely and gain the world.

In the Centre Realm of late summer and the element of earth is the Buddha Vairochana. He sits surrounded by four roaring lions, smiling and serene with a golden wheel in his hand. His prayer is, **om tathagata vairochana hum.** He is the illuminator buddha and with his golden wheel we can be helped to transform ourselves and those around us. The Buddhas are said to be kings among people with the most noble lineage devoted to helping all beings obtain enlightenment. This golden wheel has the message of setting out on the spiritual path that may one day put into motion the enlightenment of all beings. It is also the symbol of the golden sun who shines on everything without preference or exception. This enlightened centre is where we are both centered but also have a panoramic awareness of all things.

Vairochana's mudra is that of putting the golden wheel into motion setting us on the path of the teaching of the Buddha. Within our own mind there is now the possibility of transformation. We do this by identifying with all our experiences and by relating to the world with loving kindness. We try and not use even the subtlest of force or manipulation to obtain what we want. We relate to the world with the best of co-operative spirit. It is through care and loving kindness that we can subdue the lions of our acquisitive territorial nature and harness their energy to support our mother earth. When we open our hearts to people then we can see through egotism and embrace loving kindness towards others nourishing all.

It is then we receive Vairochana's gift of the golden wheel. We turn it and set it into motion and teach by passing on what we have gained. We share what we have learnt with others. No experience is complete until it has been communicated to help other beings. In this way the wheel can keep expanding planting seeds of its transcendence never finishing its endless turning cycles. We can imagine Vairochana both spinning the golden wheel as well as being in the centre of the wheel and spinning the whole mandala on the path of continuing evolution where all mandalas can be transcended. In this way we find our inner peace and are able to nourish others.

In the Western Realm of autumn and the element of metal is the Buddha Amitabha. Here is the place of the setting sun in the west, where we relax at the end of the day. His prayer is, **om padma amitabaha hum**. Amitabha sees and loves the minute differences in things and appreciates their uniqueness.

RECEIVING SPIRIT

This gentle time of sunset is when the light turns into the higher state of meditative concentration. Amitabha helps us change the passions that attach themselves to a particular object into discriminating wisdom. By becoming devoted to finding the beauty in all things we arrive at an egolessness where loving all of life we become one with all things.

Amitabha is surrounded by peacocks that can swallow poisonous snakes without being harmed. In this sense even our darkest most venomous aspects can be transformed into beauty where we go from a restless unfulfilled state to a deeper satisfying level. Here we gradually unfold our petals of spiritual potential with a longing desire to embrace heaven until we ripen into who we are just like the great lotus.

Amitabha is like the statues of timeless buddhas simply sitting silently deepening their concentration for thousands of years. The stone Buddhas is centered, content with deep connections to earth and sky finding the treasure of the inner oceans and vast universe. There is a story told of a monk who lived with beggars. In those days a samurai would test a new sword on a human victim. One evening a samurai was seen with a new sword. All the beggars were terrified he would come and test his sword on one of them. The monk told them to hide and he sat calmly in mediation on the road. The samurai came and told the monk to prepare to die. There was no reply, but the monk sat giving off a feeling of vast gentle harnessed energy coming from deep meditation. The samurai faltered and finally slunk away into the night. Later he too became enlightened.

Amitabha has the hand mudra of the union of opposites. His thumbs touch in the center making the shape of an empty egg. It is in this emptiness that all things become one. If we look at thoughts in this empty space we can see how those thoughts create the world, but we can also see how we can change. Out of this empty space can come sweet flowing rivers, and beautifully feathered birds. We too can be cradled in this empty space and see eternity in a single seed and the world in a fragrant rose.

In the Northern Realm of winter and the water element is the Buddha Amoghasiddhi. He is the buddha of unobstructed success. His prayer is, *om amoghasiddhi an hum*. He is said to fly on a chariot pulled by eagles and clashing symbols. He transforms the night so everything is bright and clear. In his right hand is the mudra of a powerful gesture. This is the hand mundra of the gesture of fearlessness. Amoghasiddhi's whole presence removes terror and fear. In the left is the double diamond thunderbolt that has an awesome power to cut through anything while always remaining unaffected. This double vajra reminds us that fearlessness comes from a full and balanced development of all sides of ourselves. When we have fear, we have a vulnerability that we have to protect. Our work in overcoming fear is to search out our weakest point and mobilize our inner resources. In this way we will gain trust, confidence, wisdom, concentration, energy and mindfulness. We then become spontaneous and totally present.

This double vajra is the symbol of total psychic integration. It is the harmony, balance and equilibrium found when we have journeyed to the most profound depths of existence for out of that deep unconsciousness comes the greatest potential for life. But also within the double vajra is the cosmos and the universe of all eons. Here are formed the deep midnight patterns of our own psyche where the universe and our consciousness are one and the same thing. Amoghasiddhi has the ability to fuse different levels of existence where the inner and outer unite and the visible and invisible become one. It is said his chariot is pulled by the shang shang birds that are half eagle and half man, symbolizing this very union of nature and man. Meditation on Amoghasiddhi helps to order energy on a deep level and profound conflicts can begin to resolve releasing energy as if from a deep spring. Here the paradoxes of spiritual life bring true wisdom enabling us to have full compassion. Here we can find the psychic integration to be able to move in all directions.

TARA

Tara is known in various forms all over the world. She embodies all that is helpful, compassionate, fearless, and healing. She is the protectorate of those who are ill. Her healing prayer is, *om tare tutare ture soha.* She represents the feminine aspect of the Buddha nature. Tara is understood to be the Buddha mother, 'she who saves', and the protectress of the sick. According to legend, Tara was a human woman who vowed to work towards liberation of all sentient beings. She vowed to achieve enlightenment in female form and to remain in this form to be a helpful and healing mother figure for all beings in need. She is directly accessible to all who request her help, not simply those initiated into her practice tradition. One simply has to call on her sincerely.

Imagine in the space before you a white lotus and on it a moon disc. In front sitting on the lotus appears the love and compassion of all the Enlightened Beings in the form of the Noble Wish-Fulfilling Tara. Her right hand makes a gesture of invitation to liberation. Her left hand holds an utpala flower indicating the protection of the three jewels that gives courage and assurance to those dominated by fear. At her crown is the white Om, at her throat the red Ah, at her heart the white Tam and the blue Hum. Light radiates from the heart inviting the wisdom beings and empowering deities. A Buddha of infinite light adorns her crown. Energy streams forth from Tara's heart cleansing and revitalizing all beings enabling them to obtain the realization of enlightenment.

As we say the blessing of *om tare tutare ture soha* we engage in the following. Om, I bow down to the liberator, and the fully realized goddess Tara. Tare, I bow down to the glorious mother who liberates me from attachment. Tuttare, I praise the mother who eliminates all the eight fears. Ture, I praise the mother who grants all success and liberates from all illnesses. Soha, I offer the greatest praise. As you repeat the mantra visualize the energy rays going out from Tara's heart, reaching in every direction in the universe. The light rays then return to Tara bringing with them the purity, vigor and capability of each of the five elements in their natural state. Imagine these rays bathing you in brilliantly coloured light and liquid.

The golden yellow rejuvenate the earth element and works with bodily strength, nourishing our organs, flesh and bones.

The liquid blue rejuvenates the water element and works to revitalize all the body fluids, blood and emotions.

The red rejuvenates the fire element and works with vital energy to bring laughter, heat, joy and compassion.

The emerald green rejuvenates the wood element and works to clear anger and open our vision.

The crystal white rejuvenates the metal element allowing us to let go and bring in the vital essences of the heavens.

Imagine this healing light protecting, healing and helping others who are ill. Imagine the light and liquid streaming from Tara's heart reaching these people bathing them, as well as you, and granting all, Tara's compassionate aid.

HEALING PRAYERS AND HEALING WISDOM

This is a collection of healing prayers and stories of wisdom from all over the world that I use with patients who come to me. I may say them silently during the session, but I may also give them to patients for inspiration and comfort particularly during a difficult time in their lives. For children I often give them a hand coloured medicine buddha with his blessing written on the back. When I begin a session, I pray for the higher beings to send their healing light through my hands. I feel this is important. We as healers are simply allowing the healing energy of nature to flow through us to help the patient. It is nature herself and our own spirit who heals us.

A MIRACLE

A miracle may touch many people you have not met,
And produce changes undreamt in situations
Of which you are not even aware.
In you is all of heaven.
Every leaf that falls is given life in you.
Each bird that sings will sing in you again.
Every flower that blooms has saved
Its perfume and beauty for you.
Healing is the effect
Of our minds joining together
And sickness comes
From minds that separate.

PRAYER OF ALBERT SCHWEITZER

May I follow a life of compassion
For the suffering of all living things.
Teach me to live with reverence for life everywhere,
To treat life as sacred, and respect all that breathes.
O Father, I grope amidst the shadows of doubt and fear,
But I long to advance toward the light.
Help me to fling my life like a flaming firebrand,
Into the gathering darkness of the world.

RECEIVING SPIRIT

BUDDHIST PRAYER
May I be a protector for those without one
And a lamp for those desiring light.
May I be a bridge, a boat, a ship
For all who wish to cross the water.
May the forest of razor sharp leaves become
A beautiful pleasure grove,
And may the trees of knives and swords
Grow into wish fullfilling trees.

May the regions of hell become
Places of joy with vast and fragrant lotus pools
Beautiful with exquisite calls of wild ducks, geese and swans.
May the heaps of burning coals change to heaps of jewels,
May the burning ground become a polished crystal floor,
And may the mountain of the crushing hells
Become celestial palaces of worship filled with Buddhas.

May the rains of lava, blazing stones and
Weapons become a rain of flowers.
May all battling with weapons
Become a playful exchange of flowers.
May the naked find clothing and hungry find food.
May the thirsty find water and delicious drinks.
May the poor find wealth,
Those weak with sorrow find joy.
May the forlorn find new hope
Constant happiness and prosperity.

May all who are sick and ill
Quickly be freed from their illness
And may every disease in the world never occur again.
May the troubled wanderers
Who have lost their way meet with fellow travellers
And without any fear of thieves or tigers
May their going be easy without fatigue.

May those who find themselves
In trackless, fearful wilderness
The children, the aged, the unprotected,
Those stupefied and insane
Be guarded by beneficent celestials.

May the land everywhere be pure, smooth
And devoid of any rocks
Level like the palm of the hand and the nature of lapis lazuli.
May the celestials bring timely rains
So that the harvests may be bountiful.
May kings act in accordance with the Dharma
And the people of the world always prosper.
By the merits I have accumulated
May every single being abandon all forms of evil
And forever engage in virtue.
For as long as space endures and
For as long as living beings remain
Until then may I too abide
To dispel the misery of the world.

RECEIVING SPIRIT

CELTIC PRAYER FOR HEALING
*I wish healing upon you,
The healing of Brighid, angel Michael and Mary,
Be with me all three
Your pain and sickness
Be in the earth's depths,
Be upon the grey stones
For they are enduring,
Fly with the birds of the air,
Fly with the wasps of the hill,
Swim with the sea-going whale,
For they are swiftest,
Be upon the clouds of the sky
For they are the rainiest,
Be upon the river's current
Cascading to the sea.*

NATIVE AMERICAN WISDOM
*To honour and respect means to think of the land
and the water and plants and animals
Who have lived here as having a right equal to our own.
We are not the supreme and all knowing beings
Living at the top of the pinnacle of evolution,
But in fact we are member of the sacred hoop of life,
Along with the trees and rocks, the coyotes and the eagles
And fish and toads that each fulfills its purpose.
They each perform their given task
In the sacred hoop and we have one, too.*

ARCHIE FIRE LAME DEER
To be a medicine man you have to experience everything
Live life to the fullest.
If you don't experience the humans side of everything,
How can you help teach or heal?
To be a good medicine man, you've got to be humble.
You've got to be lower than a worm and higher than an eagle.

CHIEF SEATTLE
If all the plants and beasts were gone,
We would die from loneliness of spirit,
For whatever happens to the plants and beasts happens to us.
All things are connected.
Whatever befalls the earth befalls the sons of the earth.

JESSE CORNPLANTER
The patient must be in a certain frame of mind,
a flexible mind,
He must work in conjunction with the medicine.
He must have faith in its power in order to help it.
In the Indian philosophy of sickness,
It is thought that one's mind must be freed
from worry and distrust
In order that the patient may get well.

RECEIVING SPIRIT

ZEN WISDOM
A samurai warrior was walking through the mountains
He met Master Hakuin and asked,
'What is hell and heaven?'
Master Hakuin looked at the warrior and began insulting him,
'You are so unclean and your clothes so tattered,
you would never understand.'
The samurai became furious and pulled out his sword.
'There!' said Hakuin, 'That is hell.'
The samurai was overcome with gratitude
and bowed before the master.
Hakuin said, 'And that is heaven.'

DOGEN (1200-1253)
The moon
Resting in the midst of
The stillness of mind
Clouds break
Into light.

TRADITIONAL BUDDHIST CHANT
Just as the soft rains fill the streams,
Pour into the rivers and join together in the oceans,
So may the power of every moment of your goodness
Flow forth to awaken and heal all beings,
Those here now, those gone before, those yet to come.

By the power of every moment of your goodness
May your heart's wishes be soon fulfilled
As completely shining as the bright full moon,
As magically as by a wish-fulfilling gem.
By the power of every moment of your goodness
May all dangers be averted and all disease be gone.
May no obstacle come across your way.
May you enjoy fulfilment and long life.
For all in whose heart dwells respect,
Who follow the wisdom and compassion, of the Way,
May your life prosper in the four blessings
Of old age, beauty, happiness and strength.

THE SUFI PRAYER OF LIGHT

O God! Grant me Light in my heart, Light in my grave,
Light in front of me, Light behind me,
Light to my right, Light to my left,
Light above me, Light below me,
Light in my ears, Light in my hair,
Light on my skin, Light in my hair,
Light within my flesh, Light in my blood, Light in my bones.
O God! Increase my Light everywhere.
O God! Grant me Light in my heart,
Light on my tongue, Light in my eyes, Light in my ears,
Light to my right, Light to my left,
Light above me, Light below me,
Light in front of me, Light below me,
and Light within my self, increase my light.

BAHA'I PRAYER

Thy name is my healing, O my God,
And remembrance of Thee is my remedy.
Nearness to Thee is my hope, and love for Thee is my companion.
Thy mercy to me is my healing and my succor in both this world
And the world to come.
Thou, verily art the All-Bountiful,
The All-Knowing, the All-Wise.

JEWISH PRAYER

Heal us, Lord, and we shall be healed.
Save us and we shall be saved, for it is You we praise.
Send relief and healing for all our diseases,
Our sufferings and our wounds.
For You are a merciful and faithful healer.
Blessed are You Lord, who heals the sick.

CHRISTIAN PRAYER

Lord, the one that I love is sick and in great pain,
Out of your compassion heal him and take away his pain.
It breaks my heart to see him suffer,
May I not share his pain if it is not your will that he be healed?
Lord, let him know that you are with him,
Support and help him that he may come to know you more
Deeply as a result of his suffering.
Lord be our strength and support in this time of darkness and
Give us that deep peace which comes from trusting you.

PRAYER FROM THE VEDAS

May the Wind breathe healing upon us,
Prolong our life-span, and fill our hearts with comfort!
You are our father, O Wind,
Our friend and our brother.
Give us life that we may live.
From that immortal treasure, O Lord,
Which is hidden in your abode,
Impart to us that we may live.

WISDOM OF THICH NHAT HANH

Our true home is in the present moment.
To live in the present moment is a miracle.
The miracle is not to walk on water.
The miracle is to walk on the green Earth
In the present moment,
To appreciate the peace and beauty that are available now.
Peace is all around us, in the world and in nature,
And within us, in our bodies and our spirits.
Once we learn to touch this peace,
We will be healed and transformed.
It is not a matter of faith
It is a matter of practice.

PRAYER OF RABBI RAMI SHAPIRO
There are moments when wellness escapes us,
Moments when pain and suffering
Are not dim possibilities
But all too agonizing realities.
At such moments we must open ourselves to healing.
Much we can do for ourselves,
And what we can do
We must do
Healing,
Not less than illness,
Is participatory.
But even when we do all we can do
There is
Often
Still much left to be done.
And so we turn as well to our healers
Seeking their aid in our struggle for wellness.
But even when they do all they can do
There is
Often,
Still much left to be done.
And so we turn to Life,
To the vast Power of Being that animates the universe
As the ocean animates the wave
Seeking to let go of that which blocks our healing.
May those
Whose lives are gripped in the palm of suffering

Open even now
To the Wonder of Life.
May they let go of the hurt
And Meet the True Self beyond pain,
The Uncarved Block
That is our joyous Unity with Holiness.
May they discover through pain and torment
The strength to live with grace and humour.
May they discover through doubt and anguish
The strength to live with dignity and holiness.
May they discover through suffering and fear
The strength to move toward healing.

SIOUX PRAYER

O our Father, the Sky hear us
And make us strong.
O our Mother the Earth, hear us
And give us support
O Spirit of the East send us your wisdom.
O spirit of the South,
May we tread your path of life.
O spirit of the West,
May we always be ready for the long journey.
O Spirit of the North, purify us
With your cleansing winds.

MANITONGQUAT

Hear, O Humankind, the prayer of my heart.
For are we not one, have we not one desire,
To heal our Mother Earth and bind her wounds
To hear again from dark forests and flashing rivers
The varied ever-changing Song of Creation?

O humankind, are we not all brothers and sisters,
Are we not the grand children of the Great Mystery?
Do we not all want to love and be loved, to work
And to play, to sing and dance together?

But we live with fear. Fear that is hate, fear
That is mistrust, envy, greed, vanity, fear that is
Ambition, competition, aggression, fear that is
Loneliness, anger, bitterness, cruelty…and yet,
Fear is only twisted love, love turned back on itself,
Love that was denied, love that was rejected, and love…..

Love is life, creation, seed and leaf
And blossom and fruit and see, love is growth
And search and reach and touch and dance.
Love is nurture and succor and feed and pleasure,
Love is pleasuring ourselves, pleasuring each other,
Love is life believing in itself and life,
Life is the Sacred Mystery singing to itself, dancing
To its drum, telling tales, improvising, playing
And we are all that Spirit, our stories all

But one cosmic story that we are love indeed,
That perfect love in me seeks the love in you,
And if our eyes could ever meet without fear
We would recognize each other and rejoice,
For love is life believing in itself.

SAINT MARY MAGDALEN DEI PAZZI
Spirit of truth,
You are the reward to the saints,
The comforter of souls,
Light in the darkness,
Riches to the poor,
Treasure to lovers,
Food for the hungry,
Comfort to the wanderer,
To sum up,
You are the one in whom all treasures are contained.

AZTEC PRAYER
Mother of gods, father of gods, Ancient God,
A mere appendage of the realm, a common man, has come.
He comes crying, he comes in sadness, he comes with guilt.
Perhaps he has slipped, perhaps he has stumbled,
Perhaps he has touched the bird of evil,
The spider's web, the tuft of thorns.
It wounds his heart, it troubles him.
Master, Lord, ever present, ever near
Take it from him, hear the pain of this common man.

RECEIVING SPIRIT

PRAYER OF ANNE BARING
Beehive source,
Trellised womb
Mother of all beginnings
Hold me
Gather me
Feed me
With the honey-nectar
From the hive.
Nourished
I will sing
The Bee-song
The long-forgotten melody
Of praise to thee

SAINT AUGUSTINE
God of life, there are days when the burdens we carry
Chafed our shoulders and wear us down
When the road seems dreary and endless,
The skies grey and threatening,
When our lives have no music in them and our hearts are lonely,
And our souls have lost their courage,
Flood the path with light, we beseech you,
Turn our eyes to where the skies are full of promise.

PRAYERS AND HEALING

PRAYER OF THE UTE TRIBE

Earth teach me stillness as the grasses are stilled with light.
Earth teach me suffering as old stones suffer with memory.
Earth teach me humility as blossoms are humble with beginning.
Earth teach me caring as the mother who secures her young.
Earth teach me courage as the tree which stands all alone.
Earth teach me limitation as the ant
which crawls on the ground.
Earth teach me freedom as the eagle which soars in the sky.
Earth teach me resignation as the leaves which die in the fall.
Earth teach me regeneration as the seed which rises in the spring.
Earth teach me to forget myself as melted snow forgets its life.
Earth teach me to remember kindness
as dry fields weep with rain.

NAVAHO CHANT

May it be delightful my house,
From my head may it be delightful,
To my feet may it be delightful,
Where I lie may it be delightful,
All above me may it be delightful,
All around me may it be delightful.

RECEIVING SPIRIT

SANTIDEVA

May I become a medicine for the sick and their physician,
Their support until sickness come not again.
May I become an unfailing store for the wretched,
And be first to supply them with their needs.
My own self and my pleasures, my righteousness,
Past, present and future,
May I sacrifice without regard,
In order to achieve the welfare of beings.

WENDELL BERRY

When I rise up
Let me rise up joyful
Like a bird

When I fall
Let me fall without regret
Like a leaf

SAINT FRANCIS DE SALES

Be patient with everyone, but above all with yourself.
Do not be disheartened by your imperfections,
But always rise up with fresh courage.
How are we to be patient in dealing with our neighbour's faults,
If we are impatient dealing with our own?
They who are fretted by their own failings will not correct them.
All profitable correction comes from a calm and peaceful mind.

PRAYERS AND HEALING

RABINDRANATH TAGORE
Let me not pray to be sheltered from dangers
But to be fearless in facing them.
Let me not beg for the stilling of my pain
But for the heart to conquer it.
Let me not crave in anxious fear to be saved
But hope for the patience to win my freedom.

ARABIC PROVERB
Write the wrongs that are done to you in sand,
But write the good things that happen to you on a piece of marble.
Let go of all emotions such as resentment and retaliation, which diminish you,
And hold onto the emotions, such as gratitude and joy, which increase you.

AFRICAN-AMERICAN SPIRITUAL
Precious Lord, take my hand.
Lead me on. Let me stand.
I am tired. I am weak. I am worn.
Through the storm, through the night,
Lead me to the light.
Take my hand, precious Lord and lead me home.

CHINESE PROVERB
*You can go halfway
into the forest, then you are coming out
the other side to the light.*

AN AFRICAN CALL FOR LIFE
*Busy normal people, the world is here.
Can you hear it wailing, crying, whispering?
Listen, the world is here. Don't you hear it?
Praying and sighing and groaning for wholeness?
Sighing and whispering, wholeness, wholeness, wholeness?
An arduous, tiresome, difficult journey towards wholeness.
God, who gives us strength of body make us whole.
Wholeness of persons, well-being of individuals.
The cry for bodily health and spiritual strength
Is echoed from person to person, from patient to doctor.
It goes out from a soul to its pastor.
We, busy, 'normal' people, we are sick.
We yearn to experience wholeness in our inner most being,
In health and prosperity, we continue to feel un-well,
Un-fulfilled, or half-filled.
There is a hollowness in our pretended well-being,
Our spirits cry out for the well-being of the whole human family.
We pride ourselves in our traditional communal ideology,
Our extended family.
The beggars and the mad people in our streets,
Where are their relatives?
Who is their father? Where is their mother?*

PRAYERS AND HEALING

We cry for the wholeness of humanity.
But the litany of brokenness is without end.
Black and white,
Rich and poor,
Hausa and Yomba,
Presbyterian and Roman Catholic,
We are all parts of each other,
We yearn to be folded into the fullness of life together.
Life, together with the outcast, the prisoner,
The mad woman, the abandoned child,
Our wholeness means healing the hurt,
Seeing and feeling the suffering of others,
Standing alongside them.
Their loss of dignity is not their loss,
It is the loss of our human dignity, we busy, 'normal' people.
The person next to you, with a different language and culture,
with a different skin or hair colour,
It is God's diversity, making an unbroken rainbow circle,
Our covenant of peace with God,
Encircling the whole of humanity.
There is no wall, there is only God at work in the whole,
Heal sores on feet, salvage the disintegrated personality,
Bind the person back into the whole.
For without that one we do not have a whole.
Even if there are ninety-nine, without that one,
We do not have a whole.
God, who give us strength of body, make us whole.

RECEIVING SPIRIT

MAORI WISDOM

*In the Light there is life and compassion
In the Darkness there is only darkness.
In the light the dream knows no bounds,
In the Darkness the dream distorts,
And fails to find its beginning and fears its end.
The children of peace are like saplings
Nurtured by the Earth Mother.
Seeking the light, they reach ever upwards to the sky
To become the tall trees of the forest.*

ST. FRANCIS OF ASSISI.

*Lord make me an instrument of your peace
Where there is hatred, let me sow love,
Where there is injury, pardon, where there is doubt, faith,
Where there is despair, hope, where there is darkness, light,
Where there is sadness, joy.
O Divine Master, grant that I may not so much seek
To be consoled, as to console, to be understood, as to understand,
To be loved, as to love,
For it is in giving that we receive,
It is in pardoning that we are pardoned,
It is in dying that we are born to eternal life.*

AMADO NERVO

*I am only a spark, make me a fire.
I am only a string, make me a lyre.
I am only a drop, make me a fountain.*

I am only an ant hill, make me a mountain.
I am only a feather, make me a wing.
I am only a rag, make me an angel.

A PRAYER OF THANKS OF THE IROQUOIS TRIBE

We return thanks to our mother, earth, which sustains us.
We return thanks to the rivers, which supply us with water.
We return thanks to all herbs,
Which furnish medicines for the cure of our diseases.
We return thanks to the corn, which give us life.
We return thanks to the bushes and trees, giving us fruits.
We return thanks to the wind, moving air, banishing disease.
We return thanks to the moon and stars,
Giving us their light when the sun was gone.
We return thanks to our grandfather, He'no,
Protecting his grandchildren and giving us his rain.
We return thanks to the sun, and its warmth.
Lastly, we return thanks to the Great Spirit, and his goodness
And who directs all things for the good of his children.

BLESSING FOR SOMEONE WHO PASSES OVER

Heal this spirit Lord, from all wounds that this heart has
suffered through this life of limitation upon earth.
Purify this heart with Thy divine light and send upon this spirit
Thy mercy, Thy compassion and Thy love.
Amen

RECEIVING SPIRIT

PRAYER FOR THE DEAD
O thou the cause and effect of the whole Universe,
The source from whence we have come
And the goal toward which all are bound:
Receive this soul who is coming to Thee into Thy parental arms.
May Thy forgiving glance heal his/her heart.
Lift him/her from the denseness of the earth,
Surround him/her with the light of Thine own Spirit.
Raise him/her up to Heaven,
Which is his/her true dwelling place.
We pray Thee grant him/her the blessing
Of Thy most exalted Presence.
May his/her life upon earth become as a dream
To his/her waking soul,
And let his/her thirsting eyes behold the glorious vision
Of Thy sunshine.
Amen

PRAYER OF REMEMBRANCE
In the rising of the sun and in its going down,
we remember them.
In the glowing of the wind and the chill of winter,
we remember them.
In the opening of buds and in the rebrith of spring,
we remember them.
In the blueness of the sky and in the warmth of summer,
we remember them.
In the rustling of the leaves and in the beauty of autumn,

we remember them.
In the beginning of the year and when it ends,
we remember them.
When we are weary and in need of strength,
we remember them.
When we are lost and sick at heart,
we remember them.
When we have joys we yearn to share,
we remember them.
So long as we live, they too shall live,
For they are now a part of us, as we remember them.

GRIEF ON ANOTHER'S DEATH, NATIVE AMERICAN TRADITION

Farewell, my younger brother.
From the highest places
The Gods have come for me.
You will never see me again.
But when the showers pass over you,
And the thunder sounds,
You will pray:
There is the voice of my elder brother.
And when the harvests ripen,
And you hear the voices
Of all the small beautiful birds, and the grasshoppers chirp.
You will pray:
There is the voice of my elder brother,
There is the trail of his soul.

ARTEMESIA VULGARIS
MOXA

THE ENERGY AND SPIRIT OF EUROPEAN MEDICINAL PLANTS

Flowers open our eyes with wonder, enchant our hearts and have been given as offerings of sacred love for centuries. Each spring they bring alive the world with their promise of new life in the most vibrant colours and with the most fragrant perfumes. Wild plum trees fill our sense with sudden hope in clouds of white blossoms. Hidden mauve violets bring delight to our heats. The light powder-blue faces of a hundred speedwells follow the course of the sun throughout the day in vibrant devotions. Flowers brighten windows, honour sacred moments, adorn ritual and are great offerings of love and companionship. What heart does not lighten to see a field full of may poppies, or the fairy rings of crocuses around an ancient oak or the smiles on the faces of a field of sunflowers. To go into a garden in spring, or to walk through the forest or across fields of wild flowers brings life back into our spirit.

Plants have been used for centuries to heal the mind, body and the spirit. Simply walking in nature often brings a deeper sense of well being if we allow our senses to be refreshed by the green wonders that surround us. If we stop and rest by a tree or plant and spend some time simply being with it and observing it, something about its character usually reveals itself. We can learn even more by resting by the plant and

RECEIVING SPIRIT

talking to it in our imagination. When we have a good contact with the plant we can lie still, close our eyes and internally journey to the spirit of the plant. When we can see the plant spirit, we can ask it about its healing qualities. This contact gives us a rich understanding of the plant. Some people see beautiful pictures of their spirit characters. Other people have amazing imaginary journeys with the plants. Some hear music, and other learn dance patterns. Plants are our friends, so it is important to give them a gift and thank them for their help. Then we will be able to go back to the plant and ask it for its help when needed.

    I feel the local growing wild plants are the most beneficial for healing. They gather in the local energy from the seasons, the stars, the heavens and the earth, to bring healing to those around them. It is important to form contact with the plants. I always ask their permission when gathering them. I then give them an offering in return. I take very little of the actual plant, maybe a leaf or a flower because that in itself when taken with respect, imprints its healing qualities on the water, cognac, olive oil or cream that is used as medicine. I then bless these medicines with prayers. When you have a relationship with the plant by journeying to its spirit, you can then simply call on the plant to help a person. By calling on the spirit of the plant, you can then ask it to help and heal the person. Mugwort is a plant that can move energy. Nettle and Foxglove help with a fire imbalance. Evening Primrose and Great Mullein help with an earth imbalance. Plantain helps with a metal imbalance. Horsetail and Mallow help with a water imbalance. Willow

MEDICINAL PLANTS

and Celandine help with a wood imbalance. Morning Glory helps to open a person's vision so they can see further with their own spirit and also see more spirit in the world around them. How do we make this contact with the healing energy of these plants?

First you have to journey to your garden angel. Close your eyes and imagine you are in a beautiful place. You find an opening and go through the opening. You find a being waiting for you and you talk to each other. This magical being will help you find the spirits of the plants and their healing qualities. You thank this friend and ask for his or her help on your journey to the plant kingdom. You then open your eyes and rest in quiet contemplation.

To journey to a plant you begin by going out to the plant. It is best if it is a time when the plant is flowering. You greet the plant and spend sometime observing it and drawing it. Bring it something as a gift. I often bring some tobacco or dried mugwort. Sometimes the plant wants something special. I try and get in touch with the plant and what it has to offer. I then ask it about its healing qualities and finally thank it for its help. When this is done, find somewhere where you can lie down comfortably. Close your eyes and journey with the angel of the garden to the spirit of the plant. Ask it about its healing qualities and anything else you might want to know. The plant will sometimes give you a healing journey for your own energy. Again when you have asked for what you need to know, thank the plant and open your eyes and write down the journey and what you feel the healing energy of this plant is.

RECEIVING SPIRIT

There are many ways of using plants. Leaves can be used to make a medicinal tea, the fresher picked the better. You can gather leaves and place them in olive oil for twenty days and then use the oil to make a cream. You can gather the flowers and place them in a bowl of spring water in full sunshine. After a couple of hours take some of the water and place it in a dropper bottle with a few drops of cognac to preserve it. This makes a Bach flower remedy. I sometimes gather rosebuds, echinachea, elderberries and other plants and place them in boiled spring water for a day and then strain it and add some honey to the liquid, as well as more spring water and some brandy to preserve it. This makes a flu and cold syrup. All of the medicines are then blessed with Buddhist and other prayers and blessings.

There are many ways of blessing the medicines. You can simply say whatever prayer you feel will bring healing and light to the person and the medicine. Whatever higher being you believe in can be called upon to bring healing light to the preparation. Each time I make a Bach flower remedy for a person I call on the higher beings of healing to bring their light and goodness to the medicine for that person and their difficulties. I believe it helps. There is also the traditional way of blessing medicines used in Tibet with the Medicine Buddha, but any higher being can be called upon in the same way. The Medicine Buddha's Prayer which is also used for blessing medicines is:

Tayata om bekhanze bekhanze maha bekhanze bekhanze radza sumugate soha.

MEDICINAL PLANTS

The Medicine Buddha is given his healing powers from the Namgyal Tree. This is an ancient tree that no longer lives on earth but still grows in the spiritual realms. It is sometimes called the completely victorious Myrobalan, Myrobalan being another name for the same tree. The Namgyal was originally planted in the realm of the gods by Yitrogma who was an emanation of the goddess Dusolmah. As Yitrogma prayed to the Buddhas of the four directions he discovered the tree's amazing healing abilities. The tree is said to heal physical illnesses, cleanse wrongdoings, remove mental obstructions, impart long life, bring wealth and good fortune, and even make the body indestructible. In the painting of the Medicine Buddha he holds a branch of the Namgyal tree in his hand. There are five types of Myrabalan tree know as the golden, the kempo, the longsih, the seven foldings and the spiritual. Their essences can be procured from the spiritual dimension through the blessings of the Medicine Buddha. This essence is stored in his offering bowl which he holds in his left hand and will infuse any medicine with healing qualities. The realm of the Medicine Buddha is imagined as a country where there are spiritual heroes, heroines, protectors, guardians and the eight Medicine Buddhas. You imagine giving them pure and luminous gifts. Then imagine a lotus flower in the centre of which is a white moon disk. On the lotus throne imagine the radiant Medicine Buddhas, translucent blue, holding a lapis lazuli bowl overflowing with healing nectar in his left hand and a branch of the Myrobalann tree, the king of all medicinal plants in his right. Reciting the mantra imagine the healings rays of pure and brilliant light radiating out from the Medicine Buddhas to all sentient beings, purifying them of diseases, afflictions, negative karma and ignorance. Conclude by imagining the Medicine Buddha dissolving into light and then absorbing this light into your heart.

To bless the medicine, such as a Bach flower preparation or a St. John's Wort oil, begin by making a clean space on a table. Cover it with a cloth and sprinkle some rice or flour or something similar as an offering. Then place the medicine, or imagine it, in a precious bowl of some kind. Imagine the Medicine Buddha, surrounded by enlightened beings, is in front of you. Acknowledge your profound respect for the Three Jewels and your reliance on their help. Then make a sincere request for healing from the many diseases which originate from the three poisons of anger, attachment, and ignorance.

Now recite the Medicine Buddha mantra, *tayata om bekhanze bekhanze maha bekhanze bekhanze radza sumugate soha.* The prayer is roughly translated as, Homage to the Highly Realized Lapis Lazuli Healing Guru Medicine Buddha, to the Great Realized Ones, Homage to the Healing, To the Healing, to the Supreme Healing, So Be It. This prayer sanctifies the medicine itself and honours the sacred nature of the healing process. This blessing can be used by anyone who has a sincere belief in the healing powers of the Medicine Buddha. The selfless intentions and visions surrounding the ancient practice of the Medicine Buddha are of benefit in the struggle against illness in all of its manifestations.

As you recite the mantra, you also imagine brilliant lights emanating from the heart centres of the Medicine Buddha and any other enlightened beings. Visualize that these lights are absorbed by the medicine and acknowledge that they impart to it enhanced ability to alleviate suffering, disease and illness. Then visualize the assembly of enlightened beings dissolving into the medicine. Put a small portion of the medicine on your tongue and taste it as a blessing. From this eternal centre within ourselves comes healing. From this eternal centre the great teachers look deeply into the conditions of humanity and prescribe healing medicine to remedy its ills. By thinking about misfortune and illness, we then motivate ourselves to improve our lives and the lives of those around us. We have a choice to suffer or to relieve that suffering in ourselves and others.

For any illness, we can call on the Medicine Buddha himself to send healing light energy to where it is needed. The Medicine Buddha can also enlighten our spirit giving us the understanding to heal ourselves. When we ask for help of the Medicine Buddha he sends his healing to us.

Let us now explore forty of the common wild plants of Europe, some of their myths, healing energies and medicinal uses. All of these grow around you. You can find them in cities like Paris or London, in the street cracks or in wild parts of the parks or along the river banks. These plants are very generous and are constantly healing our world and energy. When you begin to know them, you can use them to send their energy to help heal others.

WILD FLOWER PLANT SPIRITS

Violet, *Viola*, is a precious small flower desired for its scent. Once when Zeus was in love with the beautiful Nymph Io, Hera, his wife, came to find Zeus. Zeus turned Io into a beautiful calf and asked the earth to create the violet for Io to eat. Hera was not convinced and sent a gadfly to chase Io into the sea. Zeus confessed and promised not to look at Io. Hera changed her back and the violet has remained in meadows ever since. The violet is the spirit of the fertility of the spring as it is one of the first flowers to appear after the winter. The flowers have for centuries been mixed with medicines to comfort and strengthen the heart. They are often used for treating colds and coughs. Violets have the energetic ability to brighten and renew our spirits after the long cold winter. It is like a tiny precious gem from which comes the hope, joy and purpose of life. Bashô honoured them by saying, 'Violets – how precious on a mountain path.'

Willow, *Salix,* is one of the first trees to flower with its catkins. There is a lightness and grace in the willow trees. They dance among the other trees of the forest with an unhindered spirit that rekindles the life force in spring. Willows easily regenerate even when heartily cut back in the winter. The bark has been used for centuries to relieve pain, bring down fevers and give anti-inflammatory relief for arthritic and rheumatic conditions. The Celtic goddess, Brighid carries a white willow wand in spring to fertilize the land. In ancient times women would bring gifts to her shrine to bring them fertility, intuition and inspirations. In spring willow trees are celebrated and gifts and ribbons are tied to their branches to bring fertility and blessings and answers to questions. The willow brings us flexibility, new growth and vision. When life is full of old unbendable dead wood, we become irritated, angry and frustrated. When we go to willow for healing she brings us fresh vision. We then have the flexibility and excitement to bring new experiences, hope and adventure into our lives. The spirit of willow gives us hope, ease, flexibility and playfulness.

Wild Plum, *Prunus Domestica*, is one of the best wild fruits. The tree gives our spirit and body nourishment in the spring. The Indians of North America used the branches to make prayer sticks. They were made to heal a sick person and as offerings to the gods. The leaves in a tea, can be used to lower fevers. In Bach flower remedies it is used for desperate deep depression to return the person to a state of calm quiet courage. The wild plum is one of the first trees to blossom in the spring. It seems to know the exact moment of when to announce its fresh growth. In the same way it reaches our deepest darkness and out of it brings light and hope. In this way we feel the sun's return, the sap rising up our veins and we are filled with light and vision. The wild plum give our life the faith and courage to live life to its fullest. Izami Shikibu honours the wild plum by saying, 'I cannot see which is which, the glowing plum blossom is the spring night's moon.'

Lesser Celandine, *Ranunculus Ficaria*, comes with the arrival of the swallows. It is said to be the messanger of spring. The Celts named the flower after the sun because the flowers shut if it is raining but open in the full sunshine. For centuries the roots have been used for haemorrhoids. Traditionally it was thrown on the fire to celebrate the return of spring and used to bath the forehead to open vision and intuition. It is a herb of protection and gives the person who wears the flowers good spirits and joy. The flower covers the earth in spring like fresh open eyes seeing the world afresh in all its splendours. It gives us a freshly renewed vision so we can move forward enriched by what has gone before and change with what needs to come. Celandine brings to us the flowering out of the richness of the old.

Cherry, *Prunus Avium*, blossoms inspire the poetic heart. The cherry tree needs space to grow and is often found on the edge of forests or in clearings. The Japanese wait for the day when the cherry tree blossoms and on that day everyone comes with poems, songs and offerings to celebrate its flowering. They say that if you tie a strand of hair to a blossoming cherry tree you will find love. Its wood is beautiful and often made into wonderful objects finely polished. Its bark is used for coughs, colds and fevers and to ease labour pains. The fruit is a soul delight. When we lie under the beautiful blossoming cherry tree we are filled with an expansive beauty. We enter a place of deep calm and wonderful images fill our hearts. Each blossom seems to inspire the special artist within us enabling us to create in our own special way. Bashô honours the cherry when he says, 'Spring night, cherry blossom dawn.'

Cowslip, *Primula Veris,* has the most delicate green leaves and charming lantern shaped flowers of delicate yellow. They express the fragile delicate life that comes into being each spring with all its fresh sensual pleasures. It is said that young maidens can see their future husbands by holding the flowers in their hands and closing their eyes. The Celts believed the flowers grew in places where there was fairy enchantment. The Druids would initiate young bards and open their vision with an infusion of cowslip and vervein. If you hold a flower of cowslip in your hand it will help you find hidden treasure. It is a plant that awakens the fullness of the senses. The tea helps with colds, coughs, calms the nerves, relieves nightmares, and eases the back. If the flowers are added to bath water it is said to increase beauty. Cowslip bathes us in golden sunshine and opens our senses to the rich sounds, smells and colours that surround us.

Nettle, *Urtica Dioica*, is known for its sting. It is said that the Great Lightening Serpent gave the nettle her sting. But it has its own cure. If the leaves are boiled in water and then cooled, the juice when placed on the skin takes away the sting. The nettle is full of vitamins and minerals and since ancient times has been used to enrich and flavour stews and soups. It was said that if one placed nettle under the bed of a sick person they would recover quickly. A tea of nettle is full of restorative ingredients and helps stimulate milk in nursing mothers, regulates menstruation, helps gout and rheumatism, tonifies the blood, relieves high blood pressure and cystitis. An infusion can be used for eczema, itchy skin, diaper rash and insect bites. The dried leaves slow and stop the bleeding of wounds. Cloth and paper are made from their strong fibres.

Nettle is a fiery plant and her energy and fire power help the heart and small intestine meridians. Her spirit sends warmth, joy and love flowing into our hearts so we can fully enjoy good friends, good food, laughter and the joys of life. This joy and warmth is the spirit of nettle whose vibrant energy brings alive our very heart strings as we too become an exquisite flower of love. As James Percival says, 'They talk in flowers and tell in a garland their loves and cares.'.

Foxglove, *Digitalis Purpurea,* is an enchanted flower with her beautiful bell shaped flowers. For centuries she has been planted to give protection to the gardens and home. Fairies are thought to hide in the bell flowers. Foxes are said to wear the bells on their feet to walk silently. Foxglove is used to help circulation when the heart's ability to maintain normal circulation decreases. It enables the heart to beat more regularly, strongly and slowly. It also stimulates urination which lowers the strain on the heart. Foxglove is said to bring the entire garden into harmony. The spirit of Foxglove protects our heart and gives it the warmth it needs to function well. Its vibrant energy gives harmony, balance and strength to the meridians of the heart protector and triple burner. Close your eyes and imagine Foxglove standing in front of you. Ask it to harmonize the strings of your heart and give you joy and love. Feel this nourish your heart allowing it to open. Thank Foxglovefor her gifts. Foxglove uses the warmth and light of the sun to bring balance, harmony and protection to our hearts. As Robert Frost says, 'A flower unplucked is but left to the falling and nothing is gained by not gathering roses.'

Evening Primrose, *Oenothera Biennis*, blossoms in the height of the summer with stocks of rich yellow flowers. It is one of the grand culinary wild plants of the garden. Her flowers are used in salads and cakes. The leaves were eaten in sandwiches and called garden ham. The roots are pickled or made into a relish. The leaves were soaked and then used for wounds, bruises and other skin problems. Teas are used for digestion and as a mild sedative. The oil is used for itchy skin and taken internally for the menopause, rheumatoid arthritis and multiple sclerosis. Energetically it helps keep the meridians of the stomach and spleen in balance and harmony. Imagine you are in a golden field of wheat at harvest time surrounded by rich golden sunshine. Gather into yourself this rich abundant harvest of energy. Ask the spirit of Evening Primrose to give you a harvest fruit and taste its delights. Imagine what you have harvested over the past year and use that to nourish yourself until the next year. Thank Evening Primrose for her basket of goodness. The energy of Evening Primrose gives us the bounty of the kingdom where we feel the great oneness of our mother earth enveloping all with her great care. The abundant spendour of earth's great granary and full house is the spirit of Evening Primrose. In the words of Oren Lyons, 'The earth does not belong to us, we belong to the earth, and we have a sacred duty to protect her and return thanks for the gifts of life.'

Great Mullein, *Verbascum Thapsus,* is a tall plant with lemon yellow flowers and deep orange centers. The long stem was dipped into suet in olden times and made into sacred candles. Hermes gave Ulysses a sprig of mullein to protect him from Circe's enchantments. It has always been used for protection in sacred rites as well as hung over doorways to protect the house. Soaking its leaves and flowers in oil for twenty days and then straining the mixture produces an oil for ear infections, skin infections, frostbite, bruises, and is a general destroyer of germs. The leaves can be used for wounds and placed in the shoes to keep the feet warm. Mullein is a great circulator of nourishment and energy. It helps keep the meridians of the stomach and spleen in balance and harmony. Mullein helps the body transport nourishment where and when it is needed. Its spirit helps us to be nourished from the great harvested reserves of mother earth.

Plantain, *Plantago*, is a very humble herb that grows close to the ground. It seeds are like a magic wand dancing above rich green finger leaves. It a plant that is used all over the world for healing. It can also be eaten as a salad herb. Plantain leaves are used to staunch the blood flow and encourage the repair of damaged tissues. The leaves or oil made from the leaves can be used for bruises, burns, ulcers, haemorrhoids, and broken bones. An infusion can help ulcers, diarrhoea, dysentery, bowel syndromes, and respiratory congestion. Plantain helps keep our lung and large intestine meridians in balance. It helps us take in the heavenly breaths of inspiration and let go of what we no longer need. With plantain we find our connection to our heavenly father and our own inner essence. We are able to let go of what is no longer needed and breath in the welcome fragrances of the heavens.

Heather, *Erica,* is a magic carpet of flowers in the spring and autumn. A sprig of heather is worn by travellers to protect them. It is one of the first plants to return after a forest fire because of the durability of its seeds that can germinate even after ten years or more. Heather is a flower that is sacred to goddess Venus and the Celtic goddess Garbh Ogh. Its flowers have been used since ancient times to brew ale. The flowers made into a cream or oil can help joint pain and flexibility. Its tea helps to disinfect the urinary tract and is an overall tonic for the system. Heather helps to deeply restore our inner vitality. It helps us let go of the old in order to take in the new. It also helps us to easy move through the changes that come in the spring of energy emerging and in the autumn of energy descending. Heather helps us remain balanced no matter what life bring. She helps us blossom through all the changes in life. As Lao Tzu says, 'Who can wait quietly while the mud settles? Who can remain still until the moment of action? Observers of the Tao are not swayed by desire for change.'

Horsetail, *Equisetum Arvense,* loves water. Its segments have hairs that look like green fountains. It is a very primitive plant from the paleozoic era. In Roman times the young shoots were fried with flour and butter. Whistles made of the stems were thought to call snakes. From ancient times it has been used as wound healing plant. It is good for clotting blood, staunching wounds, and can reduce the coughing up of blood. It speeds up the repair of damage to connective tissues and improves strength and vitality. It can help heal sprains, fracture, eczema, rheumatic and arthritic problems, emphysema and chronic swellings of the legs. Horsetail has the ability to fill our reserves and reservoirs with vitality. It helps keep our bladder and kidney meridians in balance. The spirit of Horsetail refreshes us like a bubbling spring, a great mountain steam, a returning current and a valley full of river waters. It gives us the fluidity, vitality and constant flow which is our water element. As Lao Tzu says, 'Under heaven nothing is softer and more yielding than water, and for attacking the solid and strong, nothing is better, it has no equal.'

Mallow, *Malva Sylvestris,* dances in all directions as it wildly grows in the garden. It has the ability to soften and mend. It has been used since ancient times for healing and is said to strengthen the soul on its way to the spirit world after death. All of the plant can be eaten and the roots are often pickled or fried. The ancient Greek healer Pliny said, 'Whoever shall take a spoonful of Mallow each day shall be free from disease.' Mallow soothes and protects the mucous membranes. The roots when boiled produce a juice which helps sore throats, irritation of the alimentary canal, urinary and respiratory organs. Used externally it also helps with bruises, sprains and aches in muscles and sinew. The fresh leaves steeped in hot water can be used for insect stings. The flowers in an infusion can be used for inflamed skin. The peeled root was traditionally given for teething babies to chew. Mallow like Horsetail has the fluidity and vitality of water. It helps keep the bladder and kidney meridians in balance. It fills our energy with vibrant spring waters and rejuvenates the body and spirit. When our resources are full we too can dance around the garden like Mallow. As Lao Tzu says, 'The highest good is like water. Water gives life to all things and does not strive, it flows everywhere and so is like the Tao.'

Yarrow, *Achillea Millefolium*, has delicate green feathery leaves and lacy flowers. Chiron the centaur showed Achilles how to make a salve out of Yarrow to heal the battle wounds of his soldiers. Since ancient times it has been used to help with divination and clairvoyance. It was used at Delphi for the trance state of the oracle and the stems are used to make up the I Ching sticks of fortune telling of the Taoist temples. It has traditionally be used to heal wounds as it slows down the blood flow and fights infection. It arrests both internal and external bleeding. It helps to regulate the menstrual flow. A tea is used to help colds, flu, digestion, colic, hay fever, to lower blood pressure and to improve venous circulation and help varicose veins. It helps with infection both internally and externally. The spirit of Yarrow gives us strength and direction to achieve our goals. We feel a strength and swiftness with fresh insight to bring our dream into being. As Pam Brown says, 'The work of a garden bears visible fruits in a world where most of our labours seem suspiciously meaningless.'

Mugwort, *Artemisia Vulgaris*, grows in some form all over the world. She is a prehistoric plant and the great energetic mover of the garden. She holds the harmonic force of balance of all the energies of nature. She is often placed near a woman when giving birth to protect the mother and baby. Travellers carry mugwort for protection and also put leaves in their shoes to keep their feet from tiredness. It is plant that provides protection and increases fertility. A tea of mugwort is used as a tonic to improve appetite, digestion and the absorption of nutrients. It helps eliminate worms and can help regulate menstruation. Used externally it can help ease pain. Used in a bath it will refresh and revive. Dried crushed leaves are made into tiny cones and lit to warm acupuncture points. Sticks of dried crushed moxa when lit to form a gentle heat are used to ease pain and tension as well as help with circulation of energy. Mugwort is the vibrant green man of the garden. She knows the patterns of the energy of life and helps balance that energy. She has the ability to grow and change, to be always in motion and never still in the constant changes that move and create life in every instant. Mugwort moves energy back into balance again.

Herb Robert, *Geranium Robertianum*, is the wild geranium full of delicate pink or mauve flowers. Herb Robert was used by the Celts to contact the greenman of the woods or the spirit of nature. It is used as a tonic for the blood, skin irritations mouth sores, eye irritations, and as a general antiseptic and wound healer. Herb Robert is the magical messenger of nature. She knows no boundaries and is in contact with every other plant in the garden. She is the wholeness of nature and its vast network co-ordinator. In healing, every plant can be contacted through her. She is the keeper of the garden riches.

Oak, *Quercus*, is the strength and father of the wilderness. Many great oaks are known to be over 800 years old. The festival of oak is traditionally celebrated at the end of May when the oak and other trees are decorated with presents. It is said to be a tree of oracles. This wisdom can be heard in its rustling leaves or the murmurings of the sacred springs near its roots. The oak is said to open the door to great knowledge. Crushed dried bark in water helps burns, skin irritants and haemorrhoids. The tea can help diarrhoea, and dysentery and a sore throat or to bathe eczema. The oak gives us great strength to pass through despondency and despair. It brings back hope, courage and stability. The oak tree puts us in contact with the great wisdom and knowledge of the ages. It is like finding our spiritual ancestors who can be asked for their wisdoms and insights. In the words of John Ruskin, 'We cannot fathom the mystery of a single flower, nor is it intended that we should.'

Morning Glory, *Convolvulus*, announces the day with its large bell flowers. It brings beauty to the most derelict places where it climbs and adorns old walls with its vibrant flowers. When it is grown in the garden, it brings peace and happiness. The plant is poisonous but a tincture made from the flowers is used for headaches, rheumatism and inflamed eyes. The spirit of morning glory washes our vision clear and opens our senses. We are able to leave old thoughts and the past behind and see the world with a vivid freshness. We are filled with curiosity and inspired by what is possible in life. We suddenly see the beauty all around us and new possibilities emerge out of this wonder. This open vision is the spirit of morning glory. As Walt Whitman says. 'A morning-glory at my window satisfies me more than the metaphysics of books.'

Self Heal, *Prunella Vulgaris*, is a small plant with almost orchid like flowers. It is said to help all internal and external wounds. It was used for sores everywhere in ancient times including gangrene. A little of its juice mixed with roses is said to cure a headache. It has a strong antibiotic effect on infections both internally and externally. Its spirit brings light, hope and joy when there is a deep emptiness inside or a deep depression. When the world has gone grey, this plant brings back the excitement and inspiration to life. Self heal brings back the spirit of life when illness has been long, when suffering has been great and when hope has been lost. As Mevlana Jelaluddin Rumi says, 'The garden of love is green without limit and yields many fruits other than sorrow or joy, love is beyond either condition.... It is always fresh.'

Chicory, *Cichorium Intybus*, blooms in the height of summer with beautiful blue flowers that open with the sun and close at midday. The leaves are always aligned with the north. It is believed that if you carry a sprig of Chicory it will make your way in life easier and with less difficulties. Its tea is good for the spleen, gallbladder and liver and helps with digestion, and acts as a tonic. The bruised leaves help with swellings and skin problems. The dried ground root is added to flavour coffee. All of the plant can be eaten. The flowers can adorn salads, the leaves used as a boiled vegetable and the root pickled or roasted like parsnips. Bach used the flower essence when he felt someone had difficulty trusting and allowing love to flow outward. When love flows there is care and concern for others without the slightest thought of return or possessiveness. The spirit of chicory helps when someone has had a difficult times in relationships. When they have been rejected or repeatedly put down or even injured. It eases the bruises, rejections and losses in life and returns the heart to a place of trust, joy, love and understanding. We then are courageous to again love what comes in life. As Mevlana Jelaluddin Rumi says, 'Just as the heart becomes carefree in a place of green growing plants, goodwill and kindness are born when our souls enter happiness.'

Agrimony, *Agrimonia Eupatoria*, has rich ripe yellow flowers with purple-red or deep yellow centers. Her leaves are a deep rich green. Agrimony is said to repel all forms of negative energy that might lead to depression, lethargy or physical and spiritual energy drain. Agrimony has the ability to staunch bleeding and encourage clotting. The tea is a tonic for the stomach, sore throats, coughs, and bladder infections. Bach used a tincture of agrimony for people who appeared calm on the surface but underneath are restless with thoughts that churn over and over again. It helps people realistically see their worries and see how unimportant they are. They then can become optimistic and peaceful within themselves. The spirit of agrimony soothes our worries and takes us to a place of inner calm where we can see the essentials of life. It brings a refreshment and reawakening to the spirit gently enticing it back to the full enjoyment of what life can bring to the heart and all its senses. As Clara Balfour says, 'What a desolate place would a world without flowers! It would be a face without a smile, a feast without a welcome.'

Broom, *Cytisus Scoparius* is a riot of rich yellow flowers in the spring. When sheep eat the tops of the plant they become slightly intoxicated. Broom is full of an abundance of energy. It was used in ancient times to clear sacred spaces for ceremonies, calm the winds, and placed in houses for protection and to help with psychic powers. The branches were used for making brooms, baskets, thatching and fencing. Its shoots were used for paper and cloth making. Broom tea is used for irregular or fast heartbeats. It also counteracts fluid retention. It is used to prevent blood loss after childbirth because of its ability to cause the muscles of the uterus to contract. The spirit of broom lightens our load and sweeps our inner house clear of its dust and debris. We then find our inner essence and its joy and elegance. Broom enables the dullness of our being to blossom with brightness and life comes to us in all its fullness. As Hsien Ling-Yun says, 'I have banished all worldly care from my garden, it is an innocent and open place.'

Sage, *Salvia,* has a strong odour and orchid shaped leaves of blue, red or mauve. Sage is believed to give long life. It is a herb used to purify sacred spaces and temples. If you want a wish to come true you should write it on a sage leaf and leave it under your pillow. It can be eaten as a sandwich between two slices of butter bread. The tea helps with sore throats, poor digestion, sore gums, menstruation, menopause, and asthma. Fresh leaves can help with stings or bites. It both calms and stimulates the nervous system. The spirit of sage gives us great courage and strength. It gives us our warrior energy to bring about changes and take up new adventures and challenges. There is no holding back with sage. It gives a leap into new directions with a fullness of purpose and the strength of firmly being able to stand our ground. Here we can fly straight and true to the very centre of our goals. As Martin Luther says, 'Even if I knew for certain the world would end tomorrow, I would plant an apple tree today.'

Cornflower, *Centaurea Cyanus*, is delicate and charming with its blue flowers. It is said the cornflower can be asked directly about love. It also represents the gifts of the harvest. Water distilled from the petals is used for weak eyes. The tea can be used for hay fever, to bathe the eyes, for digestion, for infection, and to treat wounds. The spirit of cornflower gently washes away our old hurts, bruises, fears and anxieties. We can feel a lightness and wealth of energy bubble up and refresh life. Cornflower is the blue sky on a sunny summer's afternoon, calm and tranquil. It is the blue sea with gentle breezes moving the sails without effort. It is a blue pool full of silent brightly coloured fishes. Cornflower is full of blueness to calm our fear, sooth our bruises and ease our anxieties. As James Douglas says, 'It is good to be alone in a garden at dawn or dark so that all its shy presence may haunt you and possess you in a reverie of suspended thought.'

Poppy, *Papaver Rhoeas*, has delicate silk petals and slender stems. It is said the God of Sleep created the poppy to help Ceres the goddess of the harvest, to sleep when she had worn herself out. Ceres slept and then refreshed, she created an abundant harvest. The poppy is a plant of fertility, abundance, and harvest. Each plant has the capacity to produce around 17,000 seeds. The seeds and flowers are used in mixtures to help induce sleep. It is also useful to bring rest to invalids.

Syrup made from the seeds and flowers helps with colds, hoarseness, consumption and the loss of voice. The tea will help asthma, bronchitis, and angina. It also induces sleepiness and brings relief to pain. The spirit of Poppy brings us great joy. Poppy awakens our desires like the rosy red sunrise full of promise for the new day. Poppy brings us a deep relaxation and fills us with joy, love and happiness.

Harebell, *Campanula Rotundifolia*, is a most delicate blue bell flower. The young plant can be boiled and eaten with a nob of butter. The leaves can be cooked and taste like spinach. The root can be roasted or pickled. It is said that under the harebell are magical staircases leading to magical places in the earth. A tea of the flowers can be used for inflammations and the strained liquid is said to be good for the complexion. The spirit of harebell brings grace and elegance to our life. Our inner essence is refined and we become special as our talents emerge. It gives us the strength to be who we are and to move forward in our own way whether we become a polished diamond or a delicate soft flower. It helps us find the truth of who we are.

Wild Rose, *Rosa Canina*, is a flower of love created by Chloris the goddess of flowers and Aphrodite the goddess of love. Its oil is made into the most delicate perfumes. Roses have been used in love potions for centuries. Roses planted in the garden are said to attract fairies. It has been used since ancient times for helping with depression, strengthening the heart and refreshing the spirit. When we become resigned to the dullness in life, it is the rose that can again awaken our joys and pleasures. Then we have a lively interest in all that is happening and this interest and vitality attracts excellent conditions where we are able to enjoy friends, happiness and good health. The tea helps treat chest problems, alleviates gastric inflammation and reduces thirst. Rose water is used for conjunctivitis and for dry inflamed sensitive skin. The spirit of the rose puts us in touch with our own rose garden of beautiful flowers and delightful scents. In this garden our relationships and companionships deepen and mature. Our heart strings find their harmonies in others. The love within relationships is the very heart and spirit of the rose. As Mevlana Jelalludin Rumi says, 'If your thought is a rose, you are a rose garden.'

Shepherd's Purse, *Capsella Bursa-Pastoris*, has heart shaped seeds. It grows all over the world feeding birds and animals alike. Its tea helps stop hemorrhages of all kinds including bleeding from the kidneys. The leaves softened in water are used for bruises, sprains, inflammations and to help heal wounds as it is very effective in stopping bleeding. The spirit of shepherd's purse gives us a little heart shaped pocket of vitality. It helps nourish our spirit when the way has been filled with difficulties. It gives confidence when we lack courage. It gives us the resources we need to expand our life and helps us to grow. It brings a lightness, brightness and hopefulness to the new day. The spirit of shepherd's purse gives us a fullness of hope that gets us over and through all of life's bumps and difficulties.

Star of Bethlehem, *Ornithogalum Umbellatum*, is an exquisite white star shaped flower. The bulbs are eaten as food often roasted over a fire. As a Bach flower remedy the flower essence is used for any kind of shock. When our energy has been deeply affected by some illness, emotional upheaval or other shock, the Star of Bethlehem brings us back into balance. Imagine the rains of winter softening the seeds within you. Feel the spring sunshime bringing that seed to life. Bathe in the summer sunshine and grow into a mature being. Harvest the fruits and flowers of the year. Allow the leaves to fall back into the soil with the seeds of the next spring. Find the inner contemplation of the winter and feel its resources deep inside. When something weakens our energy through these natural cycles, it is the Star of Bethlehem that can revive our energy and bring it back into balance so that each season once again enhances life and enables it to flow smoothly. As Lao Tzu says, 'Bamboo bends before the storm, while the pine is broken in two. The difference is the living centre.'

Valerian, *Valeriana Officinalis,* grows in old walls, along steep banks and any tiny place there is a bit of soil. Her leaves are designed to catch water. The entire plant is edible. The flowers are eaten in salads, the leaves used as a vegetable and the roots added to soup or pickled. It is often used in charms and potions for love. Its tea is used to help bring about sleep and to relax the mind and body. It can also relieve pain. It helps palpitations of the heart, nervous complaints, eases pain and tranquilizes without side effects. It reduces mental over-activity and nervous excitability. The spirit of Valerian give us our dreams. It clears our worries, relaxes our body and expands our vision. It brings us back to the quiet calm source of our being washing away our cares and worries. In this way we are again receptive to the world and all its gifts.

Gorse, *Ulex Europaeus,* has spikey leaves and bright golden flowers. It grows in rocky places and on waste-land. Gorse tea is said to bring hope and positive thoughts. Its flowers make a sweet wine and are used to flavour whiskey. The seeds are very nutritious and were used in breads and cakes. The Back flower essence is used for those who have lost heart to bring back hope and joy. If given at the beginning of a long illness it brings the hope of recover which helps the healing. The spirit of Gorse gives us faith and hope and the certainty we will overcome all difficulties. Gorse protects wild exposed places so trees can take root. It gives our spirit its strength and belief that goodness will always be with us even in the most difficult circumstances. As Jesse Cornplanter says, 'In the Indian philosophy of sickness, it is thought that one's mind must be free of worry and distrust in order that the patient may get well.'

Saint John's Wort, *Hypericum,* is said to protect against enchantments, and spirits and to frighten witches and goblins. The tea is used for coughs, neuritis or neuralgia. The ointment is used for wounds, boils, ulcers and inflammations. A flower tincture is used for depression, anxiety, tension, and the menopause. Steeped in oil, it is effective against many viral infections and is used for wounds, burns and nerve pain. The spirit of St. John's Wort helps us come back to our centre when we feel pulled in many directions. It helps us sort our priorities out and brings space back to life. All the diverse ways become united into one stream so we are able to move from our essence and are not torn apart by demands and distractions. As black Elk says, 'Then I was standing on the highest mountain of them all, and round about me was the whole hoop of the world. And while I stood there I saw more than I can tell and I understood more than I was, for I was seeing in a sacred manner the shapes of all things in the spirit, and the shape of all shapes as they must live together like one being. And I saw that the sacred hoop of my people was one of many hoops that made one circle.'

Hemp Agrimony, *Eupatorium Cannabinum,* is a large plant with rose coloured flowers. It was used for snake bites, wounds and to keep bread from moulding in ancient times. Its tea is used as a tonic for fevers, colds, flu and other acute viral conditions. It give us resistance to infections. The spirit of hemp agrimony open our spirit so our inner core can shine forth. It is like a candle producing a glimmer of light in the dark nights and passageways of life. We find the compassion and forgiveness to move out of old patterns and to free our emotions and goals. From these depths our compassion can give us the means of helping others from a place of love and understanding.

Buttercup, *Ranunculacea Aeris,* is the brightest and most friendly flower ever to be found. A field of buttercups waving their sweet smiles of bright yellow flowers is like being in a field of friends. The roots are boiled and eaten with various sauces. The leaves can be used to draw a blister. The plant is considered toxic and not used in herbalism today. The spirit of buttercup brings us back to our convivial nature. We are open to friends and enjoy occasions to share lives together. It puts us back in contact with those people dear to us and with whom we can share our tender feelings and intimate beliefs.

Elder, *Sambucus Nigra*, berries make a wonderful strong wine that is good for health, bringing warmth to the heart. The Druids used the wine for clairvoyance and inner vision. The leaves and berries are used to bless sacred spaces and the home. Its wood has been used for musical instruments, combs and small toys. Elder is said to be the medicine chest of country people. The leaves are used in an ointment for bruises, sprains, and wounds. Elder flower water was used as an eye and skin lotion. Teas are used for lung infections, fevers, measles, flu and influenza. The flowers placed in oil are used for joint pain, wounds, burns and scalds. The berries are full of vitamins and are used in a syrup as a tonic. The spirit of Elder is the wisdom of the elders within ourselves. It is our connection with our ancestors and their experiences. With Elder we can find the wisdom of the wise to help us with any disharmony or disorder.

Vervain, *Verbena Officinalis*, is a delicate sky blue flower. She has been used for charms of protection since ancient times. The Romans sprinkled vervain water around the room to make people merry. It was used to cleanse the temple and carried for protection. It was said to inspire eloquence, inspiration and prophecy in Celtic bards. It is a herb sacred to poets and singers. Its tea is used to help digestion, to relieve stress and tension, to help with infection, to relieve colds, coughs and diarrhoea and to relieve headaches. The spirit of Vervein is like a shining star that puts us in contact with our special gifts in life. She can help us find what we need to nourish our spirit so like a star we can shine in the dark and move with the constellations around us. She brings to us great light and stillness that illuminates our path in life.

Campion, *Silene Latifolia*, is like a Japanese lantern. The shoots can be eaten as vegetables and are good sauteed with various sauces. The spirit of Campion helps us to mature and grow. When someone does not have the courage to move forward or is worn out from too much disappointment, then Campion can come along and be their champion, their friend and a person to walk with them. It helps us take the first steps in a new direction and gives us the confidence that all will be well. She helps our shyness to grow into wonder, our hurt to become compassion and understanding, our fear to become delight and our sadness to become strength. As Mevlana Jalluddin Rumi says, 'The clearest sign of grace is that from dung come flowers, from the bulbous sludge, buds and then sweet pears. The ground's generosity takes in our compost and grows beauty! Try to be more like the ground. Give back better, as a rough clod returns an ear of corn, a tassel, a barley awn, this sleek handful of oats.'

Birthwort, *Arstolochia Clematitis*, is a primitive flower of prehistoric times. It was used to keep away the evil eye and snakes in monastic gardens. It is not in general used medicinally. The spirit of birthwort can help when there are difficulties in family relationships. It enables the person to calm their own reactions and to also see the other person's viewpoint. Birthwort is like a grandmother who arrives with a cake and makes tea and has everyone in the family sit down and share their points of view. This offers a time for each person in the family to see each other in their fullness. The difficulties then seem more distant and everyone can bring their needs and strengths to helping each other rather than remaining with the conflict. When one person changes and is able to see the value of the other person then everyone benefits. By changing one energy, all the energy around also changes. These changes are in the spirit of Birthwort. As Chief Seattle says, 'Every part of the earth is sacred, every shining pine needle, every sandy shore, every light mist in the dark forest, every clearing, and every winged creature is sacred to my people. We are part of the earth and it is part of us. The fragrant flowers are our sisters, the deer and mighty eagle are our brothers, the rocky peak, the fertile meadow, all things are connected like the blood that unites a family.'

Flax, *Linum Perenne*, is a rich deep blue flower lighting up fields with deep blue gem droplets. It is used to make linen. It is the sacred plant of weavers and sewers. The seeds are very nutritious and used in breads and cakes. It is said that if children dance in a field of flax when they are seven, they will receive the gift of beauty. Flax tea and oil is used for intestinal problems, and chest problems. The oil mixed with red wine is used as a wound healer. The spirit of Flax is able to weave the strands of our life together into a great rich tapestry. When we need to reflect and see more of the potential of our life, Flax

RECEIVING SPIRIT

can give us the necessary expanded vision. We can also feel the connectedness with all things and how they help to guide our life. In this way we see ways of using our gifts to benefit others.

All of these forty plants you can find growing around you. Use them to help when you and others you know are unwell. Go out into nature and feel her healing energies. Sit by a tree and feel it give its strength to your body. Look deeply into the centre of a flower and smell its nectar. Take a petal of clover blossom and taste the nectar on the end. Sit with any of these plants and ask them to reveal their healing energy. Some people receive images of healing energy. Others hear healing music. Still others learn healing dances. The local plants work with the energy around us all the time to balance the world. This alive energy is what we use in healing others. The plants that live around us also know what energy is needed to help us. In this way the local plants are always the strongest. Explore the natural world around and begin to sense the dynamic energy of the plants you live with. You will then begin to see the heavenly spirit in each wild flower. When you touch this essence it brings goodness and health to our entire being.

MEDICINAL PLANTS

'We are all flowers in the great spirit's garden.
We share a common root, and the root is Mother Earth.
The garden is beautiful because it has different colours in it,
and those colours are different traditions and backgrounds.'

GRANDFATHER DAVID MONONGYE

Path of herbs
Carpet of red moss,
Window in the mountains
Brimming with greenery
I envy your wine
In the midst of the flowers
Those butterflies that flutter in your dream

QIAN QI

WATERWHEEL

IN WINTER
THE SEVEN STARS
WALKD UPON A CRYSTAL FOREST
SOEN NAKAGAWA (1907-1984)

INNER ALCHEMICAL HEALING CYCLE

This is a healing cycle for both ourselves as well as the earth. Ya Hu means the breath of God. This healing cycle is a combination of both the Chinese and Sufi traditions of inner meditative healing. First we breath this goodness through a cycle of points on ourselves and then we send this healing energy through the earth chakras. It makes a difference to our own wellbeing as well as helping to rebalance the energy of the earth that has suffered from our misuse of her.

The earth is a wonderful magnificent being giving us life. Earth gives us all that we need to survive. She is filled with vast energy networks of water, wind and sunshine. There are many places on the earth where there are wells of energy that bring great healing. Like us she has energy meridians and points of wells of energy that constantly flow, bringing harmony and balance to the seasons. Just as we work with our own energy meridians and acupuncture points to bring balance and harmony back into our lives, we can also work with the earth to help heal her from the pollutions and industrial stresses that she is experiencing at this time.

The earth has three lower chakras. The first is for all plant life. The second for all animal life. The third is for all ocean life. There are then the four middle chakras. These are earth, air, fire and water. Each of these chakras has an angelic guardian. The earth chakra has the guardian of Angel Michael. The air chakra has the guardian of Angel Gabriel. The fire chakra has the guardian of Angel Uriel. The water chakra has the Angel Raphael. They can be called on to help bring healing to these elements of the earth. There are then the upper chakras of the earth. The first above the water element is the chakra of weather. Above that is the chakra of communication. On top of that is the chakra of the balance of life. At the top is the chakra of the breath of the divine.

It is very important to send goodness and positive thoughts to the earth chakras. For plants we can send love and well being. For animals we can send a calm security. For the seas loving kindness. We can ask the angels to help us with the pollutions in the air, water, earth and fire elements. We can pray for balance to come back into the weather. We can breath peace and understanding into the chakra of communication. From the chakras of the balance of life and the divine we can ask for guidance and simply allow that energy to flow through us and the earth.

We begin the cycle by bringing healing to ourselves as we breathe Ya Hu, meaning the breath of the divine, into areas of points on our own bodies. Eight of these points has a connection with one of the I Ching trigrams and one of the eight extraordinary meridians that direct the creation of life before birth. The other two help our spirit at a deep level. After we are full of healing energy we can then send our heart energy into the earth chakras in sequence beginning with the lower earth chakras and going upwards.

ALCHEMICAL HEALING CYCLE

會
陰

Hui Yin means the meeting of
the inner seas of vitality.
It is in between the legs on the
perineum

Here is the meeting point of the inner waters that form the ocean of our inner energy. *Hui Yin* relates to the conception vessel or the Ren Mai which creates life, and the I Ching trigram of earth. The Ren Mai is the sea of energy that both creates and governs our inner resources. It is the sea of the fertility of life. The I Ching trigram of earth describes how earth receives yin energy out of the yang energy of heaven by being responsive, flexible, devoted and humble. Here we master our nature by following and being gentle and strong in perserverence to get to our goals. In this way, like earth, we are able to receive nourishing pure yang and be guided by it.

Hui Yin is the meeting of our inner seas of rich life giving nourishment. *Hui* is drawn as a meeting together of many mouths or sayings. It means to meet, gather or collect. *Yin* is drawn as the shady side of the mountain. It means inner, dark, secret, mysterious and feminine. Contained in *Hui Yin* are the vast source waters of life, dark, secret, mysterious, soft and receptive. Here are both the inner springs of our inherited resources as well as the energy we accumulate each day that nourishes our lives as we grow. This point contains the profound energy and depth of our energetic sea. Here our energy is united into a rich nourishing fullness that gathers together in our own inner ocean. When it flows freely there is tremendous vitality that feeds our inner most depths. This gives us a full life force. From this source all the meridians are fed from our inner ocean of resources. By breathing Ya Hu here all the meridians are fed with goodness and vitality.

Ming Men means the gateway of life, destiny and life's unique purpose.
It is in the area between the second and third lumbar vertebrae.

Ming Men is the gateway of life, destiny and life's unique purpose. This is an opening into our fate and way in life. *Ming Men* relates to the extraordinary meridian of Yang Qiao Mai which gives us dynamic movement, and the I Ching trigram of thunder. It is said that when thunder comes there is alarm and then laughter. This means that out of the spontaneous inner movement of thunder there will come good laughter. When in life we are not startled by thunder then there is no impediment to action. We will not be startled off our path but awakened into spontaneous action. In this way we need to be careful about our inner life and make life balanced so it is not affected by changes. By looking inward we can overcome this fear. It is said we should remain calm and not run off from the startle of thunder or we lose inner treasures.

Each person is unique and what we do with our lives will be ours alone. *Ming Men* is the gate to our life's purpose. *Ming* is drawn as a written order which is placed over a mouth and a seal. It is a decree agreed between heaven and earth, directing man. Here is heaven's stamp that creates our unique way in life. It is what we may achieve to keep balance and harmony between heaven and earth. *Men* is drawn as two leaves of a door facing each other and means a doorway or gate. How we use the potential we are born with depends on how far we can open this gate during our life time. This is the purpose of our life and when we are united with that purpose then all the rest of life flows with us. It is this sense of destiny that unfolds and renews life. This gateway opens our own special way that creates a pattern of life that can grow and develop from birth until death. Here is our naturalness in harmony with life. Opening this gateway brings us back to the unique purposeful drive that is individual and special to each person. Here is our unique way forward opening opportunities that enable us to develop in the richest way possible.

神
道

Shen Tao means spirit path
It is in the area on the spine
between the shoulder blades

Shen Tao means spirit path. This point is associated with the extraordinary meridian call Chong Mai which sparks life into action and also holds the pattern for the development of life. It relates to the I Ching trigram of water. The Chinese say that when heaven and earth interact, one point of original yang returns to earth and earth is filled with water. Then heaven is filled with one yin point and becomes fire. Water represents danger. Here the mind gets involved with all the distractions that happen with coming into the world. We can become good or bad. By good practice we become good and if there is truthfulness the mind develops and can return to the mind of the Tao. When this unity happens we are no longer distracted by yin and yang. In this way the trigram for water is called mastering pitfalls. If we fall into a pit but are not influenced by bad habits or distracted by the dust of the world, then we can emerge from the pit. We should use simplicity, sincerity and openness to find the light. If we do not practice goodness then it is like being tied with a rope in a briar patch. With a positive attitude we can transform dangerous situations. By maintaining confidence, soothing the mind with assurance and having faith, caution and trust, we can pass through any difficult situation. By seeking understanding in the very centre of our being we can cultivate goodness even in difficult times. In this way we return to our place between heaven and earth, living in harmony and flowing without obstruction just like water.

Shen Tao is our path of spirit. *Shen* is drawn as two hands extending a rope towards the heavens where are the sun, moon and stars. The rope represents our invisible connection with the heavens. It means spirit. Tao is drawn as a person running along a path and means a true path, a way, to lead, and to guide. As we become more present within ourselves and the world, everything begins to reveal its spirit. The ancients would watch the fields grow and would look to the heavens for sun and rain, searching the vastness of heaven and earth for divine guidance. They would see the divine signs in daily life that would reveal the Tao. In the same way a diviner would look at a cracked tortoise shell and see the entire universe. They would open their senses to this vast wisdom. When we can listen deeply within ourselves, then we can hear this wisdom. It can guide and lead us along our true path.

風
府

Feng Fu means the palace of the winds. It is in the centre of the base of the skull on the back of the head

Feng Fu is the palace of the winds. It relates to the extraordinary meridian of the Yang Wei Mai which is said to be like a great net that joins together and supports the harmonious growth of all the yang meridians. In this way it supports and protects all the Influences that move and circulate between the yang meridians. It is said to be like a bird cooked to perfect harmony in love and warmth. *Feng Fu* also relates to the I Ching trigram of wind. Wind is said to be small but developmental like the gentle winds of spring reaching everywhere. It is said that like the wind, we gradually make progress by flexible obedience. By making gradual progress and by keeping going with both firmness and flexibility, we will eventually arrive at the essence of the great path. We do this by striving to deepen into the Tao gradually, by having the correct flexibility like growing plants, and by holding faithfully to the virtue of the centre. We should proceed humbly, gently and flow easily wherever the wind goes. It is said that to gently proceed is the most effective way of influencing events. If we proceed humbly and gently we gain friends and their support. Like the wind, proceeding humbly, sincerely and with trust, brings good fortune.

Feng Fu is the palace of the changing winds. *Feng* is drawn as an insect that is surrounded by motion. It means wind, influences, climate and atmosphere. *Fu* is drawn as a building where something is given and means, a store house, treasury or palace. Here is a palace of the winds. It is a storehouse of influences, distinguished airs and ambiances of spirit. Here the winds of the eight directions give us the flexibility to move in harmony with the Tao. It is where our vision can be swept clear so we can once again see with the fresh innocent eyes. Here our house of spirit is aired and filled with the brightness of sunshine.

百會

Bai Hui means the meeting of grand unity
It is at the top of the head

Bai Hui is a meeting place of unity where our meridians are united in harmony. It relates to the extraordinary meridian of the governor vessel or the Du Mai. The Du Mai is the director that keeps an eye on the other meridians and supervises how they are run. It guides and directs all the other meridians so that they work in a masterful way. It directs all activity from a unity of power with skill, authority and flexibility. *Bai Hui* relates to the I Ching trigram of heaven. It is said that in strength nothing is stronger than heaven. There is nothing that heaven does not cover and in this way nothing can harm it. It is the ultimate of soundness and strength. When there is this positive energy, all things prosper. As this positive energy expands all things develop and flourish and then mature and finally rest quietly returning to their roots. Heaven acts unceasingly with great strength and this original innate nature is called the true yang. It is referred to as the dragon energy. If we are able to use strength and are not used by it, we can develop a pure unadulterated vitality in which this yang strength is properly balanced. By cultivating this hidden dragon, our living potential subtly emerges and the light within us grows brighter. We can then see the Tao in all things and at every turn, just like sunlight illuminating all beneath it.

Bai Hui is this unity. It is a point of balance between the light and dark, the moon and the sun and between the yin and the yang. Here is where the river of the meridians can be united together to work together directed from the original source of all life. The grand unity for the Chinese was the number one hundred called *Bai*. *Bai* is drawn as the number one over the sun. *Bai* means one hundred and unity. *Hui* is drawn as a meeting of words brought together under one roof. *Hui* means to meet, assemble, collect, co-operate, to understand and to be in the habit of. *Bai Hui* is a place that calls on the wisdom of the ancients to bring the entire life of the individual back into harmony and balance. It is at the top of the head, the point nearest to the heavens and their influences. Here is the unity of our being and a place of great inner wisdom, calm and harmony.

印堂 *Yin Tang* means the hall of our inner seal
It is in an area called the third eye in the middle of the forehead.

Yin Tang means the mysterious pass or hall of seals. It is located where the third eye is said to be. It relates to the extraordinary meridian called the Yin Wei Mai which is said to be like a great net that joins together and supports the harmonious inner growth of all the yin meridians. Here all the yin is maintained in good, constant proportions to make a harmonious unity. It is said to be like an inner dove of peace that is cooked to perfection with all the warmth and love that it needs. Its I Ching trigram is valley. A valley is said to receive all things by simply being and in this way is said to be joyful. We receive great joy in finding the Tao. Those who follow the Tao do not delight in the senses or in wealth and gain, but instead find joy in benevolence, justice and happiness. When we are trustworthy, sincere, and have inner harmony then we are joyful and bring joy to others. If we are lured in the wrong

ALCHEMICAL HEALING CYCLE

direction, try to please people, or are seduced by worldly objects then there is only craving.

Yin Tang is this mysterious pass. It is where a mark of blessing is traditionally placed for various religions. *Yin* is drawn as taking a badge of authority by the hand. It means a seal or stamp. *Tang* is drawn as dry even soil under a roof. It means a hall, meeting house, court or church. *Yin Tang* is the sacred hall of our inner intuitive vision. It is the vision of our third eye. Here we can see beyond the mundane into the spirit of all things.

人
中

Ren Zhong means the middle of man
It is in an area in between the nose
and mouth

This point and the following point do not relate to an extraordinary meridian or an I Ching trigram but unite the meridians into a whole. *Ren Zhong* means the middle of man. It is man's inner centre where he can live in balance harmony and with simple modesty. If we lose our way then life becomes a struggle, but if our aim is straight and true then we will reach our target. *Ren* is drawn as two legs of a man and means the one who stand upright and mankind. *Zhong* is drawn as a whole split into two halves.. These different halves are said to always balance each other, in the same way that day balances night, or light balances dark. It is also said to be drawn as an arrow that flies straight and true and hits its target. *Zhong* means middle, among, inside, within, in between, to attain and to be affected by. When there is harmony, then life can be lived in great simplicity. Above this point our nose takes in the fragrances of the heavens and below our mouth is nourished by the earth. We are between in perfect harmony between heaven and earth nourished by both. Here we can rest and live in balance, simplicity, modesty and harmony with all around us. From this inner core of wisdom we can return to our purpose and direction along the path of life.

Tian Tu means the sudden opening of the heavens
It is in an area at the level of the adam's apple on the throat

Tian Tu is the sudden opening of the heavens. It gives us glimpses of the wonders of the heavens and opens our eyes with visions of wonder. By uniting all the meridians, this point gives us great inner illumination. *Tian* is drawn as a man with the heavens above him. It means sky, nature, the heavens, the supreme ruler, the seasons and weather. *Tu* is drawn as a dog that rushes out of his kennel to attack an intruder. It means suddenly or impetuously. This point is a window that opens to the heavens. It opens our vision to both what our life is and what it can be. These heights can be frightening or unuseful unless we have the courage and ability to see the way forward. We need to be able to see beyond what has gone before in order to be able to move forward. The sky itself is vast and ever changing. It inspires us each day as we walk our path. This point contains the vastness of the heavens that can help our inner vision to grow greater so we can more fully experience the world we live in. Here we can see beyond who we are with great vision and unity.

巨
闕
Ju Que means the great palace gateway
It is in the area at the level of the heart
in the middle of the chest

Ju Que is the gateway to our inner heart palace. It relates to the extraordinary meridian of the Dai Mai. This meridian is like a rope that ties a bundle of sticks together to keep them in good order. It is also like the sheep dog who brings all the sheep safely into the barn. It ensures the good continuous flow of the ordinary meridians so they can act for the same purpose by being directed from the warmth of the heart. Its trigram is fire. Fire is said to be both our inner and outer illumination. This illumination is beneficial for correctness and development. This heart fire is said to embrace the female within. Here we are heartful, centred, joyful and our intuition is nourished. When we nourish our inner fires of warmth and illumination then we mature. When we are sincere and wholehearted, we are able to distinguish appropriateness and rightness. The true mind is then said to be like the radiance of a king. If we are filled with illumination within, we will be able to illuminate others. Great people are said to illuminate

RECEIVING SPIRIT

the four quarters with continuing light. It is said that in times of darkness, people should cling to one another. When they do, things get brighter.

Ju Que is the great palace gateway or the grand door of the palace. It is the gate to the our great inner palace of spirit. *Ju* is drawn as a large carpenter's square that is used to measure large pieces of wood with great precision. It means very large, forceful and big. *Que* is drawn as a doorway in which there is something that obstructs. It means void, and a lookout tower above the gateway to the palace. The supreme ruler of the body is the heart. Great for the Chinese represented the emperor or this supreme ruler. Here is the opening into the wealth, riches and inner calm of the emperor's private chambers where life is ruled by love and joy. When we put our hearts into what we do then our work flowers with life. The opening of our hearts is sometimes not an easy task but here is a place where we can find our own inner palace of heart warmth, love and joy.

There are two different points described in the texts for this last point and I use them both together.

神
闕

Shen Que means the inner gateway of spirit
It is on the navel

Qi Hai means the sea of abundant Qi
It is just under the navel

氣
海

Shen Que is the inner gateway of spirit. *Qi Hai* is the sea of Qi. They both relate to the extraordinary meridian called the Yin Qiao Mai which gives us dynamic movement. It helps us to dance in a vital, powerful and graceful way through the constant flowing changes of life's energies. It relates to the I Ching trigram of mountain which represents stillness. Mountains are places of contemplation to reflect before moving forward. It is said to be like walking in a beautiful garden. Here our energy is nourished in quietness where the good can be discerned and developed in a place of rest. This stopping helps us maintain correctness by being humble and not daring to act arbitrarily. In this way we are not self willed and know when to take action and when to be still. It is by stopping, that strength and weakness can be balanced. Here we can rest in the realm of the ultimate good like a lofty mountain. The Chinese say that when we stop our jaws, our words become orderly and we speak both to benefit other and to induce others to goodness. Here is time for careful deliberation so we can harvest what we have and see our goal open before us.

Shen Qui is a gate to our soul. *Shen* is drawn as two hands reaching upwards extending a rope and the sun, moon and stars above. The rope represents the invisible connection between man and the heavens. The ancients would go out into nature and observe the world to find spiritual guidance. Whether they worked the soil or observed the heavens, spirit was everywhere and contained what they needed to know. *Shen* is the invisible inspiration that comes from truly being a part of the whole. The *Shen* spirits come at night when the heart is empty to fill the heart with goodness. It is through the heart that all understanding comes. *Que* is a doorway where something blocks the breath. It means both a void, as well as a lookout tower above the city gate of a palace. This point is on the navel. The Chinese describe the navel as a lotus flower. They believe that during conception the fetus begins development with the kidneys that then produce the liver, which produces the heart, which produces the spleen which produces the lungs. At the tenth month of conception everything is complete. It is then that the breath of the *Shen* enters the foetus at birth through the *Shen Que*. This gives the foetus its humanity. This point is the complete flowering of the greatness of our spirit. Here is the gateway to the palace of the body. This point connects our spirit within to the world of spirit that is all around us. Here the great spirit mother nourishes our inner essence so we live in the world with wholeness and joy.

Qi Hai is a sea of abundantly flowing Qi. This is the sixth point on the Ren Mai where there is great fullness. *Qi* is drawn as the steam that comes from boiling grains of rice. It is the energy that creates and nourishes all life. *Hai* is drawn as a mother's breasts and the abundance with which grass grows. It means sea. Grains of rice provide the main nourishment for the people of China in the same way Qi nourishes all life. It is said that by growing rice we learn humility and experience the vitality of life in all its cycles. We have to carefully store the rice seeds in winter and then bend down to plant them

ALCHEMICAL HEALING CYCLE

in the spring. We have to stand in the mud to transplant the small shoots. Then we have to accept what the seasons bring in the way of rain and sun. We have to wait with patience for the ripening and harvesting and gather the rice at the precise moment it is ready. In this way we learn about the seasons and the abundance of energy in all cycles.

This point is a vast expanse of prolific Qi energy in all its forms able to nourish all cycles of life. It can give our entire system a full boost of vitality. It is this energy that is contained in the smallest seed as well as the most vast ocean. This is also the place of what the Chinese call the *Shiah Dan Tien* or the lower elixir field. It is a centre made out of the essence we are given at conception by our parents or our inherited Qi. It is said that by meditating in the area of the *Dan Tien* both the heart Qi and spirit Qi can be generated to bring harmony to life and develop a depth of spirit. *Qi Hai* bathes us in a sea of abundantly flowing Qi. It builds our Qi energy and brings a surge of vitality that give us warmth and passion to strengthen our spirit.

Having touched each of the points with light and love we now do a cycle of the points eight times to build the energy beginning with REN MAII, *Hui Yin,* and going up the centre of the back, over the top of the head and down the centre of the front. This builds and unites our inner energy. Doing this fills our inner core with light, love and joy. Next breathe this united energy still saying Ya Hu into the legs from the hips down sending circles of energy down to the knee joints, then the to the ankle joints and finally into the feet. This fills our direction in life with light, love and joy. Then breathe Ya Hu into the arms from the shoulders down sending circles of energy down to the elbow joints, then to the wrist joints and finally into the fingers. This fills our actions in life with light, love and joy. Feel this energy throughout your entire body. Now we can breathe this rich heart loving energy into the Earth.

Begin by breathing Ya Hu filled with energy and love from your heart into the earth chakra of plants. Give them any good wishes you feel you want to give them. Then do the same for the second chakra of animals. Then go on to the chakra of the creatures of the oceans.

Next go to the middle earth chakras. Begin with the earth chakra and call on Angel Michael with any wishes you have for the earth. Next comes the air chakra with the help of Angel Gabriel. Following this breath Ya Hu into the fire chakra with the help of Angel Uriel. Finally breath Ya Hu into the water chakra with the help of Angel Raphael.

Then go to the upper chakras beginning with the chakra of weather. After that is the chakra of communication. Then the chakra of the balance of life where you may find insight and greater understanding. At the chakra of divine blessings simply allow the energy to flow through yourself and all the chakras of the earth. At the end spend a bit of time in the quietness and the well being of life. Use this cycle each day and you will be healthy, peaceful and well.

ALCHEMICAL HEALING CYCLE

Who can wait in quietness as the mud settles clearing the waters?
Who can rest in stillness until the moment of action?
Those who walk the Way do not want fullness,
Although seeming to be empty they are ever full.
Not seeking fulfillment,
They are not swayed by a desire for change.
Though seeming to be old,
They are beyond the reach of life and death.
LAO TZU

You understand that there are certain things
One should not talk about,
Things that must remain hidden.
If all was told then there would be no mysteries left,
And that would be very bad.
Man cannot live without mystery
He has a great need of it.
JOHN FIRE LAME DEER

The word is like the nest,
The meaning is the bird,
The body is the river bed,
And spirit, the rolling water.
MEVLANA JELALUDDIN RUMI

RECEIVING SPIRIT

I have three treasures that I dearly cherish,
The first is love.
The second is moderation.
The third is humility.
From love comes brave courage and one is fearless.
With moderation comes generosity and abundance.
From humility comes leadership to fulfill the highest position.
If one is fearless without love,
Has abundance without moderation
And leads without humility,
Then this is certain death.
Love is an impregnable defense conquering all attack.
Heaven does not send an army,
It protects with love of all equally.
The virtue of not confronting,
Working with your own abilities
And complying with heaven
Is the the ancient path of love.

LAO TZU

FURTHER READING

Birrell, Anne, *Chinese Mythology*, Hopkins University Press, 1993
Burber, Martin, *Chinese Tales*, Humanities Press International, Inc., 1991
Cheng, Francois, *In Love with the Way*, Shambala, 2002
Cleary, Thomas, *The Taoist Classics, Vols. 1-4*, Shambala, 1991
Connelly, Dianne, *All Sickness is Home Sickness*, D. Connelly, 1986
Connelly, Dianne, *Traditional Acupuncture*, D. Connelly, 1979
Cooper, J.C., *Chinese Alchemy*, The Aquarian Press, 1984
Chevallier, A., *The Encyclopedia of Medicinal Plants*,
  Dorling Kindersley Ltd. 1995
Cowan, E., *Plant Spirit Medicine*, Swan Raven & Co., 1995
Deng Ming Dao, *Chronicles of Tao*, Harper Collins, 1993
Deng Ming Dao, *Everyday Tao*, Harper Collins, 1996
Deng Ming Dao, *367 Tao*, Harper Collins, 1992
Ellis, Wiseman, and Boss, *Grasping the Wind*, Paradigm Publ., 1989
Franglen, N., *Keepers of the Soul*, Five Element School Ltd., 2006
Franglen, N., *The Handbook of Five Element Practice*,
  Five Element School Ltd., 2004
Gerard, J., *The Herbal*, Dover Publications, Inc., 1975
Harrison Tu, Xinshi, *The Wisdom and Art of Chinese Calligraphy*,
  Lingnan Art Publishing House, 1998
Helminski, Kabir, *The Rumi Collection*, Threshold, 1998
Huang, Alfred, *The Complete I Ching*, Inner Traditions Inter, 1998
Jones, Wayne Lee, *Weave a Garment of Brightness*, Berkley Books, 1997
Kaatz, D., *Characters of Wisdom*, Petite Bergerie Press, 2005
Kaatz, D., *The Alchemical Path*, Petite Bergerie Press, 2006
Kaatz, D., *Wild Flower Plant Spirits*, Petite Bergerie Press, 2005

Keh Ming, Peng Tuah, *Calligraphy et Peinture Chinoise*, Fr. Loisirs, 1998
Khor, Gary, *Reflections on Qi*, New Holland, 2004
Kohn, Livia, *The Taoist Experience*, State University Press of N.Y., 1993
Kohn, Livia, *Taoist Meditation and Longevity Techniques*,
    Michigan Monographs, 1989
Larre, C. and Rochat de la Vallee, E., *The Eight Extraordinary Meridians*,
    Monkey Press, 1997
Larre, C. & Rochat de la Vallee, *The Secret Treatise of the Spiritual Orchid*,
    Monkey Press, 1991
Larre, C. and Rochat de la Vallee, E., *The Seven Emotions*,
    Monkey Press, 1996
Lao Tzu, *Tao Te Ching*, trans. Addiss, Lombardo, Hackett Pub. Co.1993
Lao Tzu, *Tao Te Ching*, trans.English and Gia-Fu Feng,
    Wildwood House Ltd., 1973
Lao Tzu, *Tao Te Ching*, trans. Star, Jonathan,Penguin Group, 2003
Levering, M., *Zen Inspirations*, Duncan Baird Publishers, 2000
Mabey, Juliet, *Book of Prayer*, Oneworld Publications, 2009
Mantak, Chia and Tao Huang, *Secret Teachings of the Tao Te Ching*,
    Destiny Books, 2005
Maoshing Ni, *The Yellow Emperor's Classic of Medicine*, Shambala, 1995
Olson, S., *The Jade Emperor's Mind Seal Classic*, Inner Traditions, 2003
Olson, S., *Qigong Teachings of a Taoist Immortal*, Healing Arts, 2002
Oman, Maggie, *Prayers for Healing*, Conari Press, 1993
Parachin, Victor, *Prayers from Around the World and Across the Ages*,
    ACTA Publications, 2004
Raheem, A., *Soul Lightning*, iUniverse, Inc. 2005
Ricard, Matthieu, *Rainbows Appear*, Shambala, 2002
Rossbach, Sarah and Lin Yun, *Living Colour*, Kodansha Int, 1994

FURTHER READING

Smith, F., *The Alchemy of Touch*, Complementary Medicine Press, 2005
Thich Nhat Hanh, *Cultivating the Mind of Love*, Parallax Press, 1996
Vogel, V., *American Indian Medicine,* Univ, of Okalahoma Press, 1970
Weeks, Nora &Bullen, Victor, *The Bach Flower Remedies*,
    C. W. Daniels Company Litd. 1964
Wieger S. J., Dr. L., *Chinese Characters*, Dover Publications, Inc., 1965
Wong, Eva, *Cultivating Stillness,* Shambala, 1992
Wong, Eva, *Cultivating the Energy of Life*, Shambala, 1998
Wong, Eva, *Harmonizing Yin and Yang*, Shambala, 1997
Wong, Eva, *Holding Yin Embracing Yang*, Shambala, 2005
Wong, Eva, *Nourishing the Essence of Life*, Shambala, 2004
Wong, Eva, *Seven Taoist Masters*, Shambala, 1990
Wong, Eva, *Tales of the Taoist Immortals*, Shambala, 2001
Wong, Eva, *Tao of Health, Longevity and Immortality,* Shambala, 2000
Wong, Eva, *Taoism*, Shambala, 1997
Wong, Eva, *Teachings of the Tao*, Shambala, 1997
Wu Jing-Nuan, *The Spititual Pivot*, The Taoist Centre, 1993
Worsley, J.R. *Classical Five-Element Acupuncture, Vols 1-3,*
    Worsely Inc., 1998

RECEIVING SPIRIT

The ancient masters were subtle,
Mysteriously profound, responsive.
The depth of their knowledge was unfathomable,
Baffling all inquiry.
So deep that they can only be described by appearance
That tell their outer signs.
Wary and watchful of one crossing a stream in winter,
Cautious and alert, as men aware of danger.
Courteous, like guests.
Reverent as if receiving an honoured guest.
Relaxing like ice about to melt, selfless.
Simple as uncarved wood, pure.
Open and accepting as the valley,
Where the course of nature clears muddy waters.

LAO TZU

THE AUTHOR AND ILLUSTRATOR

DEBRA KAATZ is a Chinese medicine healer, writer, musician and gardener. She lives in southern France in a stone house she built herself. She wrote her first story at the age of three and has never stopped writing and researching. Her current books include, *Characters of Wisdom-Taoist Tales of the Acupuncture Points, Wild Flower Plant Spirits* and *The Alchemical Path*. She gives workshops at her home and beautiful gardens as well as teaches in various countries around the world.
To contact her please email: debra@cmhealing.com

XINSHI HARRISON TU, as a devoted artist, has created numerous works of calligraphy, many of which have been selected for exhibition in the United States, China, Japan, Korea and Singapore. Mr. Tu has three calligraphy artworks that are in permanent collection at the Denver Art Museum. His other exhibitions have included:

2005 Naropa University Art Gallery Exhibition Boulder, Colorado,
2000 Personal Exhibition on Shanghai Library, Shanghai, China,
1998 Personal Exhibition on China National Art Gallery, Beijing,
1997 American Biographical Institute, International Cultural
          Achievement Award

Mr. Tu is a devoted proponent of exchange and mutual understanding between the East and West. Since 1994, he has been Editor-in-Chief of the Chinese American Post. He is a visiting professor of The Naropa University and Colorado College, USA, teaching Chinese Calligraphy & Culture.
To contact him please email: tuxinshi5@yahoo.com

MAY YOUR PATH BE BLESSED WITH LIGHT